A LIVE THING IN THE WHOLE TOWN

THE HISTORY
OF THE
INDIANAPOLIS-MARION COUNTY
PUBLIC LIBRARY
1873-1990

COMPILED AND WRITTEN
BY

LAWRENCE J. DOWNEY

Library of Congress Number 91-058046

ISBN 1-878208-06-3

This book was designed by Steven D. Armour
of Alexander Typesetting, Indianapolis.

Color cover the gift of Alexander Typesetting
and Guild Press of Indiana, Inc. in loving
appreciation of Hilton U. Brown and old Broadway
Branch libraries.

DEDICATED TO

THE PEOPLE OF INDIANAPOLIS AND MARION COUNTY

FOR MAKING THE PUBLIC LIBRARY TRULY
"A LIVE THING IN THE WHOLE TOWN"
AS ENVISIONED BY
ELIZA GORDON BROWNING
IN 1896

AND

TO THE LIBRARY STAFF, WHO SINCE
1873 HAVE PROVIDED THOUGHTFUL
AND DEDICATED SERVICE
TO ALL

Table of Contents

CONTENTS

Preface

A history of the Indianapolis-Marion County Public Library was begun in the late 1960s by Ernestine Bradford Rose in anticipation of the Library's centennial in 1973. The project however, was never completed in time for the Library's one hundredth anniversary.

Mrs. Rose, a former member of the Library staff, and author of *The Circle*, a history of Monument Circle in Indianapolis, published in 1971, researched the Library's history up to 1973. A working draft was subsequently completed in the mid 1970s with the editorial assistance of Miss Frances Stalker, Coordinator of Adult Services, Miss Pauline French, Supervisor, Central Services, and Miss Marian McFadden, Director of Libraries, 1944-1956. The project lay dormant until 1978, at which time the Board of the Indianapolis-Marion County Public Library Foundation, at the request of Library Director Raymond E. Gnat, authorized completion and publication of the history.

It was not until 1989, however, that work was once again begun on a manuscript suitable for publication. Lawrence Downey, Associate Director for Management Services prior to his retirement in December, 1988, began a major verification, editing, and re-writing of much of the earlier research and working drafts. Mr. Downey completed the library's history up to 1990, including a chapter on the history of the Public Library Foundation.

The Library's archives proved to be an invaluable source for the information contained in the history, but appreciation goes to Catherine Gibson, Adult Services Coordinator; Christine Cairo, Children's Services Coordinator; Carolyn Wheeler, Personnel Services Office; Susan Ebershoff-Coles, Supervisor, Technical Services Department; and Beth Steele, Public Relations Office, for their special assistance in providing data and in editing pertinent copy.

Special thanks must go to Ernestine Rose for her personal insights and humorous comments on events during the administrations of Charles Rush and Luther Dickerson from 1923 to 1938 while she was a member of the library staff.

The advice of Jacqueline Nytes, Associate Director for Management Services; Laura Johnson, Associate Director for Public Service; Harold J. Sander, former Director; Marilyn McCanon, former Associate Director for Extension Services; and Raymond E. Gnat, Director of Public Libraries, has been a major source of inspiration and guidance in the completion of this work.

And finally, we are deeply indebted to the Public Library Foundation for providing the necessary funding for the publication of this history of the Indianapolis-Marion County Public Library.

Sketched from an Old Print

The Beginnings

The heritage of the public library in the United States is one of which all citizens may be proud. Despite the fact that European nations owned vast repositories of books, the United States deserves the credit for starting the free public library movement.

The first book depository in Indiana which might be designated as a public library was established in 1807 in Vincennes, the capital of the Indiana Territory, and at that time the home of many of the state's most influential and educated men. It was natural that they would influence the Constitutional Convention in 1816 to make provisions for books and reading in the new state.

As a result, the 1816 Constitution, Article IX, Section 5, stated, "The General Assembly, at the time they lay off a new County, shall cause, at least, ten percent to be reserved out of the proceeds of the sale of town lots, in the seat of Justice of such County for the use of a public library for such county . . ." In 1818 a law was passed providing for the incorporation of public libraries in Indiana. The first to be established was in Pike County. Marion County itself did not exist as yet.

A subscription library was established in 1844 under the provisions of the 1816 Indiana Constitution. Although it was little used by the public, the Marion County Library lasted the longest of all the county libraries established in the state after 1816. The Marion County Library was in existence a span of eighty-six years, until 1930; then, by an act of the Indiana General Assembly in 1931, its books, documents, and funds were transferred to the Indiana Historical Society.

There were several reasons that this Marion County Library did not fulfill all expectations. When the state legislature passed an act creating Marion County and enabling it to have a library, it allowed only two percent of the sale of town lots to be used to fund the library, rather than the ten percent as provided by the Constitution and allowed other counties. Other ambiguities of the 1821 law delayed the library's start. Finally, not the least of the factors was the political situation in frontier Indiana. Backwoods politicians seemed dilatory and uninterested in a library for their constituents.

So, the library was late in getting underway. The proceeds from the sale of lots were placed in a fund known as the "Indianapolis Fund," but by an act of the state legislature in 1831, money from the fund was used for a state prison at Jeffersonville and for a new state house instead of books. Year after year the money accumulated in the library fund, but no group or individual attempted to use it for the purpose for which it was intended.

It was not until 1841 that Henry P. Coburn, a lawyer and clerk of the Indiana Supreme Court, finally asked permission of the legislature to investigate the status of the fund with a view of finally implementing a county library.

Early Libraries in Indiana

Long before free public libraries, families enjoyed the popular McGuffey Readers.

Facing page — The Public Library occupied one room of the high school when it opened in 1873.

1

The legislature empowered him to do so in an act approved January 31, 1842 and the Board of County Commissioners was ordered to appoint seven trustees whose duties were to establish the library as provided by statute.

Mr. Coburn worked with patience and shrewdness and got the funds to start the library. At his instigation it opened April 22, 1844, with a sum of $600 to buy books. By 1853 the board's treasury held $2,438, so it is presumed that the library had gained control of the outstanding funds previously collected and due to it. Mr. Coburn was a member of the library's first board of trustees and its treasurer.

Still, the library did not gain popular acceptance and usage. The county library was housed in the county courthouse as stipulated in the law. It was open only on Saturdays during its entire existence to all adults and children upon payment of an annual fee of fifty cents per person or seventy-five cents per family. In 1870 the subscription fees were changed to $1 and $1.50, and in 1898 the subscription fees were abolished and the county library became free to all persons over ten years of age who were guaranteed by persons owning real estate.

The librarian's salary was meager—reaching $85 per annum by 1874, so none stayed very long. Between 1844 and 1896 there were eighteen "librarians" appointed, none professionally trained or knowledgeable about libraries.

The library held from 2,000 to 7,000 volumes during its long history, all on open shelves for browsing. However, the number of subscribers was few and the number of books borrowed was small. For example, according to the Librarian's Annual Report for 1896, only 506 books were circulated that year. The inconvenient location in the courthouse contributed to this low usage, as did the shifting nature of the collections: the library was moved repeatedly within the courthouse from the basement to the attic, as space needs of other county functions dictated. The library was always hampered by the indifference and often outright enmity of county officials.

In 1926 the order was given to move the library to the "Bum Room," a storeroom on the fourth floor of the courthouse. The librarian refused to go with the books. Most were soon boxed and sent to the county infirmary, the rest were stored in the courthouse attic. The boxes of books remained unopened and soon deteriorated. There were no funds to rent a place for them because the County Commissioners had for some years neglected to collect the tax. The library was officially closed by the county on February 22, 1930.

In spite of its low circulation and usage, the Marion County Library fulfilled a need in its early days, particularly prior to the establishment of the Indianapolis Public Library in 1873.

It is prophetic that as early as December, 1922, Indiana historian George Cottman wrote a feature article in the *Indianapolis News*, which stated that the county library had served its usefulness and "has no place in the present system." He urged that the county library be merged with the city library and that the services of both be extended to the whole county and city, an idea clearly before its time. It would be another forty-six years, in 1968, before a city-county library was eventually established.

County libraries were not the only ones being established in the State.

Township libraries were set up through a school law passed by the Legislature in 1852 under the guidance of Robert Dale Owen and Caleb Mills. Although the plan for distribution was inadequate, resulting in an unequal allotment of books to the townships, township facilities were at least partially successful and popular. The little library in Indianapolis, however, never assumed much importance, and the same was true of several other small collections, including the above described Marion County Library, and one in the YMCA.

One of the best known early efforts to foster libraries in Indiana was the creation in 1838 of the Working Men's Institute in New Harmony. William Maclure, its founder, worked closely with Owen in improving the welfare of the working man. Maclure died in 1840 and his will provided a sum of five hundred dollars to any society of laborers who would establish a reading room with a library of one hundred books. The money did not become available until about 1855; after that societies and reading rooms were quickly established in eighty-nine counties. However, for the most part, these actions were taken primarily to receive the five hundred dollar donation. Old books were gathered together and few, if any, of the collections remained when modern public libraries later came into being.

None of these early efforts to bring books to the people ever really amounted to much. They were poorly housed; frequently there was no one responsible for their care, and no money was provided for their maintenance or expansion.

One library that did survive was the State Library, established in the new capital, Indianapolis, in 1825. In its early days it did not circulate materials, and its function was primarily to serve the officers of the State. Therefore, many of its volumes were duplicate titles or government publications, and it was too specialized in subject matter for the general public. Under the jurisdiction of the Secretary of State, the State Library was jointly operated with the Law Library, and its first librarian, John Cook, was not appointed until 1841. At that time, according to existing records, only 2,000 volumes were in the collection, but by 1867 its general collection exceeded 10,000 volumes.

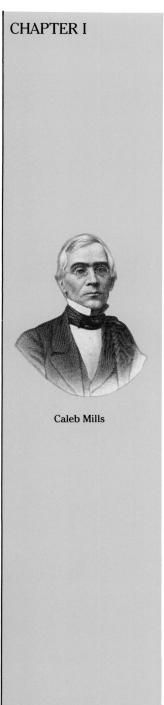

Caleb Mills

Washington Street, East from Capitol, 1862. Glenn's Block with fire alarm tower, right center.

ROOTS OF THE
INDIANAPOLIS
PUBLIC LIBRARY

Calvin Fletcher

Thus, despite the noble intentions of educators and legislators, even after the beginning of the second half of the nineteenth century there were few books available on a free basis to the average citizen of the state or of Indianapolis.

However well intentioned State action had been, it provided little help in developing free library service. This was of particular importance in the capital city. Indianapolis, a town that by mid century had moved beyond its log cabin pioneer days, was growing up and creating a cultural life of its own.

Although in the early days of Indianapolis there were few provisions for libraries, the private libraries of some leading citizens were generously opened for the use of interested friends and neighbors. Mr. James Blake, a civic leader for many years, was reputed to have the largest non-professional library in the city. Calvin Fletcher tells of reading from Mr. Blake's library and remembering especially Goldsmith's *Animated Nature* and the *Arabian Nights Entertainment*. Calvin Fletcher had his own collection as did Samuel Merrill, Obed Foote, and Dr. Harvey Gregg. Another pioneer, David Turpie, stated that his father had thirty books, "a large collection for the time and place," which contained *Pilgrim's Progress,* a *History of the United States,* Hume's *English History*, Weems' *Life of Washington*, and Cowper's *Poems*, a rather varied fare. Mr. Turpie was appointed United States District Attorney in 1884 and was elected to the United States Senate in 1887.

An important movement which was closely related to the need for books started with the forming in 1821 of the Indiana Sabbath School Union, which held its first annual meeting in Indianapolis. At the time it was estimated that only 2,000 of the 50,000 children in the state attended Sunday Schools. The purpose of the Sabbath Schools, beyond their religious influence, was to pave the way for common schools and to act as a substitute until they were available. One of their most important duties, therefore, was to teach children to read and spell, and they became depositories for books which were lent to the pupils as rewards for their Sunday work. The children were fined for a dirty mark or grease spot, a leaf turned down or torn, or a book overkept a week. Among some of the picturesque titles were *The Dairyman's Daughter*, and *Little Jack, the Circus Boy*.

Dr. Isaac Coe, the town's first college-trained physician, was the real founder of the Union Sabbath School in Indianapolis. In announcing its beginning Dr. Coe said, "The Indianapolis Sabbath School will commence on next Sabbath, the 6th of April, 1823, at 9 o'clock in the morning at Mr. Caleb Scudder's shop. A general and punctual attendance of scholars is requested and that they will bring with them the testament, spelling books, or such other school books which they may have."

Dr. Isaac Coe is credited with doing much to overcome the malaria epidemic during the first winter of the wilderness settlement. A descendent of his, Evelyn Sickels, was a long-time member of the Library staff, an author of books for children and young people, and was Supervisor of Work with Children when she retired in 1958. She stated that Dr. Coe was very much interested in encouraging people to read and in providing books for them. He lent books freely from his own library.

The need for a free library accessible to the general public had long been felt by the residents of Indianapolis. What was desired was a true public library with books covering the wide interests of all the citizens. Although there had been many discussions on the subject, the real impetus for the movement came from a Thanksgiving Day sermon, delivered in 1868 by the Reverend Mr. Hanford A. Edson, pastor of the Second Presbyterian Church. Reverend Edson was a graduate of Williams College, had studied two years at Union Theological Seminary, and had been an instructor in Greek at Genesee Academy in New York. He was so highly respected and admired by his congregation that his text on that Thanksgiving day was bound to make a real impact on his listeners.

Mr. Edson's sermon was primarily "a plea for a Public Library." After telling of the growth of the city and its many improvements, he also described its deficiencies, stating the many things needed "if our aim is not so much to have many citizens as to give all just reason to say that ours is 'no mean city.'" He then continued,

> *The great want of the city, the deficiency that is really fatal to its character—is the want of a public library. No community can be respectable without books . . . Without a library the best results in scholarship and in professional life are absolutely unattainable . . . the people, the whole body of citizens, gain more than indirect benefit from the proximity of a public library . . . It makes readers of the multitude and leads them to the reading of better things . . . The simple fact then is that we have no public library. We have nothing that materially aids the student and absolutely nothing to satisfy and educate the tastes of the great reading public. Most of our 50,000 people are greatly limited in their use of books and many are wholly denied the pleasure and benefit of reading . . . How can the needed library be secured?*

After outlining the possibility of a public grant or a private gift, Reverend Edson suggested as his third alternative "the establishment of an association, as was done by Benjamin Franklin in Philadelphia. We must naturally look to the Young Men's Literary Association. This will be a true Thanksgiving for me if I have induced any to strive for, or even ardently desire, a Public Library."

Following Edson's impassioned plea, in December a group of citizens met and on March 18, 1869, the Indianapolis Library Association was formed by 113 citizens who each contributed $150 in capital stock, to be paid in annual installments of $25, for a subscription library. Approximately four thousand books were acquired by purchase or gift. The Association had its quarters on the second floor of the Martindale Building, located on the east side of Pennsylvania Street between Washington and Market Streets. The librarian was Mrs. Eliza McCready and the first officers were John D. Howland, president; William P. Fishback, vice president; D. W. Grubbs, secretary; and William S. Hubbard, treasurer. Among its members was Benjamin Harrison, later President of the United States.

Although creation of the Indianapolis Library Association was a significant step, this private group fulfilled only a small part of Reverend Edson's

. . . our aim is not so much to have many citizens as to give all just reason to say that ours is 'no mean city'. . . The great want of the city, the deficiency that is really fatal to its character — is the want of a public library. . . .

— Rev. Hanford Edson
Thanksgiving Day Sermon
"A Plea For a Public Library"
November 26, 1868

Abram C. Shortridge, Superintendent of Schools. He was instrumental in the passing of legislation in 1871 which permitted school-controlled public libraries in Indiana.

hope for a public library. By 1870 there was an urgent need for expansion and improvement of public schools in Indianapolis, as well as for a free library for the use of the general public. Abram C. Shortridge, who had been chosen Superintendent of Schools in 1863, had done a great deal to develop the schools. He was the type of individual who not only could see the needs, but also had the ability and foresight to find ways to meet them. Feeling that school children had few of the things needed for their proper progress, he called together a group of leading citizens for advice and planning.

The members of the committee were Judge Elijah B. Martindale, Judge John Caven, Dr. Harvey G. Carey, Judge Addison L. Roache, Austin H. Brown, Simon Yandes, and Dr. T. B. Elliott. Two were invited who could not attend—W. A. Bell and Clemens Vonnegut. The committee met in Judge Martindale's office to formulate a plan to divide the city into districts, to select a commissioner from each district in a non-partisan election, and to create a free public library to be controlled by this duly elected board of school commissioners.

A law for this purpose, drafted by Judge Roache, Dr. Carey, and Mr. Brown, was presented to the Indiana General Assembly and was passed on March 3, 1871. The law authorized the establishment of a Board of School Commissioners for any city of thirty thousand or more inhabitants with the power to levy its own taxes (under certain restrictions) for the purpose of governing the schools within the district.

Section 4, paragraph 3 of the law read, "To levy a tax each year of not exceeding one-fifth (of one mill) on each dollar of taxable property assessed for city taxes by the City Assessor for the support of free libraries in connection with the common schools of such city, and to disburse any and all revenue raised by such tax levy in the purchase of books for and in fitting up of suitable rooms for such libraries, and for salaries for librarians; also to make and enforce such regulations as they may deem necessary for the taking out from and returning to, and for the proper care of all books belonging to such libraries, and to prescribe penalties for violation of such regulations."

Admittedly, two cents on each one hundred dollars of assessed valuation did not allow for excess spending. In the first years of the library it amounted to about $14,000. However, Judge Roach frankly admitted, "The idea was suggested . . . to levy an annual tax so small no one would feel it."

This law has frequently been called the measure which brought larger benefits to the citizens of Indianapolis than any other school legislation passed by the Indiana Legislature. At last a public library could be started. So it seems fair to say that although Reverend Edson's sermon doubtlessly gave purpose and enthusiasm to the movement, it was the efforts of Abram C. Shortridge and his committee which profited the city most. Their actions created the impetus for the legislation passed in 1871 which permitted school-controlled public libraries in Indiana.

The determination and wisdom of that original committee of prominent citizens to establish a good, free public library for the community are well exemplified by a statement written by Judge Daniel Wait Howe, a member of the Marion County Superior Court from 1876 until 1890. "The people of Indiana wove into their public 'enactments' the virtues of their private character," he said "and we have grown up in the shadow of their achievements."

In order to understand the Indianapolis Library and the people who established it in 1873, it is important to recall the scenes and activities of those early days and look at the economic, social and cultural growth of the town itself. Indianapolis was no longer the rugged frontier village which had been founded by the Assembly in 1823 near Indian campsites. By 1830 it had become an urban community with a developing culture. In the 1870s it was still in the middle of the horse and buggy era, and of course it was quite different from today's city. Life did not move at the rapid pace it did even one hundred years later. Still Indianapolis was on the move.

Following the Civil War Indianapolis had grown at a feverish rate. According to the 1870 census the population was 48,244, made up chiefly of native-born Americans. However, 10,657 were foreign-born, mostly German, but also many Irish. In spite of the financial panic of 1873, which was severe and prolonged, the Hoosier capital was manufacturing twice as much as any other town in the state. By then a thriving railroad center, Indianapolis saw railroad lines continue to open despite the panic, and by 1874 twenty-seven lines crossed the state.

Indianapolis was also a center of journalism, with four daily newspapers, the largest and most influential being *The Sentinel* and *The Journal*. Some of Indiana's outstanding authors gained national prominence during the era. *The Hoosier Schoolmaster* by Edward Eggleston was published in 1871 and *The Fair God* by Lew Wallace in 1873, followed in 1880 by his more famous and perennial favorite, *Ben Hur*. John B. Dillon, who was called the "father of Indiana history," was contributing his invaluable work, and the Indiana Historical Society had also been founded.

Churches played an important role in the community. By 1870 there were ten Methodist Churches, and Methodism was the largest denomination. Although Presbyterians were not such a large group numerically, they were influential, having more highly trained ministers than any other denomination. Their members were active in every phase of civic life. Church influence was strong in school development, in the temperance fight, in prison reform, and also in attitudes which influenced the approved recreation of the day. Theatrical performances were considered "beyond moral toleration" and circuses "the devil's device."

Music, however, was most acceptable. Indianapolis had many visiting musical events, both opera and concerts. There was a Philharmonic Society and an orchestra. Parlor concerts had come into vogue, and the quality of music performed seemed to be at an increasingly high level. The Hoosier capital offered two schools of music and five dealers in musical instruments. The musical talent of the large German population was in part responsible for this early love of the arts, but the 1870s saw a flowering of the performing and visual arts all over America and Indianapolis was part of a larger trend.

In 1870 the Academy of Music and the Metropolitan School of Music were in operation; and soon after, in 1880, the Grand Opera House and several other public halls opened. As prejudice against the theatre began to relax, plays became more popular. There were stock companies, and many visiting

CHAPTER I

Lew Wallace, noted Indiana writer, the author of *Ben Hur*.

troupes established schedules in the years 1873 and 1874.

It was into this thriving, though depression-slowed community, that the Indianapolis Public Library was born. The new institution was destined to become an increasingly important part of the city's cultural life itself.

The Board of School Commissioners had been appointed. The next step in creating a library was taken on May 24, 1872, when a Public Library Committee was appointed, consisting of Dr. Harvey Carey, Dr. Thomas Elliott, Mr. Austin Brown, and Judge Addison Roache, all members of the School Board. These men visited libraries in other cities to study their methods, to get assistance in organizing the new library, and to find a librarian.

Their search led them to Cincinnati, and to its chief librarian, William F. Poole, one of the most distinguished and able men in the field, and former librarian of the famous Boston Athenaeum. Most librarians remember Mr. Poole as the author of the massive *Index to Periodical Literature*, or as the originator of the Poole system of classification. Besides all this, he was a genius at organizing libraries, the inventor of the dictionary catalog principal, an expert in library architecture, and an historian of such repute that he was President of the American Historical Association. In his earlier days he had written about Cotton Mather and witchcraft in Salem, Massachusetts. Later, while librarian in Cincinnati, he wrote a history of Ohio and of the Northwest Territory. He was also to become a noted literary critic.

On July 5, 1872, the committee secured Mr. Poole's services, at a cost of $300, to compile a list of at least eight thousand titles which would be purchased to form the nucleus of the library collection. The list was received on September 20, 1872. He was also asked for advice as to the arrangement of the library, the method of lending books and, perhaps most important of all, names for a possible librarian.

He immediately recommended his protegé, twenty-two-year-old Charles Evans from the Boston Athenaeum. Charles Evans had worked under Mr. Poole at the Athenaeum, and Poole described him as conscientious, capable, and scholarly. The Board agreed to employ Mr. Evans at an annual salary of $1,200. Mr. Poole became the foremost person to befriend and advise Evans in the ensuing, and often stormy, years.

Second Presbyterian Church.
Sermon by the Pastor, Hanford A. Edson.
Thanksgiving Day, November 26 1868.

The New England holiday has become national. Made one people by the war, we are called by the President to united thanksgiving, & the States readily fall into line, South Carolina with the rest. It is good for us so to be reminded of our obligations to God, & thus with one mind to praise Him. We have reason to thank Him. He has blessed our families, making the light to shine even in our darkness. To this church, both in its temporal & spiritual

A page from Rev. Hanford Edson's sermon, "A Plea For a Public Library."

The Early Years

Charles Evans arrived in Indianapolis in November, 1872. A handsome young man with red hair, almost six feet tall, he carried himself with dignity. He was energetic and filled with enthusiasm for his new position.

The town, which suffered from the typical Midwestern provincialism of the time, took a dim view of bringing in an outsider, especially an easterner. John H. Holliday, publisher of the *Indianapolis News*, who was to become one of Evans' closest friends, commented in his paper that a "Boston import" was not needed. The press gave him a hard time, making frequent disparaging references to his extreme youth. But with his superior knowledge of literature and his unusual persistence, the young librarian set to work to prepare for the opening of the Library. He ordered, catalogued, and classified the book collection with the aid of only three assistants.

Before long, Evans' very obvious attributes of brilliant mind and experience, the latter of which he had gained from dealing with men of culture during his years at the Athenaeum, won over many of his most insistent and articulate critics. Even before opening day, *The Sentinel* had changed its tune and was saying that the choice of books and the plan of the Library showed the ability of the young librarian who had come from so far away.

Born in Boston in 1850, Charles Evans had a childhood marked by tragedy. His family had moved five times in eight years, which provided him no real feeling of a stable life. Left an orphan at age nine, he was sent to the Boston Asylum and Farm for Indigent Boys, a school and home for boys who had lost their parents. The home was located on Thompson's Island, which was a beautiful spot overlooking Boston Harbor. Here the boys learned a love of nature and the practical skills of gardening and farming. Charles received a good academic education in reading, writing, geography and grammar under teachers devoted to the welfare of their pupils. The outdoor work on the farm and the strict, regular hours provided a clean, healthful life. More importantly in Evans' case, the boys were also allowed the privilege of reading from the many books in the institution's library. Sunday was given over to Sunday School and religious services, from which the boys gained a knowledge of the Bible and respect for moral integrity, industry, and self discipline.

After young Charles had spent seven years at the Farm School, one of the members of its Board, Dr. Samuel Eliot, took him under his wing. Dr. Eliot, a scholar, educator, and philanthropist, became his guardian until Charles, then only sixteen, became of age. In addition, he offered him a position as assistant at the Athenaeum of which Dr. Eliot was also a trustee. It was a rare opportunity for a boy from the Farm School to be employed in a distinguished library. It marked the beginning of Charles Evans' lifelong interest in books and was the best possible education and training for his future profession. At

CHARLES EVANS, *The First Librarian,* 1873-1878

A Boston import was not needed.
— *Indianapolis News,* 1872

Facing page — Charles and Lena Evans and two of their children.

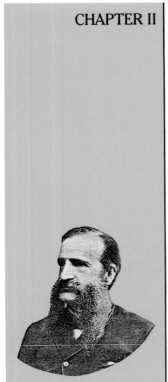

Dr. William F. Poole, Librarian of the Boston Athenaeum, author of the *Index to Periodical Literature*, and long-time friend to Charles Evans.

Obedience, fidelity, individual character and industry. Possessed of these, there is nothing which may not be obtained in life. Genius is only the capacity for hard labor.

— Charles Evans

the Athenaeum he was to learn of many of the leading scholars and writers of the day—Ralph Waldo Emerson, Julia Ward Howe, Francis Parkman, Charles Francis Adams, Gamaliel Bradford, and Charles Sumner, the United States Senator, who was to become a close friend.

He also worked with outstanding librarians who exerted a great influence on him. Chief among them was Dr. William F. Poole, the librarian of the Athenaeum, already famous as the author of the *Index to Periodical Literature*. Poole was greatly interested in training young men to become librarians, which he considered a high calling. It was he who gave young Charles Evans a chance to develop as an historian and bibliographer.

It was also Evans' ambition to attain a college degree, but after he failed to be admitted to West Point, he never tried again. Instead, he bent all his energies towards self-education, using the wealth of literary material available to him and the exceptional opportunities for contact with the literary people who surrounded him. Nevertheless, among the honors he later received, the one that pleased him most was a Doctor of Literature Degree conferred upon him by Brown University.

He himself described as "the cardinal virtues" taught him at the Farm School, "obedience, fidelity, individual character and industry. Possessed of these, there is nothing which may not be obtained in life. Genius is only the capacity for hard labor." Throughout his life, Charles Evans lived up to those virtues.

Although the years spent in Indianapolis were filled with many difficulties, there were pleasurable compensations. His family life was happy, even though it was punctuated by periods of poverty and of forced separation from his wife Lena (Young), who always worked with him and supported his endeavors. The couple suffered the loss of a little girl, Constance, but were proud of their other children, Gertrude, Eliot Howland, and Charles. Young Charles became well-known as "Chick" Evans, champion golfer in the late 1910s and 1920s.

The Indianapolis Library Association, which was almost three years old, disbanded shortly before the opening of the new Library and transferred to the Library its entire collection of 3,649 volumes. The members of the Association, interested in the library movement from the beginning, continued to work for it as members of the Board, or on the Citizens Library Committee. Mr. Evans was enthusiastic in his praise of their gift, saying that the books had been selected with care and discrimination and showed the good taste and knowledge of literature of the purchasing committee.

On April 1, 1873, the Library was opened to the public for the registration of borrowers. The next day the *Indianapolis Journal* said, "Notwithstanding the inclemency of the day which kept nearly all within doors who were not driven out by dire necessity, upward of 100 certificates were filled and extra employees engaged by Mr. Evans were kept busy. The library committee will meet every evening this week for the purpose of passing upon the certificates." By opening day 500 borrowers had been registered.

On April 9, 1873, the doors of the first Indianapolis Public Library, located in the High School at the northeast corner of Pennsylvania and Michigan Streets, were opened to the public.

The formal dedication took place in the High School building on the previous night, April 8. In spite of a downpour the hall was filled to capacity. To quote the *Indianapolis Journal* of April 9, "The flood which poured from heaven deluged the streets and saturated the crowd . . . it is a most encouraging sign and exceedingly complimentary to the people of Indianapolis that they came and kept coming until High School Hall was well filled." With the entire building lighted and the library thoroughly thrown open to inspection, the exercises began promptly at half past seven. John R. Elder, president of the Board of School Commissioners, presided. The following is the program:

Anthem - "The Glory of the Lord" from the Messiah - Euterpian Society

Invocation - Dr. H. R. Naylor

Historical and Business Statement of the Library - Judge A.L. Roache

Response - The Reverend Mr. H. A. Edson
       Honorable J. D. Howland on the part of the Indianapolis
       Library Association

Music - "Sweet and Low" - Banby - Amphibian Club

Addresses - Governor Thomas A. Hendricks
       Honorable Daniel Macauley
       Senator Oliver P. Morton

Music - "Achieved is the Glorious Work" - Creation-Euterpian Society

Benediction - The Reverend Mr. H. A. Edson

Governor Hendricks, who described Indianapolis as the "City of the Plains," spoke emphatically of the importance of information and culture.

> *Here in the midst of this great valley, surrounded by an unbroken country of most valuable land on every side of us, scarcely an acre that will not yield men comfort and wealth and happiness, of this great country drained by these great railroads and pouring wealth into this city every day, shall the information of the people not keep step with the progress of material prosperity? Shall Indianapolis be less cultivated than she is successful in business? As we become a great city, we become 'observed of all observers' and I should like to have it said always that Indianapolis is as elegant in her culture as she is successful in her business and her development.*

The *Indianapolis Journal* the following day carried a flowery review of his speech.

> *The soul of every Indianapolitan, nay of every Indianan, will glow with honest pride as he reads the magnificent oratorical effort of our Governor at the opening of our library last evening . . . the sparkling sentences, the glowing periods, the profound philosophy and the eloquent tribute to books and to histories in particular are enough to thrill a graven image with feelings never felt before.*

I should like to have it said always that Indianapolis is as elegant in her culture as she is successful in her business and her development.
— Governor Thomas A. Hendricks
Dedication of the Opening of the Indianapolis Public Library, April 8, 1873.

CHAPTER II

. . . The largest use . . . is made by young men who usually are led to grace the corners of the street, or other public places, for want of better employment; should find here a place congenial to their tastes, and instructive to their minds. . .

— Charles Evans
First Annual Report
April 9, 1874

Also included in the program were the Reverend Mr. J. P. E. Kuemler, pastor of the First Presbyterian Church, and Mr. Austin H. Brown, who read a long letter from Mr. Michael Haggerty, a stone cutter, setting forth the advantages which his fellow workmen might derive from the Library. Why Charles Evans was not included in the program is not known.

The first home of the Library had been the residence of Robert Underhill, a Quaker, who came to Indianapolis in 1834 and became one of the earliest iron manufacturers and millers in the city. The story is told that he drove with his family in a carriage all the way from New York and upon arrival, traded his carriage for a town square bounded by Pennsylvania, Michigan, Delaware, and North Streets.

On the southwest corner he build a large and beautiful frame house facing Michigan Street, occupying three quarters of the square. Shaded by tall forest trees, the yard was laid out with gravel paths, shrubs and rosebushes, all surrounded by a picket fence.

Underhill sold the property to the Baptists in 1858, and it became the Indianapolis Female Institute. The school closed in 1871, and the residence was purchased by the Indianapolis School Board for $41,000. The Board erected an additional building and made improvements costing $53,000.

The high school was moved from Circle Hall, the former Second Presbyterian Church on the Circle where Henry Ward Beecher had preached, into the remodeled residence. It used the front rooms for the offices of the Board of School Commissioners and the high school principal. The classrooms were in the new addition at the rear. The Library occupied the double parlors and dining room at the left of the wide entrance hall. Through the center of the front parlor ran a long counter and the remainder of the space housed the books on wooden bookshelves destined to move with the Library for forty-five years to each new location. Upstairs there was a small work room.

After many, many months of planning and hard work the Library on its opening day had 12,790 volumes ready on the shelves for the use of the 500 registered borrowers.

The Library Committee of the Board of School Commissioners, doubtlessly aided by William F. Poole, had issued a pamphlet giving the "Rules and Regulations of the Public Library of Indianapolis." The Library was to be open daily from 9 a.m. to 9 p.m., including Sunday, although no books could be borrowed on that day. The librarian was to have complete responsibility for the books and property and for "the quiet and orderly use of the Reading Rooms." Each resident who gave satisfactory information was to be supplied with a library card. Books could be kept for two weeks and renewed once, except those labelled "Seven Day Book." Overdue fines were to be three cents a day. Encyclopedias, dictionaries, and atlases were for reference use only, and the complete rules were published in the newspapers. At a time when very few libraries over the country had a reading room open on Sunday, this feature received favorable comment in the newspapers and from the public in general.

Mr. Evans' first annual report expressed pleasure with the extensive use of the reading room, especially by young men who otherwise "would be led to grace the corners of the streets." Mr. Evans' image continued to improve as the new library pleased the public. Contributing factors were the popularity of the Library with young people, the Sunday hours, his emphasis on collecting Indiana historical material, the printed catalog, which had been issued in the fall after his arrival, the growing number of borrowers, and the continuing increase in the use of books.

The first catalog, listing the Library's holdings by author, title, and subject was issued in November, 1873. In addition, once a month the daily newspapers printed a list of the new books which had been added to the collection. Many books were purchased abroad, as European book prices were cheaper. The type of reading matter selected always concerned Mr. Evans. Although the percentage of fiction circulated was high, he felt strongly that a library supported by taxes was for the use of all the people and that all tastes in reading should be satisfied. While discarding the worst sort of fiction, which was "vicious and immoral," he felt that novels by such popular authors as Mrs. Southworth and Mrs. Holmes "which are merely feeble," should not be eliminated. The publication of the catalog not only increased an already flourishing circulation but also raised the percentage of non-fiction issued. In spite of carefully selected titles on a great variety of subjects, some reflect the period and are amusing by today's standards, such as *Good Morals and Gentle Manners; What Will the World Say; Only a Woman; What Katy Did at School;* and *Fun Better Than Physics.*

By the end of the first year, 101,281 books had been circulated, a figure surpassed by only three other libraries in the country. The book stock consisted of 14,560 volumes, 10,177 obtained by purchase, the remainder through donations. Never before had the literary activity of the town been so lively. Several reading and social clubs were formed to discuss literary topics. There were few households in the city not reached by the educational materials and entertainment provided by the Library.

Mr. Evans was a leader, and his ability was widely recognized. He was considered not only a hard worker, but a man of keen intellect, capable of conceiving original ideas in various intellectual fields. Indianapolis was proud of the new, constantly growing Library which was flourishing under his supervision.

Five years later, in 1877-1878, the circulation had reached 192,076. The small staff of assistants had been enlarged, the number of volumes had increased to three times the number at the time of opening, and almost 15,000 borrowers were registered.

Stressing that it was a matter of great importance that the fleeting literature of our Hoosier heritage should be carefully collected and preserved, Mr. Evans had started a fine collection of books and documents of the early history of the state. He influenced the giving to the library of many valuable items of Indiana history.

When visiting the library in Cincinnati, Mr. Evans had been greatly impressed with a literary club which Mr. Poole had started and wanted to organize a similar one in Indianapolis. After discussing the plan with his friend, John Howland, Mr. Evans and a few other men whom they thought would be interested were asked to meet at Mr. Howland's residence on January 10, 1877. This group initiated The Indianapolis Literary Club. Besides Mr.

By the end of its first year the circulation was surpassed by only three libraries in the country.

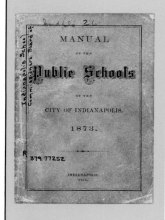

Evans and Mr. Howland those present were William Bartlett, Jonathan Gordon, William Fishback, and George H. Chapman. Mr. Evans was chosen as secretary. Other charter members were Albert Fletcher, Walter Q. Gresham, Livingston Howland, Theophilus Parvin, Ebenezer Sharpe, Luther Waterman, William B. Fletcher, Albert G. Porter, Hanford Edson, J. Henry Kappes, and Addison C. Harris.

The Indianapolis Literary Club has always counted in its membership the leading citizens of the city—governors, senators, judges, artists, such literary men as James Whitcomb Riley, and President of the United States Benjamin Harrison. During Charles Evans' years in Indianapolis, perhaps the brightest spot of all was his association with the kindred spirits whom he met once each week in the Literary Club.

In October, 1876, Mr. Evans received a call to attend a national conference of twenty-eight librarians to be held in Philadelphia. Melvil Dewey was the leading figure behind this meeting, marking the formal organization of the American Library Association. The noted librarian of Boston, Justin Winsor, became the first president. A. R. Spofford, William F. Poole, and Henry Homes were elected vice-presidents, and Melvil Dewey, secretary. The following spring Charles Evans was chosen to be the organization's first treasurer. The news that he had been asked to give a paper at this first conference was favorably received by the Board and the public.

In October, 1951, the American Library Association celebrated its seventy-fifth birthday in Philadelphia. Marian McFadden, Director of the Indianapolis Public Library, and Second Vice President of the Association, was an honored guest and proudly wore the blue ribbon presented to the representatives of those libraries whose librarians had attended the 1876 meeting.

Charles Evans' demeanor, which was usually serious when he was with strangers, was sometimes misunderstood and interpreted as aloofness and arrogance, even though he had a reputation for gaiety among his friends. His drive to accomplish and his terrific energy led him to spend long hours on his job, often day and night, which resulted in his having little time to make friends with members of his Board or with the public. He failed to understand the necessity of cultivating these personal ties. The fine relationship which existed with the advisory committee and the School Board, marked by their ready agreement to almost his every suggestion, began to change. The death of John D. Howland, one of his most loyal supporters, who had been a member of the Citizens' Library Committee from the beginning, was another blow to Charles Evans and accelerated a process of dissatisfaction with his performance that was setting in.

The situation worsened. From the beginning it was apparent that the Library would soon need more space, and a battle ensued over the selection of a new site. When the Sentinel Building was chosen by the Board, Charles Evans vociferously objected and lined up with those who disapproved. This did not endear him to the Board. To add to his difficulties, at this same time he felt it necessary to enforce more stringent rules for library card registration and borrowing and for eliminating noise in the reading rooms. Library patrons became indignant and complained that he was insulting the public.

In a politically-minded city, he antagonized a leading Democrat and

School Board member, Austin Brown. Evans' supporters were soon swayed by political pressure. So, even though all reports of the year 1877-1878 reflected the success of his administration, he was discharged by the Board. On August 31, 1878, he left the library to which he had given all his energy and his mind for the previous six years.

CHAPTER II

Successors to Evans and His Return

ALBERT B. YOHN:
The Second Librarian,
1878-1879

In September, 1878, Albert B. Yohn was appointed successor to Charles Evans. Although not a professional librarian, he was a member of the book-selling firm of Yohn and Porter and a genuine lover of books. Born in Indianapolis in 1847, he was graduated in 1869 from Indiana Asbury College (now DePauw University) and married Addie Ferguson three years later. His father erected a building on the northeast corner of Washington and Meridian Streets known as the Yohn Block. It was here that Albert Yohn established his book-selling business.

The Yohn family had always been active in civic affairs. Albert Yohn's father served both as city commissioner and as a school trustee. The younger Yohn was a member of the Meridian Street Methodist Church, following his father in the position of steward, and serving as recording secretary almost to the time of his death. He was also secretary of the Board of Trustees of DePauw University from 1888 to 1893.

Albert Yohn was a man of many interests and local connections. At a period when the Library Committee felt that Mr. Evans' difficulty had been an over-emphasis on narrow rules and regulations, Mr. Yohn received praise for popularizing the Library. It is interesting to note that although he followed closely the policies of his predecessor and continued work on the catalog, he provided a shelf for browsing, issued book lists on varied subjects, and created for himself a more favorable image than Evans ultimately had succeeded in doing.

Mr. Yohn recommended to the Board a new classification scheme for the collection. He also placed in an accessible alcove the books on Indiana history and by Indiana authors which Mr. Evans had so painstakingly collected, and he increased the usefulness of the reference collection.

Albert Yohn possessed a likeable and pleasing personality and a genuine knowledge and love of books, which made his term a very successful one. However, on June 30, 1879, to the deep regret of the Board, he was forced to resign his position because of ill health. He returned to work in his bookstore and died on April 28, 1893. Mr. Yohn is buried in Crown Hill Cemetery in Indianapolis.

In January, 1876, the Library had moved from the Underhill residence to its second home in the Sentinel Building located on the Circle. The building had been renovated for the use of the School Board and the Library. The main entrance was on the Circle, where over the door, carved in stone, was the word "Library." From this entrance the stairway led to the Library on the second floor.

The governor's mansion was gone from the Circle, and the center was now used as a city park called Circle Park. Surrounding it were Christ Church,

The Sentinel Building on the Circle was the Library's second home, from 1876 to 1879.

On hot summer days, I used to go the the library (overlooking Circle Park), get me an Oliver Optic, a Mayme Reid, or a Harry Castleman and lie under a tree in the park and read.

—Meredith Nicholson

ARTHUR W. TYLER:
The Third Librarian, 1879-1883

The Alvord House

the William H. Morrison residence, the Episcopal dioceses residence, the offices of the *Indianapolis Journal* and the *Indianapolis Sentinel*, Circle Hall, which had been the Second Presbyterian Church, and the new English's Opera House, which was to open in 1880.

Meredith Nicholson describes his visits to the Library where "the reading room windows overlooked Circle Park." "On hot summer days," he says, "I used to go to the library, get me an Oliver Optic, a Mayme Reid, or a Harry Castleman and lie under a tree in the park and read."

The location on the Circle proved popular, but again the library outgrew its quarters, so the Board leased the Alvord residence, planning to move again in September, 1880.

In August, 1879, Arthur Wellington Tyler, a New Englander, was appointed Librarian, coming to Indianapolis from New York City, where he was an assistant in the Astor Library, now a part of the New York Public Library.

Mr. Tyler was born in Pittsfield, Massachusetts, in 1842. His parents were the founders of Maplewood Institute for Women. After graduating from Amherst College in 1867, he became a member of the editorial staff of the *New*

York Mail and later of *Moore's Rural New Yorker*. Later he became Librarian of the Johns Hopkins University Library in Baltimore, going to the Astor Library in 1876. Three years later he moved to Indianapolis as Librarian.

One of the first problems that confronted Mr. Tyler on his arrival in Indianapolis in 1879 was the prospective move from the outgrown quarters in the Sentinel Building. Several options were under consideration by the Board—to remodel and remain in the Sentinel Building, or to move to either the Academy of Music, the Pyle House, or to the Alvord residence. The final decision was to move to the house of E. S. Alvord on the southwest corner of Pennsylvania and Ohio Streets. The Board leased the property for ten years for $3,000 a year, with the option of purchasing it at the end of that period for $50,000.

The handsome, three-story brick residence, with a mansard roof and a yard surrounded by an iron fence, faced Pennsylvania Street. The School Board renovated the house for School offices and built a new, two-story brick and stone addition for the Library. The main entrance of the Library faced on Ohio Street. At the front was an entrance hall with a stairway, and back of it was a long stack room. Behind the stacks was a mending room with a stairway leading up to the office of the Librarian. Also on the second floor was a huge reading room, eighty feet long. A hand-operated book lift moved materials between the first and second floors.

The Reading Room and Delivery Room had wooden ash floors given coats of oil. The Board Room was covered with linoleum, but the office of the Librarian had the best Brussels carpet costing $1.575 per yard from the firm of Albert Gall, the lowest bidder. The woodwork was oak-grained, and the rooms were well lighted by gas fixtures.

The cost of the library addition was approximately $14,000. It made an impressive appearance externally and reportedly was capable of holding 90,000 volumes. This was three times the number actually on hand at the time the Library moved to the new location in September, 1880, its third home in seven years.

It continued to occupy the Alvord House during both Mr. Tyler's and Mr. Hooper's administrations until March, 1893, when its collection of almost 50,000 volumes had outgrown the space originally intended to be adequate for almost twice that number.

During this period, Mr. Tyler was hard at work expanding the Library. He was a born teacher and the staff learned much from him about library work. Although he never got along well with the Board or the public, he was well liked by his staff, who recognized his fine mind and his wide knowledge of books. One of his early accomplishments was the placing of reference libraries in eighteen elementary schools and the expanding of the library into the high school, making reference materials available to hundreds of school children.

He continued work on the printed catalog started by Mr. Evans. Cynthia Routh, the first assistant librarian, was of incalculable help in the work, and Eliza Browning, one of the day assistants, worked long hours on the project. The new author, title, and subject catalog was to cover all acquisitions received from November, 1873 to December, 1881. When completed, 25,000

CHAPTER III

Assistants were hired to help move the Library to the Alvord building in 1880. Standing on the right is future Librarian Eliza Browning.

In no library in the United States are there so many books read in proportion to the population . . . with less than 40,000 books, the circulation last year was 331,247. The fifth largest in the United States, I believe.

—William deM. Hooper
Library Journal
January-February, 1887

21

copies of the finding aid were to be printed. However, the catalog was only finished from A to E during Mr. Tyler's tenure, and the task was left to his successor. Although there was a card catalog, it was not for use by the public. Instead, borrowers were expected to use the printed catalog and supplements and the numerous monthly newspaper clippings, which were hung on the wall, listing the new books purchased by the Library.

Perhaps Mr. Tyler's greatest contribution was his policy of book selection. He submitted a list of books for purchase to the Library Committee and the Citizen's Advisory Committee for their examination and approval. This was generally considered a means of preventing the collection from including any "unwholesome novels."

It is interesting to note library rules and administration in these earlier days. Cards were not to be issued to children under ten years of age. Library hours were set according to the state of the weather. During the hot summer months the Indianapolis Library was open only from 8 a.m. to 1 p.m., and from 6 p.m. to 9 p.m. Mr. Tyler's salary was $1,500 per annum, while the day attendants received $400 the first year, $450 the second, and $500 the third year.

The School Board was never pleased with Mr. Tyler's administration. Despite his proven ability, his knowledge of books and the excellent training he had given the staff, the Board decided that what the Library really needed to head the institution was a business man.

Mr. Tyler resigned in 1883 to go to Plainfield, New Jersey, where he had been appointed to help organize a library for that city. The following year he was appointed Dean of the Teachers' Training College of New York, and later became Librarian at Quincy, Illinois. In 1895 he was named Librarian of the Blackstone Memorial Library at Blandford, Connecticut. Because of poor health he was forced to resign in 1898. During the last years of his life, unable to work, he lived with relatives in Plainfield, New Jersey, until his death on March 27, 1906.

WILLIAM deM. HOOPER: The Fourth Librarian, 1883-1888

William deM. Hooper, a local insurance agent, was chosen by the Board for the position of Librarian in the Spring of 1883. Born in England and a graduate of Oxford University, he was not a man without educational experience, having been Superintendent of Schools in Peru, Indiana, before coming to Indianapolis. Moreover, he had the reputation of being a good business man, the qualification the Board was seeking.

As Mr. Hooper had no experience as a librarian, the responsibility of teaching him library techniques fell to Eliza Browning. Mr. Hooper reported, "She must begin at the beginning and go through everything until I know just what is done and how to do it," and Miss Browning stated she "never did manage to make a real librarian out of him."

All descriptions of him agree that he was affable, a good mixer, and well liked by the public. He was evidently a good speaker too, for the *Indiana Daily Student* in March, 1887, tells about a talk on "Books and Beliefs" he gave "to the delight of an appreciative audience."

He was elected to membership in The Indianapolis Literary Club on May 17, 1886, and in his few years as a resident of Indianapolis he gave several papers on varied subjects— "The Evolution of the Hobby Horse," "A Conversation," "English Lexicographers" and "Flood Myths." According to an account of an American Library Association meeting which he and Mrs. Hooper attended in Milwaukee, he also gave a paper on hobbies in which he expressed the viewpoint, "What should we do if we had no hobbies? A librarian must have a hundred hobbies. Above all he must have a hobby for books—Cultivate hobbies! They are the healthy impulses which refresh one's life." Perhaps that is one reason why he developed the reputation for being an excellent chess player.

Prior to Mr. Hooper's coming, there had been several years in which book circulation had decreased in the city in common with many other libraries. During his first two years as Librarian a forty-one percent increase in circulation was recorded. Part of the credit for this was due to the completion and publication of the catalog from F to Z started by Arthur Tyler. Also, Mr. Hooper issued the first juvenile catalog, consisting of a good selection of books for young readers. Even the *Library Journal* commended Mr. Hooper for the speed with which all this work was accomplished.

Mr. Hooper's theory of book selection was that a library could not supply everything in print, but must consult the wants of its readers and rely on the principles of morality, truth, and sound sense. He felt that though a patron might start with a humble beginning, he could be guided into the habit of better reading with his tastes set on the high roads of self-improvement. Children often love best those books which are just sufficiently above their understanding to excite a wish to climb to their level, he believed. As a result of his interest in children's reading habits, he emphasized work with the schools. Librarians watched the courses of study and prepared material on related topics.

On January 28, 1887, the *Indianapolis Sentinel*, writing about the library, said,

> No busier scene can be found in the city than the Reading Room after school hours or on Saturday. The same scene is to be witnessed on Sundays but with a different class of visitors, composed chiefly of men who have been busy all the week, and of newsboys, bootblacks and urchins who seem to look forward to a quiet time on Sunday over a book with some reading and plenty of pictures.

Unfortunately, from the beginning of his administration Mr. Hooper had to deal with an inadequate budget. As stated above, use of the library had rapidly increased and at the same time the budget had decreased. New books were needed and so were replacements for those that had worn out. Loud criticism was being voiced in the newspapers. One item especially spoke of the dirty, grimy floors. A book which the writer had borrowed looked positively "smallpoxy," the article said. Mr. Hooper's reply was that the condition was unavoidable because of the large crowds constantly using the Library from the time it opened until it closed, the tracking in of dirt from the unpaved streets, the faulty building, and the lack of money for maintenance. In the *Library Journal* for January-February, 1887, he said,

> We find that as a rule the public prefers a dirty copy of a book he wants rather than to go without. In no library in the United States are

No busier scene can be found in the city than the Reading Room after school hours or on Saturday. The same scene is to be witnessed on Sundays but with a different class of visitors, composed chiefly of men who have been busy all the week, and of newsboys, bootblacks and urchins who seem to look forward to a quiet time on Sunday over a book with some reading and plenty of pictures.

—Indianapolis Sentinel
January 28, 1887

there so many books read in proportion to the population and in proportion to the number of volumes on the shelves and nowhere are the means so inadequate to the work. With less than 40,000 books, the circulation last year was 331,247, the fifth largest in the United States, I believe.

As one method of economy, Mr. Hooper established for the first time a bindery within the Library building. The Board allowed him to employ a professional binder and two assistants for eighteen months. At the end of this time, it was discovered that the cost of operation was far less expensive than using any of the local binders, so the bindery was made a permanent department of the Library.

Largely due to the persuasion and influence of Henry Jameson, Chairman of the Library Committee of the Board, a budget increase was eventually granted, but the Board was not satisfied with its choice of a businessman after all. In September, 1888, it dismissed Mr. Hooper without even extending the courtesy of allowing him to resign.

Mr. Hooper was Librarian for only six years. When he left, his next position was as secretary of the Incandescent Light Company. For the next four years he was actuary for the Railway Officials and Conductors Accident Association in Boston, Massachusetts. He later became manager of an accident insurance company in New York City and also edited a paper about accident insurance. *The Indianapolis News*, January 22, 1912, reported that he had died in New York City the previous day and that services would be held in Summit, New Jersey, where he lived. He was believed to be about fifty-five years of age and was survived by his wife, a native of Peru, Indiana, and one child.

Following Mr. Hooper's dismissal, Eliza Browning was appointed Acting Librarian, serving until March, 1889, when Charles Evans returned to take the position from which he had been dismissed in August, 1878.

Against the advice of his friend, William Poole, Mr. Evans demanded a salary of $2,000 if he was to accept the appointment. After much persuasion, the members of the Board agreed, and he returned after an absence of eleven years to again head the Library where he had served as the first librarian.

He began his second administration on March 18, 1889, in an atmosphere of friendliness, flattering notices in the newspapers, and promises of support from the Board of School Commissioners. At this time he was only thirty-eight years old. He had many staunch friends in the community, and even Austin Brown, and others who had condemned him previously, had relented.

He immediately discovered into what a sad state the book collection had fallen, and that there had not been a finding list or catalog published in several years. In order to correct the situation, he requested an increased book budget. Evidently the Board lived up to its promise of support, for they granted him $5,000 for new purchases.

However, as the Library had not been maintained according to his earlier plan, he decided that the whole collection should be reclassified—a stupendous, time-consuming task which members of the Board little understood. He felt it necessary to make new rules which he rigidly enforced. As he had done

Speaking of William deM. Hooper, a local insurance agent appointed as Librarian in 1883, Eliza Browning reported later that "she never did manage to make a real librarian out of him."

CHARLES EVANS RETURNS:
The Fifth Librarian, 1889-1892

in his first administration, he worked such long hours that he left no time to make friends with his Board members or the public. Also, in spite of his truly remarkable record for excellent book selection, criticisms began to be heard regarding his choice of fiction. There was some unhappiness within the staff also, because Miss Browning thought she should have succeeded Mr. Hooper.

During the following year there was a financial recession. The Board criticized all of the increases Mr. Evans requested and cut salaries, not only of the staff, but of the Librarian himself.

The building was again overcrowded and a movement was afloat to build one specifically planned for a library's needs. Finally, when money became available for the project, Mr. Evans turned optimistically to William Poole again, this time for advice in planning a new building. Whatever their ideas were they did not prevail. When Mr. Evans saw the architect's proposed sketches, he thought they were completely wrong and voiced strong criticism of them. The Board paid no attention to his suggestions. Never a diplomat, Evans would not give up his ideas for the building project and called the proposed plan a "botch from beginning to end." Once again he was in trouble with the Board.

Then he made the mistake of surreptitiously seeking a new library position elsewhere. The information leaked out to the already displeased Board. Even though the newspapers supported his struggle, and there was no evidence that he had not proven himself to be the best librarian Indianapolis had had, when the time came, he was not reappointed, leaving his position for the last time in 1892.

After leaving Indianapolis a second time, he went to Enoch Pratt Library in Baltimore; then to Omaha, Nebraska; then to the Newberry Library, the McCormick Theological Seminary, and finally to the Chicago Historical Society. Thus ended Evans' career as a librarian. Possessed of the characteristics of high ability, kindliness and geniality, nevertheless Evans seems to have been a man of great obstinacy who never saw the necessity to cultivate social graciousness or to make friends with his governing boards.

Throughout his years of employment he worked on his stupendous *American Bibliography*, a chronological dictionary of all books, pamphlets, and periodical publications printed in the United States from 1639-1820. At the time of his death in 1935, eleven quarto volumes had been issued, taking the project through 1798. This excellent and invaluable work is the outstanding contribution of Charles Evans to the world of books.

Charles Evans died in Chicago on February 8, 1935, at the age of 85. His much-loved Indianapolis Literary Club held a memorial service in his honor; and Luther Dickerson, then Indianapolis Librarian, summed up his life with the following words, "His long and varied career was characterized by nothing so much as sound scholarship and an innate love for fine writing."

On his eightieth birthday in 1930, the Indianapolis Public Library staff had sent Mr. Evans a telegram and received the following reply, "Warmly appreciate your greetings. I had hoped to read the New Testament in the original Greek upon this happy day; but life is so short and there is so much to do before leaving it, that all the Greek I know is *Goe mou sas agapo* - My life I love thee." Scholar and philosopher he was, even to the end.

Charles Evans called the proposed plan for the new library a "botch from beginning to end— an abortion born of ignorance and prejudice, and fostered in the person of the architect, by stupidity."

His long and varied career was characterized by nothing so much as sound scholarship and an innate love for fine writing.

—Luther Dickerson, speaking at The Indianapolis Literary Club Memorial Service for Charles Evans in 1935.

Eliza Gordon Browning

For a successor to Evans the Board decided to look within the library staff and this time Eliza Browning received the appointment as Librarian. Eliza Browning, a young woman only twenty-three years old, had been first brought in on May 12, 1880, as a day assistant. She came just after the arrival of Arthur Tyler as the new Librarian and the leasing of the Alvord property. She worked without pay for many months with the exception of the week in September, 1880, when she was paid $2 a day for work involved in moving to the new library and a few other times when substituting for absent staff members.

The Sixth Librarian, 1892-1917

She was truly a native of Indianapolis from the point of view of loyalty and her contribution to the building of the community. Although her family lived in Fortville, Indiana, when Eliza was born September 23, 1856, they moved to Indianapolis soon after. Her father died when Eliza was only five years old and her mother when she was just nineteen.

At least five of Miss Browning's forefathers had fought in the Revolution, and one in the War of 1812. Her maternal grandfather, William J. Brown, was a prominent state legislator, Secretary of State, a member of Congress, and editor of the *Indianapolis Sentinel*. Her great-grandmother Brown was the first woman physician in Indiana. With this background it is little wonder that she was always interested in historical and patriotic organizations and in genealogical research.

As she expressed it, she wanted the library to be *"a live thing in the whole town . . . and a community aroused to the value of an intelligent use of the library."*

Several characteristics contributed to her success as a librarian. First and foremost, she had loved books and reading from earliest childhood. Secondly, although she was a woman of forceful personality, great energy and executive ability, she also possessed great understanding, and was kind, sympathetic, ever ready to listen to knotty problems. As an administrator she showed a ready wit and tact which often helped to solve complex situations. She could often find a humorous story to illustrate her point and to lead people to her way of thinking. Very articulate, she wrote and spoke well and was persuasive in expressing her viewpoint.

Although the Library remained her paramount interest, Eliza Browning was a member of the Fortnightly Literary Club, The Portfolio, the Indiana Historical Society and the Society of Indiana Pioneers. She was also a member of the Cornelia Cole Fairbanks Chapter of the Daughters of the American Revolution, served as its state historian and in 1903 was co-founder, with Mrs. John Newman Carey, of the General Arthur St. Clair Chapter in Indianapolis. She was on the board or council of many organizations, among them the Girl Scouts, YWCA, and the Children's Museum. An organizer of the Indiana Library Association, she was twice its president, and above all was a devoted member of Christ Episcopal Church. Consequently, she was widely known not only throughout the state but also the nation. Her many accomplishments are

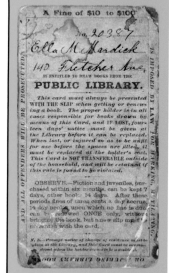

A borrower's card from 1885.

listed in the *National Cyclopedia of American Biography*.

From the time she entered library work, she began learning the rules and regulations, including how to tabulate circulation and count library visitors. In one report she related a story about the latter procedure.

There was a tin box with two compartments. One was filled with navy beans and as people came in I counted them by putting a corresponding number of beans in the empty compartment. One night the boy on duty forgot to put the lid on the box and a rat ate the beans. The worst of it was the boy had forgotten to count them. So the statistics were inaccurate for that day.

As noted earlier, at the time Miss Browning became Librarian, the Library had a book catalog which the public and staff consulted. The public was not allowed to use the card catalog, and new books were announced in newspaper columns which were clipped and hung high on the wall for people to read. Short adults and children needed a ladder to read them. She realized that a catalog system for the public was needed, and by 1907 the card catalog was opened to the public, as well as the books shelved in the stacks. A monthly bulletin was issued which listed all the new books and included a bibliography of the best books on timely subjects. It was no longer necessary to print the book catalog, and it was discontinued.

Children's Room, Central Library, 1914.

Children's books were separated for the first time in 1899 in an alcove especially set aside for their use. The improvised room was provided with low shelves stocked with 7,500 well-chosen books and was supervised by two librarians, Ella Saltmarsh and her assistant, Mary Henthorne. Story hours began, attracting hundreds of youngsters. A school reference department was also established, with responsibility for work with seventh and eighth grades and the first two years of high school.

Eliza Browning had shared in the growth of the Library from the time it moved from the Sentinel Building to the Alvord House, and as Librarian she was involved in the planning and building of another new home, a big responsibility for a new administrator.

The Library moved in 1893, this time to the first building erected primarily for its own use, although the school offices were also housed there until 1906. It stood at the southwest corner of Ohio and Meridian Streets, fronting on Meridian. When it was finished, it was considered so spacious that it would be adequate for the growth of the Library for many years to come.

The Board of School Commissioners had secured the help of Professor William Ware of New York as consulting architect. As finally conceived the library was built of Indiana oolitic limestone in the Greek classical style and was acclaimed by the newspapers as being "a model of beauty in architecture."

Above the front entrance was a large group of three figures representing the spirit of knowledge embodied in books—Science, Art, and Literature. The center male figure representing Science held high the torch of enlightenment in one hand and the palm of achievement in the other, while beside him were the owl and globe, attributes of science. At the right of the standing figure of Science was seated a female figure representing Literature, holding a book and pencil. At her feet was a bust of Longfellow. The figure of Art was seated at the left of Science, holding a drawing board; and at her side was a bust of Michelangelo. A local newspaper commented, "Cast in bronze, this statue represents allegorically the spirit of knowledge embodied in the thousands of books in the Library." The sculptor was Richard W. Bock of Chicago, who had done outstanding work in Omaha, St. Louis, and Chicago as well as in Indianapolis. He worked closely with the eminent architect Frank Lloyd Wright.

It should be noted that this bronze statue grouping was saved when the building was demolished in 1967. It was placed in the west lawn of the Central Library in September, 1981. It had been given to the Marion County Historical Society and stored at Crown Hill Cemetery at the time it was removed from the building; while in storage several of the smaller pieces were lost or stolen, so the grouping seen today is incomplete.

Although the exterior of the building was lauded as beautiful, the interior was considered "something to be lived with" in terms of functionality. Five prospective plans had been submitted to Professor Ware, and the one by the Dayton, Ohio, firm of Williams and Otter was chosen. Charles Evans, Librarian at the time, said a library should be planned from the inside out, and denounced it as "an abortion born of ignorance and prejudice, and fostered in the person of the architect, by stupidity." To his great disgust, his suggestions were ignored.

One of the gravest mistakes in the interior plan was the stairway. Leading from the center front entrance was a steep staircase to the second floor, which made it necessary for librarians to walk many extra miles each year. Besides the inconvenience, the rooms were so cut up that the library had outgrown its quarters before it moved in. In addition, no provision was made for a children's room. One of the attractive features in the new building, however, was a large fireplace which covered almost half of a wall of the circulation room.

A bond issue of $100,000 had been authorized for the building, but the final cost of the project amounted to almost $200,000.

The library building, also housing the school offices, was opened to the public on October 24, 1893, with a book collection of approximately 52,000 volumes. When the school offices moved out in 1906, the children's room was moved from the alcove on the second floor downstairs to a room of its own.

By 1909 overcrowding had become so serious that Miss Browning was begging for a new library. The wheels began to turn, and after eight years of planning and construction, in 1917 the Library prepared to move to the new Central Library on St. Clair Street. In the ensuing years the old building became the home of the Business Library (1918-1966), the Teacher's Special Library (1921-1962), and the school offices. The building was sold and demolished in 1967, when the school offices moved to the new Education Center. The Hilton Hotel currently stands on the site of the old library.

As early as 1896 Miss Browning realized the need for branch libraries to implement library expansion. The Library Committee of the Board had received a petition asking for a branch on the north side of the city, and a committee appointed to study the request reported that the borrowers found

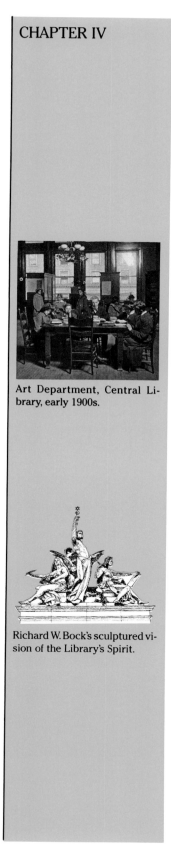

CHAPTER IV

Art Department, Central Library, early 1900s.

Richard W. Bock's sculptured vision of the Library's Spirit.

A new branch library—the gift of Andrew Carnegie.

An early storefront library, 1901.

the trip to the Library by bicycle and horse cart most inconvenient. The committee recommended the establishment of four libraries in the northeast, northwest, southeast, and southwest sections of the city and deposit stations at other convenient locations. As a result, four branches were opened in December, 1896. Branch No. 1 was located at Udell and Lulu (later Clifton) Streets; Branch No. 2 at East Tenth Street and Brookside Avenue; Branch No. 3 at Linden and Woodlawn; and Branch No. 4 at 548 South Meridian Street. Branch No. 5 was opened in April, 1897, in the newly annexed West Indianapolis, located near White River on Morris Street. Although these branches started in remodeled stores or houses, they were made as attractive as possible with displays, popular magazines and good book collections.

Eliza Browning was determined that the Library should reach out and serve the whole community. As she herself expressed it, she wanted the library to be

> *a live thing in the whole town. There should be hearty cooperation between the library and the community. In an ideal library and community, conditions result in a situation rather like a triangle; the trustees with their authority under the law to make the library possible and to maintain it; the library housed in a good building with good equipment and methods of administration; and third, a community aroused to the value of an intelligent use of the library.*

To this end she bent her energies.

There were many library procedures which concerned her, among them the cumbersome method of circulating books. During her first year as Librarian she visited libraries in the east where she found many new ideas, especially in Newark, New Jersey. The "Newark System" for circulating books was soon initiated in Indianapolis. No longer was all the information written at the time the book was taken out, but rather, identifying cards were placed in the books when they were prepared for the collection, and the attendant merely wrote on the card the borrower's number and stamped the date.

Collections of fifty books were placed in each elementary school for the use of the seventh and eighth grades, and an assistant was sent from the Central Library once a week to administer them. Also, ten delivery stations were started in drug stores and fire stations.

In 1909 Miss Browning began planning for several additional branch libraries. Her plans included a request for funds from American philanthropist Andrew Carnegie. Knowing that Carnegie was recognized as a generous donor to libraries, and that throughout his life he had carried a deep reverence for learning because of his own lack of formal education, Miss Browning decided that he was a good prospect to come to her aid. Her foresight was well justified; eventually her hard work resulted in a gift of $120,000 from Mr. Carnegie.

Realizing those fine results, however, required all of Miss Browning's originality and persistence. After many hours of work with the Educational Committee of the Commercial Club, a group of influential citizens, Miss Browning had sent a letter to Mr. Carnegie describing the Library's great need, only to receive a curt answer that Mr. Carnegie would deal only with the mayor of the city. The Commercial Club then interceded with Mayor Charles Bookwalter to make the request of Mr. Carnegie.

Subsequently, an editorial appeared in one of the local newspapers condemning the request to Mr. Carnegie, stating that his money was "tainted" because he had acquired it by way of a monopoly which had reduced his workers to a state of servitude. Miss Browning went to the editor to explain the imperative need for library expansion and to convince him of the great value of the Library as an educational institution, especially its work of teaching foreigners the customs and language of their country. As this problem was of interest and concern to him, he agreed to see the committee from the Commercial Club. As a result of this meeting, the project went forward with no further objections from the press.

The money became available very quickly with no provisions except that the Library administration was to guarantee the upkeep of the buildings. The gift of $120,000 was to build six libraries. The first, Hawthorne Branch, was built in 1910 at 170 Mount Street. The architect was August Bohlen. This same year a second branch, East Washington, was built at 2822 East Washington Street with Herbert Foltz and Wilson Parker as architects, and the third, West Indianapolis Branch, at 1926 West Morris Street, with Robert Frost Daggett as the architect.

In 1912 the fourth Carnegie branch, known as Branch No.6, Spades Park Branch, was built on ground adjoining Spades Park. The architect was Wilson Parker. In 1914 the fifth, Madison Avenue Branch, was built facing Noble Park. E. G. Graves designed the building, but was forced to discontinue because of ill health; the work was completed by Robert Frost Daggett.

The Library ultimately received only $100,000.00 of the original grant of $120,000.00 given in 1909 to build six branch libraries. The remaining $20,000 was never requested after the fifth branch was completed in 1914. The sixth branch then, was never built, reportedly due to the high cost. In 1919 Librarian Charles Rush attempted to secure the remaining $20,000.00 from the Carnegie Corporation, but Library archives indicate that it was not until 1922 that he was notified by the Carnegie Corporation that the Library had waited too long to request the funds and the account had been closed. By 1922 the Carnegie Corporation had changed its policy and was no longer granting funds for the construction of library buildings.

Miss Browning had always felt that libraries were logical neighborhood and social centers. She stated, "Where else may old and young, rich and poor, men, women and children of all ages, condition and color find a welcome at one and the same time and get as much?" Believing that bringing the public together in meetings was the best way to make people discover that the library was one of their necessities, she established auditoriums in all newly built branches.

Eliza Browning was never satisfied with the status quo, and she was always seeking to expand Library horizons. Prior to the Carnegie gift other branches had been opened—Brightwood and Irvington Branches in 1901; McCarty Branch in 1905, and Illinois Branch in 1908. By 1916, when the Library was preparing to move into its new building on St. Clair Street, it was comprised of the Central Library, five Carnegie branches, seven "sub-

Spades Park Library, one of just two Carnegie buildings still in use today in Indianapolis.

Girl's gymnastics class, Hawthorne Library, 1910.

Where else may old and young, rich and poor, men, women, children of all ages, condition and color find a welcome at one and the same time and get as much?

—Eliza G. Browning, speaking of neighborhood libraries

The life of a library attendant was by no means beer and skittles.

—Eliza G. Browning

Young men kept fit at their neighborhood branch library, 1910.

branches" (North Indianapolis, Haughville, Prospect, Brightwood, Irvington, McCarty, and Illinois) and book collections in the schools. There had been a steady growth in book stock from a total of 138,852 in 1909 to 207,200 in 1916. The circulation statistics had risen correspondingly from 451,414 in 1909 to 701,049 in 1916.

Branch libraries have always had great influence in their communities, and the ability and temperament of the librarian seem to have been great factors in bringing this about. As Miss Browning herself said, the life of a library "attendant," as they were then called, was "by no means beer and skittles." In her branch library she was responsible for the care of the building, and she must see that regulations were carried out. She needed enough judgment to know how to discipline and when to call for assistance if things were too rough. In the earlier days in some localities, there were branch visitors "who persisted in confusing branch libraries with rescue missions, and there was nothing that appealed like breaking up a mission," Miss Browning commented.

As an example, Miss Browning told the story of one Saturday when a substitute was sent to take charge of a branch. During the afternoon a tough-looking young man came in and confronted her with "Be youse the new 'un?" When she said "no", he said, "Well you know the fellers allus 'nitiates a new 'un. There isn't much to youse anyway and you'd be clean snowed under." Miss Browning had told her what to do in case of trouble. Saturday came, and five big boys seventeen or eighteen years old came in, noisily demanding the *News*. The attendant explained that the library took only one issue, and took it from the rack and divided it among them. After looking it over for a few minutes, the biggest boy came over and demanded something about pirates. Again the attendant found an attractive article for him in a magazine. Soon he got up and after saying, "Gosh boys, there's nothin' doin', let's git," he led his friends out.

After the library closed and the attendant went out to catch a streetcar home, there were the boys waiting for her. They told her they worked at the stockyards. When she replied how pleased she was that after working hard all day they were ambitious enough to come to the library to improve themselves, they promised to come the next night to take out library cards. "And this was the "new 'un's" initiation," illustrating the ingenuity and courage needed by a library assistant.

Miss Browning knew the value of training her staff. One of her first acts as Librarian was to set up a personnel grading system. She worked out an examination covering general literature which was given to all applicants—a four hour written test. Despite such rigorous demands imposed upon would-be employees and those who were already "attendants," the records indicate that in 1896 assistants were paid only $300 a year and were required to work six days a week and often on Sunday.

One of this Librarian's most popular innovations during this period was the establishment of the Duplicate Rental Collection. This collection supplied the popular new fiction for the public at a rental of one cent a day. In this way as many as twenty copies of the most sought-after books could be bought without diverting too great a sum from the book fund. After the popularity waned or the books had paid for themselves, they were transferred to the open collection.

Another new service was the opening in 1898 of the first Medical Department for the use of doctors, nurses, and others in the medical field. It began with the loan of a fine collection of books from the Indianapolis Medical Association.

But, as always, space for the ever-growing collection was the most urgent concern which the Librarian must address. In her 1909 annual report Miss Browning complained that the Library, which was built to house eighty thousand books, already was packed with one hundred and forty thousand volumes. "Not only is the housing inadequate and crowded, but conditions are most unsatisfactory. The Library is getting too big for its britches."

At the time the Library was built in 1893, there had been a good deal of dissension over the architect's plans, including the objections of Charles Evans to the plans. The interior was poorly designed and not functional from the start. Many individuals, however, had thought it would be large enough for many years to come. Included among them was the author Meredith Nicholson, who, in his speech at the dedication of the new building on St. Clair Street on October 7, 1917, "ate crow" for his earlier lack of judgment in estimating the Library's space needs.

The new Library which had opened in 1893 was really outgrown before it was finished, and as early as 1908 the School Board had purchased the property at the northeast corner of Meridian and St. Clair Streets as a partial site for yet another new Central Library. Then, in 1911, James Whitcomb Riley gave the Board land which he owned at the northwest corner of Pennsylvania and St. Clair Streets to be used as part of the site for the new library.

Once more Miss Browning was involved in planning and building a new Central Library and moving to another new location, the fourth since she became a staff member in 1880. She actively participated in every phase of planning, from approval of room space allowed by the architects for the various departments, to furniture and equipment for these departments.

The move from Meridian Street to St. Clair Street was accomplished smoothly and systematically. Shelves were designed for specific subjects, and wooden crates were packed so that the books could be shelved with the least difficulty. In all of this, Miss Browning gave her wise guidance.

When at last the beautiful new building was ready to be opened, Miss Browning, who had served as Librarian for twenty-five years, decided to step down from that position and become assistant to her successor, Charles E. Rush. She continued in this role until her death on May 18, 1927, having given forty-seven years of devoted service to the Indianapolis Public Library.

To sum up the admiration expressed by many at the time of her death, Mr. Rush said, "Faithfulness, loyalty, friendship and service—with these four—a public servant can truly serve his fellow men. In proof of this, witness the life and service of Eliza Gordon Browning."

CHAPTER IV

Not only is the housing inadequate and crowded, but conditions are most unsatisfactory. The library is getting too big for its britches.

—Eliza G. Browning, 1909 Annual Report, speaking of the Central Library built in 1892

Faithfulness, loyalty, friendship and service—with these four—a public servant can truly serve his fellow men. In proof of this, witness the life and service of Eliza Gordon Browning.

—Charles E. Rush, expressed in admiration at the time of her death, May, 1927

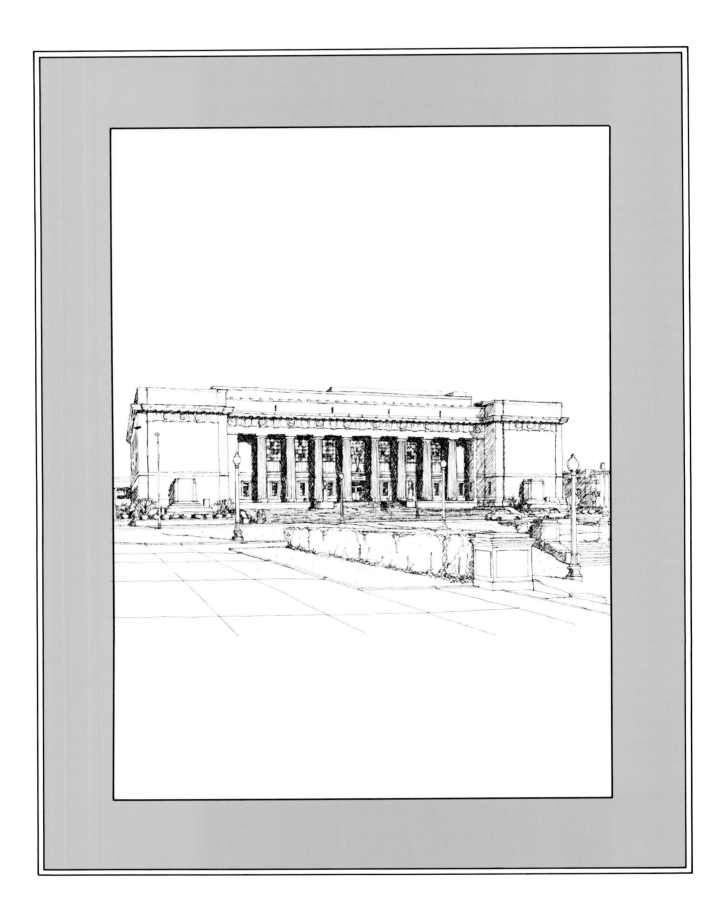

Entering The Modern Era

Acquiring the wide, well situated site on St. Clair Street for the new Central Library took several years. With acquisition of the Riley gift of land, the Board still needed to finish out the half square from Meridian to Pennsylvania Streets, and from St. Clair to the alley on the north. The Board had held a lease since 1908 on the Philander Fitzgerald property which fronted on Meridian Street, and comprised most of the entire southwest quarter of the block. They authorized a $125,000 bond issue in July, 1911, to be used for the purchase of the Fitzgerald property and the remaining houses and lots needed to complete the half square.

With acquisition of the site completed, in 1913 the Board solicited competitive proposals for a new building from interested architects. H. Van Buren Magonigle, a New York architect, was asked to make suitable arrangements for the competition. The winner was Paul Cret, a member of the Philadelphia firm of Cret, Zantzinger, Borie and Medary. The members of the Board who had worked on the project and made the final decision have been honored by a plaque placed in the entry hall of the new Central Library. It bears the names of Dr. Frank Morrison, John H. Emrich, William M. Taylor, Joseph A. McGowan, and Miss Mary E. Nicholson.

Paul Cret was already an architect of note, and besides practicing his profession, was Professor of Architecture at the University of Pennsylvania. When World War I broke out he returned to his native France, served as a lieutenant with the famous "Blue Devils" and won a *Croix de Guerre* for bravery. The plans for the Library were changed and "blue pencilled" in the trenches and crossed the ocean many times for the architect's final approval. After the plans were approved, the firm of George A. Fuller and Company secured the construction contract.

On March 24, 1916, the Library celebrated the laying of the cornerstone. A grandstand to seat three hundred guests was built for the event, and five hundred invitations were mailed to officials and prominent citizens. Members of the Board of School Commissioners, past and present, were honored guests. South of the grandstand, St. Clair Park formed a natural stadium for the audience. A chorus of 1,000 school children, under the leadership of Edward Bailey Birge, director of music for the public schools, sang "The Messiah of the Nations," written for the occasion by James Whitcomb Riley, with music composed by John Phillip Sousa. As Riley was not well enough to attend, he was represented on the program by his nephew, Edmund Eitel. Joseph Keller, President of the School Board, spoke, with the main address given by Meredith Nicholson.

The contents of the cornerstone included a list of books in the library by Indiana authors, a map of Indianapolis indicating the locations of all the

The Philander Fitzgerald House, St. Clair and Meridian Streets, 1908.

Facing page—
Sketch by K.P. Singh

35

Classically designed bronze lamps stand at the Library's entrance.

Not only Greek in form but penetratingly Greek in spirit . . . it is as perfect a piece of classical architecture as I have ever seen. I cannot think of any similar structure in any part of the world that goes beyond it. . .

—Ralph Adams Cram, speaking of the new Central Library in *Architectural Forum*, September, 1918

libraries, a plan of the new building, photographs of the uncompleted building taken prior to the time of the ceremony, pictures of all library buildings, a copy of the first printed catalog, the *Books Bulletin*, 1904-1916; book lists, and a United States flag presented by Captain Wallace Foster, who according to the 1916 Indianapolis City Directory, was listed as "Patriotic Publisher and Manufacturer Agent for High School Silk and Bunting Flags and Decorations."

Included also were an original unpublished manuscript of a poem by Riley titled "No Boy Knows" and a first edition of his *Rhymes of Childhood*, bound in blue morocco; a copy of *The Hoosiers* by Meredith Nicholson, the legislation concerning the establishment and history of the Library from its beginning, reports of its operation, and lists of its Board and Trustees, members of the advisory committees, librarians and employees in 1873 and 1916, and the first and latest library reports.

In addition, there were samples of all library supplies in use in 1916, pictures of prominent buildings, programs of literary clubs, the yearbook and constitution of the Matinee Musicale; copies of the *Indianapolis Times*, *Star*, and *News*, coins and postage stamps of the day, club papers on Indiana writers by Marietta Finley and Cora Campbell Barnett, Max Hyman's *Centennial History*, a scrapbook made by Abram C. Shortridge, and finally, an invitation to the laying of the cornerstone and a program of the event.

According to the *Indianapolis Star*, March 25, 1916, a copy of a photograph of James Whitcomb Riley and Governor Samuel Ralston was received too late as the box had already been sealed. "The picture, held down by weights, was placed on the lid of the box." The Star dramatically stated, "the box . . . is now sealed within the corner stone until earthquake, fire or deliberate design causes it to be exposed to public view." The building, which faced St. Clair Street, was placed in the center of a park-like setting with a garden at each side and a wall to give the whole charm and unity.

The design of the building was executed in Greek Doric style, described by Ralph Adams Cram, writing in the September, 1918, issue of *Architectural Forum*, as "not only Greek in form but penetratingly Greek in spirit." He continued, "I cannot recall any building in modern times that is more notable in its subtlety and its distinction. The interior is in every respect up to the level of the exterior. Nothing is overdone or wasted and the enormous success of the result follows from proportions that are fine and sensitive to the point of perfection . . . This Indianapolis library is one of the most distinctive and admirable contributions to architecture that have been made in America . . . It is as perfect a piece of classical architecture as I have ever seen. I cannot think of any similar structure in any part of the world that goes beyond it."

The building subsequently was selected as one of eighteen outstanding architectural accomplishments to be included in *Masterpieces of Architecture In The United States*, compiled by Edward Hoak and Willis S. Church, and published by Charles Scribner's Sons in 1930.

The building stands today much the same as it was designed nearly eighty years ago. The exterior is fittingly of Indiana limestone built on a base of Vermont marble, with carved stone cornices adding to its beauty. A broad expanse of steps leads up to the entrance, which is framed with impressive Greek columns. At each side of the entrance is a bronze lamp. The bronze tablets on each side of the massive wrought iron gates bear the inscription, "The gates are the gift of the children of Indianapolis in loving remembrance of their friend James Whitcomb Riley." The swinging doors into the main room read, "Friendly Books Welcome You."

Inscribed in the stonework above the windows, both inside and outside the building, are the names of seventy-six famous literary men and women. The name selection committee members were Demarchus C. Brown, Chairman; Meredith Nicholson, Evans Woollen, Carl Lieber, Thomas C. Howe, Jacob P. Dunn, Mary E. Nicholson, Grace Julian Clark, and Eliza Browning.

What a major task the choice of names was! Suggestions and advice were sought from Indianapolis authors Booth Tarkington, Meredith Nicholson, James Whitcomb Riley, and from leading citizens in other fields. The responses were as varied as the people solicited. For example, one says in suggesting the name of Victor Hugo, "Victor Hugo—the great French poet and novelist," while another replies, "Hugo—have to have, but don't want," and Tarkington speaks of "That terrible fraud Hugo." Thomas Howe said, "I should like very much to vote for Victor Hugo for one of the ten names on the front." The name Browning was included without question. In many minds it was to indicate Robert, but Riley wanted it to be Elizabeth Barrett. Riley's own name is above the door on the Pennsylvania Street side in an inscription carved in the stone, "This door opens on land given to the people of Indianapolis by James Whitcomb Riley."

Some of the comments regarding the selection of the names are most amusing. A letter from Booth Tarkington says, "In the name of Christmas presents for Village Aunts, leave off dear, good Dr. VanDyke as the sole living story-man! He's a fine little feller but has *nothing* to do with the art of writing." Throughout the period of selection, the opinions were numerous and so strong as to be almost violent. Some of the names were selected for very biased reasons, and criticism was plentiful. Many meetings and countless hours went into the final selection. The names were selected by vote. If Keats got nine votes and Shelley only eight, Shelley was out and Keats won, and then votes would be taken again. Who won the war insofar as local participants were concerned is questionable. Hoping the controversy will not start again, we present the authors who won final selection.

The frieze in the Main Room, beginning at the northwest corner, contains the following names—Herodotus, Aristotle, Marcus Aurelius, Moliere, Bacon, Grotius, Milton, Franklin, Kant, Schiller, Carlyle, Hugo, Darwin, Tennyson, Dickens, and Tolstoi.

Around the balcony corridors, beginning at the southwest corner, are these names: Aesop, Sappho, Aeschylus, Plutarch, Omar Khayyam, Luther, Descartes, Locke, Spinoza, S. Johnson, Goldsmith, Burke, Lessing, Humboldt, Austen, Moore, Grimm, Shelley, Bryant, Keats, Heine, Balzac, Bancroft, George Sand, Hawthorne, Agassiz, Stowe, Mommsen, Meredith, and Stevenson.

Those names carved on the outside of the building, beginning at the north corner on the Meridian Street side proceeding around to the north corner on the Pennsylvania Street side are—Chaucer, Burns, Wordsworth, Scott, Macaulay, Browning, Thackeray, G. Eliot, Ruskin, Homer, Isaiah, Plato, Vergil, Dante, Cervantes, Shakespeare, Voltaire, Goethe, Emerson, Irving,

A glimpse of the 1000-voice chorus performing at the cornerstone laying ceremony, March 24, 1916.

CHAPTER V

Indianapolis Public Library
Laying of the Corner stone
March 24, 1916

Program

Song—Messiah of Nations James Whitcomb Riley
    Music by J. P. Sousa
Address President Joseph H. Keller
Song—America the Beautiful Katherine Lee Bates
Laying of Cornerstone Edward Eitel
    Representing James Whitcomb Riley
Address Meredith Nicholson
Song—America

Choruses by the Children of the
Indianapolis Public Schools
Under Direction of Edward B. Birge

Longfellow, Whittier, Poe, Lowell, Whitman, Wallace, Twain, and Riley. Relegated to the north side of the building are just two authors, Bunyan and Lanier.

Included in the list are philosophers, scientists, naturalists, historians, essayists, prophets, theologians, poets, dramatists, and novelists. They are all there, drawn from all over the world, and in time from the earliest Greeks through the nineteenth century, barely spilling over into the twentieth, with Riley, a special exception being the "youngest." He died in 1916 before the new library was completed.

As one enters the building today a marble stairway to the right leads downstairs to the children's division or Riley Room for Young People. Other rooms in this area in 1917 were the Teacher's Room, used for school work with teachers, and Cropsey Auditorium, named for Miss Nebraska Cropsey, the first supervisor of elementary school work. She is commemorated by a plaque placed just inside the auditorium entrance.

From the left of the main entrance, originally a corridor led to a row of offices, facing the Meridian Street side of the building. In 1975 the administrative offices moved from this area to the new annex and the Arts Division took over this space following extensive renovation of the area to make it suitable for public service.

The great room directly ahead of the main entrance is one hundred feet in length, forty-five in width, and forty-five in height. Its walls are of Indiana limestone, Caen stone and Indiana white oak.

At either end of the room is a flight of broad stairs of Maryland marble. They lead to an encircling book-lined gallery which overlooks the spacious room below, whose walls are also completely lined with books. Two huge vases of beautiful Vermont marble crown the top of each flight of stairs.

Over the inner door at the entrance is a clock, beneath which were inscribed the words:

> Time by minutes slips away
> First the hour and then the day
> Small the daily loss appears
> Yet it soon amounts to years

The most ornamental feature of the room is its ceiling. Designed by C. C. Zantzinger, painted in oil on small canvases, it tells in color the history of Indiana. It is Pompeian in style. At the outer edge is a grape border, symbolic of the fertility of the state. Another border is of oak, representing the white oak tree, for which Indiana was at one time supplier to the world market, and also depicting the strength of the state. Between these two borders are two sets of paintings, one reproducing famous printers' colophons and the other representing typical flora and fauna of the state. Painted medallions bear the signs of the Zodiac, while others trace the development of the written language— the Rosetta Stone, a papyrus roll, the Gutenberg press, and a modern steel printing press. A series of bas-relief plaster plaques picture the early history of Indiana. At the four corners are plaques of Conestoga wagons, and at the ends and sides there are others depicting treaties with the Indians, early French explorers and early pioneers.

The beautiful circular light fixtures are of solid bronze, thirty feet in diameter and decorated with the same vibrant colors as the ceiling. Even the windows have gold leaf rosettes as decorations. The floor is of polished cork. Nothing in the room is overdone, yet no detail is undone. The total impression of the large room is a happy combination of architectural beauty and bookish atmosphere.

At the top of each staircase are large reading rooms. At the time the Library was built, the one on the west was designated the Reference Room, and since 1917 the East Reading Room has housed the art and music departments, the genealogy collection, the medical collection and the newspaper and periodical division. The rooms have beautiful wood paneling above the oak bookcases, and large leaded glass windows.

The dedication of the new building, which Arthur Bostwick described in his address as "A Temple of the Book," took place on October 7, 1917, the birthday of James Whitcomb Riley. The program was as follows:

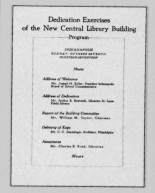

> *Music*
> *Address of Welcome*
> > *Mr. Joseph H. Keller, President of the*
> > *Indianapolis Board of School Commissioners*
> *Address of Dedication*
> > *Mr. Arthur Bostwick, Librarian*
> > *St. Louis Public Library*
> *Report of the Building Committee*
> > *Mr. William M. Taylor, Chairman*
> *Delivery of Keys*
> > *Mr. C. C. Zantzinger, Architect, Philadelphia*
> *Acceptance*
> > *Mr. Charles E. Rush, Librarian*
> *Music*

Some years later there was considerable discussion by the public because no statues had ever been placed on the pedestals in front of the building. William Taylor, Chairman of the Building Committee, said at the time of the dedication, "The building is not entirely complete until the two great pedestals on the south side are occupied by the statues originally designed to be put there."

Statues had been planned for this location, but by the time the building was completed, costs had soared. The $500,000 bond issue would not cover everything, and the statues were postponed. The last building bonds were paid off in the 1950s; in the meantime, the interest paid through the years had doubled the original cost finally to around $1,000,000. There was hope that a public-spirited citizen would donate funds to complete the statues, but to date that has not happened.

Though architecturally the building was, and is, a masterpiece, as a functioning library there are flaws which have appeared through the years. To overcome these and to provide for ever expanding services, some of the quiet beauty of the interior has had to be sacrificed. Fortunately, no changes have been made to the basic configuration of the building's exterior except for the addition which was constructed to the rear of the building in 1963.

CHAPTER V

In 1955 the Board purchased for $60,000 the large brick house just beyond the alley north of the Central Library and facing Pennsylvania Street. This old structure had quite a history of its own. In 1885 the Girls Classical School, which had been founded in 1882, occupied the building. Mrs. May Wright Sewell was the owner and principal of the school, which was attended by the daughters of many of the prominent families in the city, and she herself was probably the best known local woman of her time, engaged in every type of activity, including women's rights, letter writing, and the founding of women's clubs.

In later years the house was occupied by the Caroline Scott Harrison Chapter of the Daughters of the American Revolution. When the DAR decided to move to a new location, the Chapter offered the Library an opportunity to buy the old property. While the building was not really suitable for library purposes, it was remodeled enough to accommodate the Schools Division, which was working under very crowded conditions in the Central Library building. Then, when funds were available, the old house was razed, the alley separating it from the library was closed, and an annex, comprised of a basement and first floor, was built. The additional floors were not added to the annex until 1975.

Gates at the Library's entrance were given by the city's school children in memory of James Whitcomb Riley.

Charles E. Rush

Charles E. Rush served as Head Librarian from the time the Library moved into the new Central Library facility in 1917 until 1928. A birthright Quaker and a lifelong member of the Friends Church, he was born on a farm in Fairmount, Indiana, on March 23, 1885.

He realized early in his life that he would never make a farmer. Displaying a keen sense of humor he said, "Like all great men I was born on a farm, but from the beginning my size was against me. None as small as I am could ever make a good farmer." After graduating from Fairmount Academy, he went to Earlham College, where he received his first taste of library work while employed part-time in the college library. He turned for a while to teaching, but said, "Suddenly it came over me that I would be a librarian . . . I wonder what it is that decides things like that for us—fate, destiny, or just a whim?"

He graduated from Earlham in 1905, then went to the University of Wisconsin and, after two years library training in the New York State Library School, in 1908 he received his Bachelor of Library Science degree. In 1910 he married Lionne Adsit, and they became the parents of three daughters: Alison, Frances, and Myra. Mr. Rush had gained much practical experience in library work during his college years and immediately after receiving his professional degree became the Head Librarian of the Jackson, Michigan, Public Library. He then filled similar positions in St. Joseph, Missouri, and Des Moines, Iowa. From there he came to Indianapolis to assume the position of Librarian.

Although an intense individualist, whose motto, of true Quaker character, was "God expects every man to do his own thinking," he always enjoyed working with groups. A born organizer, he was not easily defeated, having "an unwavering assurance of victory in the midst of travail." He was highly regarded by his staff and the Board, and his friendly, outgoing manner and a love of people earned him many friends. He was a tireless worker and inspired his co-workers to do their best, stressing staff cooperation and above all, service to the public.

Mr. Rush was widely known throughout the community and was a member of two dozen or so civic, patriotic, social, and literary organizations, including the Literary Club. He also served as an advisor on reading for the National Council of Boy Scouts. He was known to have said that he especially enjoyed the men's groups, "partly because my house is filled with women and because librarians, for the most part are women." Mr. Rush belonged to the local, state, and national Library Associations and served as Vice President of the American Library Association, and as President of the Indiana and Missouri Associations. He was also a member of the Bibliographical Society of America, the American Association of Adult Education, the Society of Ameri-

The Seventh Librarian, 1917-1928

Suddenly it came over me that I would be a librarian—I wonder what it is that decides things like that for us—fate, destiny, or just a whim.

—Charles E. Rush

MODERN
ALADDINS
AND THEIR
MAGIC

CHARLES E. RUSH AND AMY WINSLOW

can Archivists, and many other comparable groups.

Within the first year after he came to Indianapolis, he took a three-month leave to accept a call from Herbert Putnam, Librarian of Congress and General Director of Library War Service in Washington, to organize a library at Camp Humphreys, Virginia and to take charge of publicity at the Library War Service Headquarters in Washington. While there he served as Camp Librarian, Camp Library Inspector, State Director and Publicity Assistant.

While still Librarian in Indianapolis, he wrote many professional papers, pamphlets, and reports on books and reading. He was joint author with Amy Winslow, of a juvenile scientific book, published in 1926, entitled *Modern Aladdins and Their Magic*.

During his administration the Indianapolis Public Library expanded in all directions. When the Central Library moved into its new building on St. Clair Street, one friend, Frederick Polley, a prominent artist, and an art teacher in the Indianapolis Public Schools from 1917 to 1941, wrote, "Charles Rush, literally as well as figuratively, rolled up his sleeves and went to work transferring books to the new building and himself into the affections of the people of Indianapolis."

After evaluating and grading the staff, Mr. Rush established a classification schedule, so that employment, salaries, and promotions might be determined more fairly. *Readers Ink*, a new house organ appeared, a successor to the *Staff News Letter*. A staff organization was formed and a special collection of professional books was set aside for the use of the staff. General staff meetings were held monthly, and weekly department head meetings were instituted.

Soon after he became Librarian, Mr. Rush recommended that the Library be organized into departments, each with its own staff. He said he wished "to place it on a par with other libraries of its size and make it the efficient organization which it should be."

Book deposit stations in fire houses—a library service continued during the Rush administration.

In order to accomplish this reorganization, it was necessary for him to recommend to the Board that six long-time employees not be reappointed to the staff. He felt that they could not meet the requirements established for instituting the reforms he proposed, which required "a different order of ability and strength" which these older employees could not possibly meet. Seven other staff members voluntarily resigned at his request rather than not be reappointed. These "dismissals" prompted some controversy and criticism, but Mr. Rush's reorganization plan and personnel recommendations were approved by the Board on September 25, 1917.

To keep the "esprit de corps" high, weekend activities such as hikes in the country were encouraged. A staff May Breakfast was initiated. Special guests were invited to teas held in the Library's staff dining room.

To help relieve the staff shortage, Mr. Rush started a library training class. Applicants were required to take a competitive examination, and most of those admitted to the class were college-trained, some already staff members, others new to library work.

The first class started on October 7, 1918, with twenty students under the direction of Miss Carrie Scott, who was in charge of work with children. Conducted for six months each fall and winter, the class had as its purpose to train students for efficient service and to develop in them the qualities desirable for library work. It covered not only the subjects connected with library administration, such as book selection, ordering, classification and cataloging, but also general literature and practice work in the Central Library and branches. The training course continued throughout Mr. Rush's administration and was not discontinued until the depression years of the 1930s when there were few vacancies on the staff to justify its continuation.

During the 1921 economic depression Mr. Rush tried in every possible way to save money. There was a shortage of "pages" to do the book shelving, so the library assistants had to do this job themselves. Mr. Rush suggested

During the 1920s collections were also placed in the city's schools.

that they wear smocks to keep their dresses clean. He himself appeared in a black sateen smock, complete with a big, black bow tie. This unique attire unquestionably provided a humorous boost to staff morale.

The Library not only grew, it continued modernizing in many ways. Although Miss Browning had attempted to change the classification of the book collection from the Poole system, she had never succeeded because of the magnitude of the project. Mr. Rush had the entire collection reclassified with the Dewey decimal system, which required the creation of a new catalog.

Mr. Rush believed strongly in the importance of cooperation with outside groups. Talks were made by staff members, and specialized book lists were made for many organizations, musical groups, the Church Federation, Scouts, the Art Museum, and the Probation Department of Criminal Court, to name just a few. Exhibits of books were sent to flower shows, and the nationally promoted Good Book Week was observed every year.

Also, systematic newspaper promotion of the Library began. Such promotional activities, probably more than any other of Mr. Rush's programs, ushered the Indianapolis Public Library into the modern era. It was proudly going forth and advertising its wares, if not in a frenzied Madison Avenue manner, at least in a way that has proven effective to this day.

Mr. Rush had personally served during World War I, and he guided the Library contribution in every possible way to local and national service during the war years and the period of adjustment following. The Library inaugurated one of the first drives to establish camp libraries and raised $9,000. It conducted three local campaigns for books, prepared the books for distribution with the assistance of volunteers, and helped at Fort Benjamin Harrison.

The Library, too, took charge of the collection and preservation of all materials relating to the Marion County War Record. This provided the information concerning the county's participation for the official history of Indiana in the war.

The Library experienced trouble in 1921 because of an inadequate budget to purchase new books, and a campaign for books was begun. Publicity was sent to more than one hundred societies, organizations and industries of all kinds, with Mr. Rush summarizing the types of books most needed. Newspaper coverage totalled 140 articles, and the need was also publicized on bill boards, electric signs and in movie theatres. A book week was set aside and public interest was aroused to such an extent that even the book stores offered a fifteen percent discount towards purchases of books to be given to the Library. A well-known musical group, the Orloff Trio, gave a benefit recital. The School Board voted an emergency appropriation of $10,000, and the campaign for books brought to the Library not only more than thirty-five thousand books, but many hundreds of dollars as well. An intangible but very real accomplishment of the campaign was the habit instilled in the public of giving books and funds to the Library.

Several new branch libraries were opened during the Rush administration. Shelby Branch was established in 1918. In 1920 the Manual Training High School Branch, an agency open only to students and faculty of the school, was established. It remained an agency of the public Library until 1948. In 1921 the

Paul Laurence Dunbar Branch was established in Public School No. 26, but was open to the public as well as students and teachers. The South Grove Branch was opened in 1922, and finally, in 1927, Attucks Branch opened in the new Crispus Attucks High School, providing service to pupils and faculty of the school as well as to the public.

Two special libraries were also organized during this period. Although the offices of the School Board occupied the old Central Library at Meridian and Ohio Streets, space was made available in the building for a Business Library, which opened February 8, 1918. It was designed especially for the use of business men and women, although a small popular collection was maintained for the general public.

Another room in the building became the Teachers' Special Library, which opened on January 12, 1921. It was hailed as an important step in cooperation between the schools and the Library, and housed a carefully planned collection of materials of interest to teachers and school officials. In 1967 the Public Library relinquished its jurisdiction when the Teachers' Special Library was moved to the new School Education Center.

Another special service was established in 1921, when library service was provided for the patients and staff at City Hospital (now Wishard), and

Central Library's Riley Room— always a mecca for eager young readers.

later for Long, Methodist, and Coleman Hospitals. In 1924, when the James Whitcomb Riley Hospital for Children was opened, a library was established there under the auspices of the Indiana Library Association and the Indianapolis Public Library. In addition, many deposit stations were placed in schools and community houses during the 1920s.

Mr. Rush, always interested in adult education, established the Out-of-School Division in 1924 for the purpose of planning reading courses for adult readers who wanted to continue their education, pursue favorite hobbies, study for a new vocation or even have directed reading "just for fun." The American Library Association published many guides to courses, and others were prepared by the Division's head, Catherine Bailey, and her assistant. One of the main functions of the new department was to help young people who had dropped out of high school or college.

Mr. Rush resigned his Indianapolis position on August 31, 1928. His record of ten years' service showed a steady development for the Library, both in methods of service and a broadening concept of the Library's function. In the ten years, circulation had increased 188 percent, the number of borrowers rose 172 percent, branch circulation more than quadrupled, and the Library's book stock increased 122 percent. Comparable statistics could be quoted not only from the departments whose responsibility was the lending of books, but also in those departments providing reference and research services. The public was steadily becoming better acquainted with the Library's resources and gaining confidence in its service.

What was the secret of his success? Mr. Rush never failed to give a large share of the credit to his efficient and well-trained staff. His Assistant Librarian, Amy Winslow, wrote in the *Library Journal* in 1928, "The secret lies in the vision of the librarian, reinforced by his dogged determination and his spirit of sportsmanship. It lies too in the loyalty of his staff members . . . staff enthusiasm and allegiance . . . are the natural products of Mr. Rush's policy of encouraging individual initiative and giving full credit for achievement . . . The personal element in any equation is, after all, the important one."

Charles Rush left Indianapolis in 1928 to become Director of Libraries and Professor of Education in the Teachers' College of Columbia University, New York City. In 1930 he was commissioned by the college to visit major libraries in eight European countries to study various methods of bibliographic research.

In April, 1931, Mr. Rush became Associate Librarian of the new $8,000,000 library of Yale University. He earned his M.S. Degree there in 1931. He was Supervisor of Personnel and Service until he left in 1938 to become Librarian of the Cleveland Public Library. He succeeded one of the nation's most prominent librarians, Linda Eastman, who resigned after forty-five years of continuous service. Unfortunately, Mr. Rush's stay in Cleveland was not an entirely happy one, and he resigned his position there in 1941.

From Cleveland Mr. Rush went to the University at Chapel Hill, North Carolina, where his administration was a dynamic one. Described as "a man of vision," he planned a splendid new addition to the library stocked partly with donated book collections. He retired in 1954, remaining in North Carolina until his death, January 31, 1958.

Facing page — Afternoon light illuminates the balanced, elegant beauty of the Library's marble staircase.

Luther L. Dickerson

Luther L. Dickerson was born in Huron, Kansas, in 1880 and spent the early part of his life in Atchison, Kansas. In 1905 he graduated from Central State College in Edmond, Oklahoma, and acquired his library training from the New York State Library School. From 1905 to 1907 he served as Librarian of the Oklahoma State Teachers' College, and from 1908 until 1917 as Librarian of Grinnell College in Iowa. During his stay there he was President of the Iowa Library Association in 1914 and 1915. During the war years he served in several capacities. He organized the libraries of Camp Doniphan, Fort Snelling, and Post Field in Oklahoma, was Camp Library Supervisor of the Southeastern states, Staff Librarian of the Library War Services in Washington D.C., and organizer and librarian of the A.E.F. University at Beaune, Cote d'Or, France. In just two weeks he organized the preparation of 40,000 books for the university library there.

In the years from 1919 to 1924 he served as chief of the library subsection of the U.S. Army and library specialist in the adjutant's office in Washington, D.C., where he had charge of the peacetime organization and operation of approximately two hundred post and special service libraries in the United States, Hawaii, Panama, the Phillipines, and Puerto Rico. In addition, he was Director of the Training School for Post Librarians in Washington. He was commissioned a Major in the U.S. Army Reserves, and was decorated by the French government.

In 1924 he resigned his position with the United States War Department to join the American Library Association as Executive Secretary of the Board of Adult Education. There he inaugurated and edited the "Reading With a Purpose" series of study guides and headed the work of publishing the notable study on "Libraries and Adult Education."

From this varied and outstanding background of work in libraries, Mr. Dickerson came to Indianapolis to assume the position of Librarian on October 7, 1928. While in Indianapolis he belonged to the library associations, The Indianapolis Literary Club, The Portfolio, Rotary, and various civic organizations. He was President of the Rotary Club, President of the Indiana Library Association, and Chairman of the National Advisory Council of Radio in Education.

Besides being a man of many social and civic interests, Mr. Dickerson was an avid reader and an enthusiastic gardener. He found time to serve on boards such as the Council of Social Agencies, Camp Fire Girls, and Boy Scouts and Girl Scouts.

Much of his administration of the Library covered the Depression years of the 1930s and the period of World War II. There was little opportunity for expansion in buildings or equipment, but there was a spectacular growth in circulation of books. Between 1927 and 1932 it increased 56.5 percent and there was a heavy increase in reference services. The enforced leisure of the many unemployed in the 1930s provided time for reading. Fifteen thousand families were on relief and many struggled to live on greatly reduced incomes. Some people used this time to improve their cultural background, some to gain vocational information. Others were seeking answers in books of religion. Many merely sought recreational reading to keep their minds off their troubles, and the Library became a place to browse and forget.

Mr. Dickerson felt that the Library should not become isolated and think only in terms of books. "The best librarians," he said, "emphasize the human touch." He tried to eliminate processes that were time-wasting so the staff could furnish more direct service to the public. The book check-out procedure was changed to a self-charging system in which the borrower was asked to write his or her own library card number on the check-out card. Mindful of special services for library patrons, Mr. Dickerson took the lead in organizing leisure hour clubs and amateur programs.

To remind people of its services, the Library produced a weekly radio program and published a book review column in the *Indianapolis Times*, under the direction of Mary Wilson, then Head of the Circulation Department of Central Library. Also, at a time when there was much demand for help, the Library attempted to act as a clearing house to provide better coordination between all the charitable, social, and cultural agencies in the city, both public and private.

The Library itself had received cuts in its budget during the Depression years, and staff salaries were lowered as well. To prevent the discharge of members of the staff and the elimination of units of service, the staff voluntarily made up the salary deficit by accepting additional cuts of five percent for employees receiving $1,200 to $1,600 annually, and 13.5 percent for those above that figure. The entire staff was working unduly hard, but displayed a fine spirit engendered by the realization of the needed service being given.

Students, businessmen and women, homemakers—all found a welcome home at their neighborhood library.

However, Mr. Dickerson refused to reduce the salary schedule. The few new people who were hired during the years of the drastic cuts were appointed at the appropriate salary set in the schedule, although they received at the time only a percentage of the money due them. This provided him with a psychological lever, for when general financial conditions began to improve, he did not immediately need to ask for "raises" but merely for a return to the salaries already set.

The schedule itself provided for salaries far below those paid school employees and other municipal workers. When the Depression years faded into the pre-war years, he succeeded in achieving a slow but steady climb to a more reasonable compensation for library employees.

During the 1930s the Library was also looking for ways to economize. Staff members watched for book sales and binding bargains, and at the same time encouraged gifts and memorials. Nevertheless, books were showing excessive wear and were cleaned and mended until they literally fell apart.

In spite of the Depression, several new branches were opened. In 1929 the Rauh Memorial Branch Library was opened at Meridian and 30th Streets when Mr. and Mrs. Samuel Rauh gave their beautiful home to the Board of School Commissioners to be used as a branch library. The Broad Ripple Branch Library opened in 1930 in rental quarters on 63rd Street, and the School No. 87 Branch in 1937, to be renamed the George Washington Carver Branch in 1944.

The Extension Department was organized in 1940, providing collections of books to large business or industrial plants. Usually, for several hours once each week, a "mini-library" under the supervision of a member of the Extension staff was open to employees of the organization.

The service to industrial plants became of utmost importance as factories began to retool for defense. As the change in national and international conditions moved the economy from a depression to a wartime footing, Mr. Dickerson, working mostly through the Extension Department, built up a collection of technical books to help the long-out-of-practice laborer, and industry itself, to turn to war-oriented production. Until management had time to develop its own training classes, the Indianapolis Public Library was ready to lend a helping hand. Because of this and other cooperative ventures, a close relationship between industry and the library has continued to this day.

Mr. Dickerson initiated a new policy requiring each staff member to make at least four visits a year to another department or agency. Its purpose was "to cultivate staff spirit of cooperation throughout the whole library system, to encourage the staff to think of the Library as a whole and as part of the life of the community, and to emphasize the danger of giving out wrong information about any unit." More staff meetings were held and bulletin boards carried notices of library activities.

During the Depression a policy was approved by the Board of School Commissioners which caused a great deal of staff dissatisfaction. On the theory that married women who worked took away possible jobs from those who were more in need of them, the rule stated that no married female librarian could be hired and that if a librarian married while employed, she would be discharged. As a result Mr. Dickerson required all supposedly

CHAPTER VII

Youngsters too enjoyed a visit to the library in the 40s.

A new branch opened in 1920— the gift of Mr. and Mrs. Samuel Rauh.

54

unmarried employees to take an oath stating that to be their true marital status. Incidentally, when the employment situation eased the rule was rescinded and Mr. Dickerson, who had refused to do what his staff could not do, was promptly married.

The Training Class, instituted by Mr. Rush in 1918, fell victim of the Depression in 1932, not so much because of a lack of funds, but due to few vacancies. Employees were holding on to their jobs despite a decrease in salaries and an increase in work loads. By 1937 the employment picture was brighter, and the classes were reactivated. It was not to last for many years, however. When World War II came there were numerous vacancies, but too few interested applicants, so the classes were ended in 1941.

In 1942, evolving from a long felt need, the Indianapolis Public Library Staff Association was formed. It was destined to become an important part of the governing and policy-forming life of the library. *Ad Lib*, a new weekly publication was started as the voice of the association.

Mr. Dickerson retired from the library in the fall of 1944, leaving the Indianapolis Public Library ranking among the top four city library systems in the nation, fourth among the largest cities in per capita circulation, and third in number of borrowers. In his final Annual Report for 1943-44 he said,

> *This public library seeks to be universal in its utility and its appeal. It asks no question except, "How can we help you?" In its service it recognizes no race, no faith, no economic level and no social position; those of every degree of economic dependency or independency are served without discrimination and to the extent that they desire assistance or guidance.*

This statement embodied his beliefs and accomplishments during the seventeen years of his administration. Upon his retirement he moved back to Oklahoma City where he died on March 24, 1957, at the age of seventy-six.

This public library seeks to be universal in its utility and its appeal—It asks no questions except, "How can we help you?" In its service it recognizes no race, no faith, no economic level and no social position; those of every degree of economic dependency or independency are served without discrimination and to the extent that they desire assistance or guidance.
—Luther L. Dickerson
Annual Report, 1943-44

Mr. Dickerson and his staff celebrated the "new" Central Library's 21st birthday in 1938.

Marian McFadden

Marian McFadden had been promoted to Assistant Librarian in July, 1944, after working at special assignments for Mr. Dickerson in 1943 and 1944. She was appointed Acting Librarian in 1944 and Librarian in 1945. At the time she was appointed to the position, she was the youngest among very few women in charge of large public library systems.

During her term of office, the title "Librarian" which had designated the top position since the days of Charles Evans, was changed to "Director of Libraries."

Miss McFadden was born in Shelbyville, Indiana, on July 14, 1904, of a family who had lived in Shelby County for more than a hundred and thirty years. Her grandfather and father were physicians in Shelbyville. Her grandfather had an extensive library and was a great reader, so Marian as a very little girl learned to browse through his many books, developing a love of reading.

After early schooling in Shelbyville, Miss McFadden graduated from Tudor Hall preparatory school in Indianapolis, and from Smith College in 1926, where she extended her interest in literature and history. She worked in the Shelbyville Public Library for almost two years following college, and then went to Columbia University Library School in New York City, completing the requirements for her B.S. Degree in 1929. She also took a year's graduate work in child psychology at Hunter College. For a year she served as an assistant and then as a children's librarian in a branch of the Queensborough Public Library, which she left in 1930 to become Head of the Children's Room in the Lincoln Library in Springfield, Illinois. While there, she lived in the home of a grandniece of Mrs. Abraham Lincoln. "It was like living in the midst of a museum," she said, becoming thoroughly imbued with Lincoln lore and history.

Miss McFadden was the high school librarian in Shelbyville in 1933, and then in 1934 joined the staff of the Indianapolis Public Library as a children's librarian, then served as Head Librarian at the Brightwood Branch Library from 1936 until 1942. After this assignment, Miss McFadden was transferred to Central Library as special assistant to the Librarian. She was designated Supervising Librarian in April, 1943, and as noted above, in 1944, became Assistant Librarian, a position which had been vacant for twelve years.

As a member of the professional library associations she served on many committees. She was Second Vice President of the American Library Association in 1951-1952 and held membership in many other social, literary and civic groups, both in Indianapolis and Shelbyville, among them the Fortnightly Literary Club and the Council of Administrative Women.

Miss McFadden assumed the position of Indianapolis Librarian at a most

The Ninth Librarian, 1944-1956

Most important of all, these were the years of the tragedy of Korea and of man's struggle to find a way to live through religion, psychology, or science, which has been reflected in the books he has read. The only hope of the individual to survive and retain his individuality lies in his ability and desire to discover for himself the truths upon which he will base his thinking.

—Marian McFadden
 Ten Year Report, 1955

Educational motion pictures became another special library service in 1948. Cerene Ohr, Supervisor of Branches, loads the projector. (*Indianapolis Star* photo).

difficult time. The war was just ending and the veterans were returning home to an uncertain future. The newly organized United Nations created an awakened interest in international affairs. An unprecedented population growth and expanded city boundaries exerted pressure on the library to extend service, especially to the over-crowded schools. At the same time, prices were soaring and salaries in a competitive labor market were rising at such a rate that it was difficult to employ or keep employees, as library salaries were controlled by the schedule set by the Board. The Library found itself without enough experienced staff to sustain needed programs.

Although faced with the prediction that television would bring an end to reading, most librarians realized that the new medium would merely arouse new interest and create a desire for further information, as had happened earlier with the advent of radio. Circulation did drop the first year television came to Indianapolis, but the novelty of television quickly waned and readers soon returned to the library.

Though circulation statistics could not compete with the Depression years of the 1930s, in 1945 the Indianapolis Public Library ranked second in per capita circulation among cities of 200,000 or over, with Cleveland being first. Indianapolis still held the same rank ten years later, in 1955.

It was a time of economic, social and intellectual change. In a special report to the Board for the years 1945 to 1955, Miss McFadden described the situation as she found it:

> *Most important of all, these were the years of the tragedy of Korea and of man's struggle to find a way to live through religion, psychology, or science, which has been reflected in the books he has read. The only hope of the individual to survive and retain his individuality lies in his ability and desire to discover for himself the truths upon which he will base his thinking.*

Numerous new services were added during Miss McFadden's administration. Through the philanthropy of Leonard Strauss and the interest of Elizabeth Ohr, Head of the Art and Music Department, phonograph records were added to the music collection. With the donation of money for records and record players, the collection grew to be a tremendous asset to the music-loving public, and noon-hour concerts were held at the Central Library for several years.

In 1944 the Library had been asked to become a depository for films of the Office of War Information and the United States Treasury Department. From the beginning the Library began to experiment with educational films, especially on travel and national and international issues of current interest. The service began to increase; a screen was purchased, projectors were borrowed, and for the first time, in the budget for 1951-1952, funds were allowed for the purchase of films. Originally the few films the Library owned had been housed in the office of the Supervisor of Branches, but in 1952 larger quarters were necessary. Films were not only loaned to the public, but also used for a variety of library educational and informational programs. The expansion of service and the use of films by the public continued to increase until the introduction of videotape loan service in 1981.

Wilma Reeve, Assistant Librarian, Cerene Ohr, and Doris Lynn, School Audio-Visual Consultant, display a poster of a new Office of War Information film, 1944.

In the fall of 1947 a series of film forums began, with a panel of experts talking about the selected film, followed by discussion from the floor. The first session was on post-war aid to Europe. It preceded by a few days a special session of Congress called to consider the Marshall Plan. Senator Homer Capehart was one of the panelists that night and said that from that experience he could carry valuable information back to the Senate.

Film programs of one kind or another followed at Central Library and at some branches during the winter of 1953-1954. Beginning in 1954, the Indiana University Extension in Indianapolis joined the Library in sponsoring the Film Forum series. The project received national attention and was the beginning of the popular "Thursday Night at the Library" film and travel slide programs held for many years.

In 1948 a staff member was assigned the responsibility of coordinating many of the community programs in which the Library had become involved. Pauline French was appointed in 1949 to the full time position of Adult Activities Librarian, which was created to carry on the increased work of heading the film section, planning the film programs and forums, and the administration of the Great Books program in which the Library had been active since 1945.

During the Dickerson administration the *Indianapolis News*, the Indiana State Library and the Indianapolis Public Library had begun a cooperative venture in microfilming back issues of the *News*. The work had progressed slowly, but after the merger of the *News* and *Star*, the project was reactivated, and back and current issues were completed. In 1949 the *Indianapolis Times* began giving the Library a microfilm copy of its current issues, and purchase of back files of the *New York Times* began. The project not only saved shelf space but also solved a bad public relations problem, making it possible for teachers, students, and others to use the microfilm without the restrictions necessitated by the wear and tear on the actual papers. By 1955 three microfilm readers were in constant use.

Due to increased problems regarding so-called "controversial" literature, and influenced by the American Library Association's "Library Bill of Rights," the administrative staff of the Library wrote its own "Statement of Policy on Printed Material," providing guidelines for the selection of material, especially if it were of a questionable nature.

The method of book selection was also changed. For many years most decisions had remained in the hands of a few capable librarians. With the ever increasing mass of printed material, it seemed prudent to widen the responsibility. Adult Book Selection Committees were appointed, with permanent members representing those departments concerned with the general reader, but also other staff members who held short term appointments to the committees. Volunteer readers from the staff were also used.

For many years children's books had been selected by committees chosen by their supervisor. "A Policy for Book Selection" was issued as a guide which stated in its introduction that,

> *The Indianapolis Public Library provides, on equal terms, free service to all individuals and groups in a community, both children and adults. Since its income is derived from taxes paid by the citizens of Indianapolis, it believes its first duty is to provide all types of library material which will satisfy the needs of all the people who help pay for its upkeep. To perform this duty the Library states that its three main functions are: (1) to provide recreational reading; (2) to provide the means of informal education and tools for formal education; and (3) to provide an orderly storehouse of recorded thoughts, knowledge and deeds.*

A big order, impossible to fill in its entirety, but one ever to be remembered as a worthy goal.

In 1955 a complete inventory of the Central Library book collection was taken, the first since the 1930s when a Works Project Administration crew did a not-too-thorough job. With the entire Library system closed, the job was completed on a Saturday and Sunday, and all employees, from pages to the Director, participated.

The increase in population after World War II and the already changing nature of many neighborhoods made it necessary for Miss McFadden to reevaluate the work done in the branch libraries. As a result, some branches became satellites of nearby larger branches, and three branches, Hawthorne, Carver, and South Grove, were closed. Also, the Manual Training High School Branch was transferred to the jurisdiction of the Indianapolis Public Schools, a logical move which marked the first step in the eventual separation of the library and school system.

During the Depression and war years, remodeling or expanding older facilities and the building of new ones had been impossible. In the late 1940s and '50s, therefore, there was imperative need for such planning and work to be done. Attucks Branch was able to expand to an unused room in the high school, and Dunbar Branch moved into larger and more attractive quarters when an addition was built to School No. 26.

In 1949 the Broad Ripple Branch moved from rental quarters in the

Students assisted in the move to the new Broad Ripple Library in 1949.

Masonic Lodge Building to its own new home, the first new library building constructed since the Central Library in 1917. In 1956 the Irvington Branch moved from the old house it had occupied since 1921 into the second new facility built during the McFadden administration. In 1949, a new branch, the Holladay Library for Young People opened at 5549 North College Avenue in a home willed to the Library in 1946 by Clara E. Holladay, a retired teacher.

In 1952 the first Bookmobile began service to areas not readily reached by any branch. The heavy use of this unit showed that a branch was needed in the fast growing northeast section of the city, and in 1956 property was purchased as a future branch site at Emerson Avenue and 37th Street.

At the same time the branch library system was under study, plans were underway to consolidate, streamline, or rearrange several Central Library departments. The Pamphlet Division, located in the west corridor leading to the administrative offices, was closed and pamphlets were shelved with the book materials on the same subjects, thus giving the user a wider choice of materials at one location. More space was made available for films, which were moved into the hallway vacated by the Pamphlet Division.

The Stations Department, which had dealt with requests for material coming from the branches since the 1920s, was placed directly under the Supervisor of Branches, where it logically seemed to belong. Then in 1947 the Order, Catalog, and Binding Departments were combined under the direction of the Supervisor of Technical Processes, a new position established to develop a simpler method of cataloging, and to achieve a smoother, coordinated flow of work between the three old departments.

Although salaries had moved up from the low Depression years during Mr. Dickerson's administration, they were still far below those in comparable fields. The old job classification plan was also out of date. As a result, a job analysis program was begun in 1947 under the direction of Helen L. Norris, who came to the Library on loan from the Oak Park, Illinois, Public Library.

From the information obtained in the Norris study, a new classification and pay plan was set up and approved by the Board of School Commissioners. The new schedule better assured "equal pay for equal work" and provided a tool which brought salaries at least nearer to those paid the public school teachers.

This job analysis project was one of the early ones done in the library field. As a result Miss McFadden and Miss Norris were requested to write several articles on the project for the professional journals. They headed an American Library Association Committee which produced a manual on job analysis, position classification and pay plans which was a standard textbook for several years in Schools of Library Science.

The new schedule also established a pre-professional position especially designed so that young college graduates could obtain experience in the library profession before making a decision to pursue graduate training. The new position provided an excellent recruiting program, which was greatly aided when Indiana University established a School of Library Science. With the Library providing space and the use of bibliographical materials, several courses were offered through the Indianapolis Extension Division of Indiana University. This enabled staff members to attend classes in Indianapolis.

In 1947 Helen Norris was appointed to the newly created position of Supervisor of Personnel, with responsibility not only for the constant revision and implementation of the classification schedule, but for the many duties revolving around a constantly changing staff.

The long sought and long fought for Public Employees Retirement Fund was established by the state legislature in 1945. On July 1, 1946, library employees, among many others, were placed under the pension plan. At the same time the staff received another long overdue benefit when it went from a forty-two hour work week to the more common forty hour week. A new staff manual brought up to date the many procedures which had evolved through the years. In 1952 the administration and the Staff Association planned the first "Library Day," an in-service training session continued bi-annually until 1972.

Marian McFadden was keenly aware of the vital needs of the future. In her final report to the Board, she pointed out the changing patterns of city living with the attendant problems of relocating old and building new branches, the growth of suburbia and the suburban communities in the county who were eager for library service. Finally she emphasized the inevitable necessity for the separation of the Library from the school system, in order that the Library could operate with more flexibility to meet these coming needs of a new age.

Marian McFadden resigned her position effective December 31, 1956, citing personal reasons, and at the age of just fifty-two returned to her hometown of Shelbyville, Indiana. During her retirement years, she was active in community affairs and wrote an outstanding history of Shelbyville, *The Biography of a Town*.

She served on a variety of boards, including the Shelbyville Board of Education, where she was president, the Tuberculosis Association, the W.S.

Major Hospital Foundation, and the Shelby County Orphans Home Board. She received the Shelby County Chamber of Commerce award for service to the community and citations from the American Legion, Robinson-Ragsdale Post, and the Loyal Legion Foundation.

Marian McFadden was recognized in *Who's Who Among American Women*. She also organized a little theater group, had a Christmas pageant published, wrote a newspaper column of children's books, and wrote many book reviews for *Library Journal* and other publications. Her own words reflect a life of joy and satisfaction, "A real lover of books is a person who will never be bored or afraid to be alone."

She continued to reside in Shelbyville until her death on September 7, 1975. In 1976-1977 the Indianapolis-Marion County Public Library Foundation received $152,042.69 from her estate. The proceeds from the investment of this principal are used to finance the annual author lecture, named in her honor, The Marian McFadden Memorial Lecture.

Marian McFadden and Dr. Luther Evans, Librarian of Congress, cut the library's 75th Birthday cake, April 8, 1948. (*Star* Photo)

Harold J. Sander

When Harold Sander assumed the position of Director in September, 1956, he too looked ahead to growth in the Library's service as an alive and lively force in the whole community.

He was born on a farm near Evansville, Indiana, on July 8, 1913, taking his first job in a flour mill following graduation from high school in the early Depression years. In April, 1932, he began working for the Evansville and Vanderburgh County Public Library, continuing there while attending Evansville College, where he received an A.B. Degree in 1938. The following year he attained his degree in library service from Columbia University, New York City. While there he worked in the School of Business Library, remaining there until he became Head of the Reference Division of the Indiana State Library in 1940.

While Mr. Sander was a student at Columbia University, he met Edna Worthington, who was also a library school student. They were married in 1941 and had three sons, Mark, Eric and Jeffery.

During World War II, Mr. Sander served as a photo interpreter with the XVIII Airborne Corps. While in service he also received training at Amherst College and the Military Intelligence Training Center at Camp Ritchie, Maryland.

Following military service, Harold Sander returned to the Indiana State Library, where he worked until 1948, serving as Assistant to the Director, and Acting Director for one summer. In 1948 he joined the staff of the Indianapolis Public Library as Head of the Business Library. In 1951 he was appointed Director of the Roanoke, Virginia, Public Library where he remained until 1956, when he returned to become Director of the Indianapolis Public Library following the resignation of Marian McFadden.

During his tenure Mr. Sander was active in civic affairs. He was a member of The Indianapolis Literary Club, serving a term as its president. He belonged to the Downtown Kiwanis Club, to both the Indiana and Marion County Historical Societies and The Portfolio and was past president of Greater Indianapolis Information, Inc. He was active in the Northminster Presbyterian Church for many years, having served as deacon, elder, and Sunday School Superintendent. A member of both the American and Indiana Library Associations, he was twice president of the State organization, in 1951 and 1969, and also served as President of the Indiana Special Libraries Association.

Mr. Sander was chairman of the 1961 Indiana Governor's Conference for Library Service and was founder and first editor of *Focus on Indiana Libraries*, a publication of the Indiana Library Association. He was listed in *Who's Who in American Education* and *Who's Who in America*.

The years which followed Mr. Sander's appointment were years of growth,

Harold Sander, while head of the Business Branch Library, attempted to see how high 275 phone books, listing 600 cities would stack. (*Star* Photo)

change and challenge. During the decade from 1950 to 1960 the city population increased only ten percent, while that of Marion County outside of Indianapolis increased seventy-seven percent. Meanwhile, borrowing of books in many of the branch libraries was declining because of industrialization of the neighborhoods and because those remaining residents were not readers or users of libraries. Mr. Sander felt it was the responsibility of the Library to take its place in the "war against poverty" and to find the means of reaching the non-users, both children and adults, in these inner city neighborhoods.

The branch libraries, using their own initiative, increased their efforts to provide activities of all kinds which might draw people into their buildings. Not only staff members, but others in the community gladly gave help to make these activities interesting and worthwhile. In the children's areas, programs were intensified with more story hours, film showings, puppet shows, special hours for pre-school children, and whatever other ideas imagination could conceive.

The "Thursday Evening at the Library" series continued, a recognized event to which many returned year after year. These programs had drawn an audience from all parts of the city, so the program was expanded and offered in many of the branch libraries. Films, concerts, and all types of programs on travel, science, health, investments, law enforcement and other topics helped to keep the Library a center of civic and cultural interest.

For too many years the library system for a variety of reasons had not been able to modernize or increase the number of its buildings. After the Depression and World War II, conditions became more favorable, and during Mr. Sander's administration, a building and modernization program began.

After years of talk, petitions, and planning, in 1958 the old house which had been the home of the Broadway Branch was replaced by a modern, attractive structure. Although the neighborhood was rapidly becoming a part of the "inner city," with its attendant problems, the new larger facility was

Bookmobiles continued to be a vital part of the Library's service during the Sander administration.

better equipped to contribute its share of help towards solving those problems.

Shelby Branch Library, which had been housed in an old frame structure on Shelby Street for many years, moved into a new building in nearby Garfield Park in the Fall of 1965, serving not only its old southside neighborhood, but also the rapidly growing area farther south. Though Brightwood Branch did not obtain a building of its own, it was moved in 1971 a few blocks from its old location on Station Street into larger, better equipped quarters in the Brightwood Shopping Center on Sherman Drive.

Other branches, after struggling with low usage for many years, reached the end of their roads. In 1959 the Attucks Branch was closed. It was turned over to the high school for student use only. Dunbar Branch ceased to exist as a public library branch in 1967, becoming also a school library. In 1971 Riverside Branch, located in a changing neighborhood, closed its doors after seventy-five years of service.

After federal funds for the project were approved, the Books-To-People service began in 1971, using a small van. It seemed the ultimate attempt to reach those who knew little or nothing about books and how they could be obtained.

Meeting the consequences of the "flight to suburbia" required an equal amount of planning, but produced more tangible results. As large, populated areas were annexed to the city, more branch libraries were essential. Emerson Branch opened in a house at Emerson Avenue and 37th Street, purchased during the McFadden administration in 1956. In 1962 the house was replaced by a new, modern structure built on the same site. Leased quarters were obtained in 1960 for Eagle Branch on the northwest side of Indianapolis, and in 1964 space for the new Northeast Branch was rented in the Northeastwood Shopping Center at Post Road and 38th Street.

In 1957 the School Services Division moved into the large brick house adjacent to the Central Library on the north facing Pennsylvania Street, which

Audio visual services expanded rapidly in the 1960s. (*Star* Photo)

had been purchased in 1955. When the building was demolished in 1962, a new addition to Central Library was built on the site, providing more attractive and utilitarian facilities for the division. However, in 1967 school library services were transferred to the Public School system along with the Teachers' Special Library and the Dunbar Branch. The building erected in 1962 subsequently became the new home of the greatly expanded Extension Services Department.

The Holladay Branch Library closed in 1958, but a "Young Adult" department was continued at Central Library until the book collection was integrated into the adult collection a few years later.

Although still under the jurisdiction of the Public Library system in 1952, the Teachers' Special Library was moved that year from the School Office building on Meridian Street to the Educational Center at 1644 Roosevelt Avenue. However, the Business Branch remained on the second floor of the School Office building until 1962, when it was moved across the street to more adequate quarters on the ground floor of the Board of Trade Building.

In 1959, with the aid of Assistant Director Nevin Raber, Mr. Sander planned and carried through an extensive remodeling program within the walls of Central Library, which expanded working space. With the addition of a fourth tier of book stacks, desperate over-crowding was somewhat alleviated. An important improvement was the installation of a new service elevator. The Central Library was fully air-conditioned in 1971. All new branch libraries were air-conditioned when constructed, and eventually summer cooling systems were added in all older buildings.

Some reorganization of the staff had been undertaken previously, but soon after Mr. Sander became Director a much more complete reorganization was done, changing and combining functions of various departments to fit expanding needs.

More employees were being hired as new branches opened, and it was essential to keep all staff members, both new and old, informed of reorganization and expansion programs as they developed. Orientation sessions and workshops were set up. "Library Day," instituted by Miss McFadden, was continued under Mr. Sander's guidance, permitting a time when the entire staff could assemble to hear talks presented by community leaders and national library administrators, and participate in discussions of a wide variety of library and community concerns.

In 1964 the Distinguished Service Award was given for the first time to a member of the staff for outstanding service to the library and its patrons. The award is discussed in detail in Chapter XXI.

Unquestionably the greatest achievement of the Sander administration was the expansion of library service to most of Marion County. Chapter XII outlines the historic events leading to the formation of the new Marion County Public Library in 1966, and then the merger with the Indianapolis Public Library in 1968 to form the new Indianapolis-Marion County Public Library District.

Mr. Sander's annual report for 1965-1966 expressed the viewpoint of those who had worked so hard and so long to bring about this wonderful accomplishment. He said, " 'Rejoice and be exceedingly glad'—This is our

"The lucky child is one whose early life has been enriched by books" believes Ann Strachan, Children's Division Librarian, shown in 1961 assisting a young reader.

feeling in reviewing the fiscal year —The giant-size good news was the establishment of a Marion County Library District, the appointment of its board, and the signing of a contract between City and County for the extension of library service."

The Board of the newly formed entity wasted no time following the establishment of the new city-county library district. It began to learn what it had inherited and to plan for the future. With the cooperation of School Board officials and the efficient work done by the Library administration and the staff as a whole, the transition from the old to the new took place without obvious difficulties. Financial, budgetary and secretarial duties became the responsibility of the Assistant Director. Another administrative assistant was appointed to take over a newly created Buildings and Grounds Department. Coordinators and supervisors had to plan for a rapid acquisition of new books and other materials, plan extended programs, and make studies of where new branches should be established. The amount spent on acquisition suddenly increased from $218,000 to $510,000, and the increase of materials awaiting processing required the leasing of more space.

County branch libraries were opened soon after the first contract was signed. Marwood, Westlane, Lawrence, and Southport Branches opened in 1967. Wanamaker and Wayne opened in 1969, followed by Nora Branch in 1971. Two bookmobiles served the county, with the third still making stops within the city. In the first year of county service 29,369 borrower's cards were issued to county residents and the circulation of books increased by 212,804, proving statistically the real need to provide free library service to all Marion County citizens.

For reasons of health, Mr. Sander resigned his position as Director of Libraries effective January 1, 1972. He remained on the staff as Manager of the Broadway Branch until he retired on July 16, 1973.

Raymond E. Gnat

Raymond E. Gnat was appointed Assistant Director by Harold Sander in 1963, holding that position until his appointment as Director on January 23, 1972, following Mr. Sander's resignation. He has served as the Library's top administrator longer than any other Librarian, with the exception of Eliza Browning.

Mr. Gnat was born in Milwaukee, Wisconsin, on January 15, 1932. He earned a Bachelor of Business Administration degree in 1954 from the University of Wisconsin at Madison. He was a page in the Milwaukee Public Library while attending college and was appointed to a full-time position as Junior Librarian shortly before induction into the United States Army. While working at the Milwaukee Public Library, he met Jean Monday, a fellow employee. They were married in 1954 and have three children: Cynthia, Barbara and Richard. Jean is also a librarian.

From 1954 to 1956 Mr. Gnat served with the United States Adjutant General Corps, serving at Fort Shafter, Hawaii. He was separated to the Army Reserve with the rank of Second Lieutenant.

Following military service he was a circulation assistant in the library at the University of Illinois and received the Master of Science Degree in Library Science there in 1958. Returning to the Milwaukee Public Library, he became a subject selector-cataloger. In 1981 he earned a Masters Degree in Public Administration from Indiana University at Indianapolis.

Besides being a member of the American Library Association and the Indiana Library Association, Mr. Gnat is a member of the Bibliographical Society of America, the Rotary Club of Indianapolis, The Indianapolis Literary Club, and The Portfolio. He served as Executive Director of Indiana National Library Week in 1965, and on committees of the American Library Association and Indiana Library Association, serving as the President of the Indiana Library Association in 1980.

The years of Mr. Gnat's administration have noted the most significant expansion and development of Library services and facilities since the administration of Eliza Browning over eighty years ago.

The advent of county-wide services in 1968 precipitated a veritable explosion in the Library's building program. Between 1972 and 1990 more new library facilities were planned and constructed or renovated than during any other period in the Library's long history.

The ever increasing demand for more space led in 1972 to the purchase of a building at 1435 North Illinois Street as a service center. The building's 21,000 square feet housed the Visual Arts Division, the Bookmobile and Extension Division operation, and the Library's supply and printing facilities.

Work was begun in 1973 on construction of four additional floors to the

The Eleventh Librarian

It is the responsibility of the library administration, working within guidelines and policies established by the Library Board, to assure that we are open a sufficient and convenient number of hours; that we provide excellent personal services; that programs and collections reflect neighborhood interests and needs; and that adequate numbers of standard and new materials are provided. The result should be an increase in the level of service to the community.

—Raymond E. Gnat
Annual Report, 1989

Staff prepare for another new branch library opening. (*Indianapolis News* Photo)

Library Director Raymond E. Gnat, with two patrons, inaugurates the computerized book check out system, at the Broadway Library, April, 1983.

one-story Central Library annex originally built in 1963. Kennedy, Brown, and Trueblood were the architects. The building was completed in 1975 at a cost of $1,715,771. Construction of the new Warren and Southport regional libraries was also begun in 1973, with completion in 1974.

The building at 815-17 North Pennsylvania Street was purchased in 1974 as new quarters for the Technical Services Department. In 1975 the last parcel of land was acquired on St. Clair Street just east of Pennsylvania Street, to provide parking for all Central Library employees and for branch personnel visiting Central. The Citizen's Multi-Service Center Library was opened in 1977 at 17th and Broadway Streets, and renovation of the East Washington Branch Library also began that same year.

The building housing the Wanamaker Branch Library, which had been leased since 1969, was purchased in 1978. That same year property adjacent to the Brown Branch Library was purchased, and eventually was used to expand their parking facilities.

After years of delay, construction began on the Flanner House Social Service Center at 2424 Dr. Martin Luther King Street, with the building planned to accommodate a public library branch. The Flanner House Branch Library was finally opened in October, 1979, the twenty-third branch of the library system.

In 1980 land was purchased at 100 South Girls School Road to be used for the building of a new Wayne Branch Library. Based on his goals for the "Long Range Plan For Library Development" approved by the Library Board in 1979, Mr. Gnat recommended a $4,500,000 bond issue to be sold in January, 1981. The proceeds were to be used for the building of new facilities for Lawrence and Wayne Libraries, the replacement of Spades Park, West Indianapolis, and Broad Ripple Libraries, the completion of the final phase of the Central Library renovation, and for system-wide computerization.

With the bond funds available, 1982 brought the start of construction of the new Lawrence and Wayne Libraries, both of which opened on schedule in 1983, the remodeling of Cropsey Auditorium at Central Library, the resetting of Central's front steps and the Central Library bookstack renovation project. This same year a new library station was opened in the Concord Community Center on the near southside of the city.

Under Mr. Gnat's guidance the city-county library system continued to grow and expand. Construction contracts for a new library in Pike Township were awarded in December, 1984, for a 13,000 square foot building to replace the Westlane Shopping Center rental unit. The new Pike Branch Library opened on May 3, 1986, following closely the opening of the new Broad Ripple Branch Library in March. On November 15th of that same year, a new 5,000 square foot West Indianapolis Branch Library opened at Morris and Kappes Streets to replace the aging Carnegie library built in 1912. One branch, the Wishard Hospital Library, was closed in early 1986 at the request of the hospital, due to a combination of substantially reduced usage and the hospital's space utilization needs.

The future of the Spades Park Branch Library, opened in 1912, was debated by the administration and the Library Board for several years. Its long utilized rooms were outmoded and poorly equipped to serve modern needs. Another suitable building site in the area could not be found. Because of its historic significance as an early Carnegie library, many individuals and groups were opposed to demolishing the building and rebuilding on the same site. The decision was made to completely renovate the building. The project was completed in 1987.

To continue with the implementation of the long range plan for library service, Mr. Gnat requested Board approval of a $6,500,000 bond issue to be sold in the Spring of 1989. The proceeds of these bonds were to be used for a new library in Decatur Township to replace the inadequate Marwood Branch Library rental quarters, a new Library Service Center to be built on land purchased at 24th and North Meridian Streets, and for renovation of several older branch libraries. Subsequently the Nora Branch Library was renovated and expanded in 1989, the new Decatur Branch Library opened in the summer of 1990, and the new 80,000 square foot Library Service Center is expected to open in early 1993.

In tandem with this phenomenal growth in the Library's physical plant, usage of library service by the public also hit record levels. From 1972 until 1990 the circulation of library materials for home use increased from 3,399,402 to over 6,630,000.

Numerous new services were begun during the Gnat administration. Database reference service was offered for the first time in 1979. Also implemented that year were the circulation for home use of a large framed art collection and the installation of the CENTREX telephone system, which greatly enhanced the speed of providing telephone reference services.

Videotape loan service began in June, 1981, followed in 1986 by the inauguration of audiotape loans. The public response to their availability was immediate, and the size of the collections and their use have grown so that video and audio tapes have become the most popular new services offered by the Library.

Mr. Gnat felt strongly that computerization of the Library's circulation and cataloging functions was the keystone to the future growth and development of the Library System. With funds available from the 1981 sale of bonds, specifications were prepared and bids taken for an on-line book acquisition, circulation, and public access catalog system. CL Systems, Inc., (CLSI) was the

CHAPTER X

When the Warren site was acquired in 1973 and the new Lawrence site was purchased in 1974, the concept was to build large, library-owned buildings in areas of potential growth and to close . . . small rental libraries . . . with the new library facilities providing a full range of services. That is, larger book collections, specialized staff to serve adults and juveniles, and adequate facilities and meeting rooms to provide a variety of programs planned for adults and children throughout the year.

—Raymond E. Gnat, 1982

Work began in 1985 on the long awaited Central Library renovation project. Artisans clean and repaint the beautiful Main Room ceiling.

successful bidder. The availability of the laser technology for the circulation functions and the touch terminals for public access to books in the library were two aspects which contributed to the selection of CLSI, together with their demonstrated ability to provide a completely operational multi-processor system which would support over 110 on-line terminals.

The computerization project moved along quickly following initial installation of equipment and software in 1982. Retrospective conversion and bar-coding of agency collections began in February, 1982, and by the end of 1984 all agencies were either fully converted to the new system or underway, one year ahead of the original conversion schedule. On April 18, 1983, Broadway Branch Library became the first agency to go on-line.

The system has continued to be modified and upgraded since 1983. A major upgrade to the on-line catalog in 1991 provided enhanced bibliographical searching capabilities using only keyboard terminals. In addition, this upgrade to the system now supports over 300 on-line terminals. The touch terminal technology for access to the Library's holdings was phased out at the time the new keyboard access system was installed.

Administrative changes and reorganization were necessitated by the rapid growth in the Library's services and usage. Mr. Gnat made a significant administrative change on October 1, 1973, when the positions of Assistant Director and Personnel Coordinator were eliminated and two new Associate Director positions were established. Lawrence Downey, formerly Coordinator of Personnel Services, was appointed Associate Director for Centralized Services, and Marilyn McCanon, formerly Supervisor of Extension Services, was appointed Associate Director for Extension Services. Carolyn Wheeler, formerly Personnel Assistant, was appointed Administrative Assistant for Personnel Services, assuming most of the duties of the former Personnel Coordinator position.

Mr. Gnat recommended a major revision of the Library's salary and classification plan in 1978 to correct glaring inconsistencies and severe overlapping of pay ranges and classifications. Further changes were proposed and implemented in 1982, 1986 and 1992.

Interlibrary cooperation and supplemental funding for library services were significant developments during the 1970s and 1980s. The Library became a member of the Central Indiana Area Library Services Authority, an eight-county library cooperative organized in March, 1974. It began serving as the organization's reference referral and interlibrary loan center in 1975.

State funds were distributed to Indiana public libraries for the first time in 1976. In 1979 Mr. Gnat recommended participation in the state-wide reciprocal borrowing program under the auspices of the Indiana State Library, and funded initially with federal Library Services and Construction Act funds. Other funding received in 1979 related to the strengthening of major urban resource libraries. These MURL grants were also federal funds received from the State Library as part of the LSCA funding. Funding for all these programs has continued into 1991.

Under the auspices of the Public Library Foundation, a Central Library Restoration Fund Drive was launched in November, 1984, following receipt of a $200,000 challenge grant from the Krannert Charitable Trust. A campaign goal of $543,000 was set using the general theme of "Recovering Buried Treasure." Volunteers were organized and contacts were made with foundations, library friends, corporations, community leaders, and the general public. The grant was matched with $229,918 received from 1,061 contributors.

In working on the "Long Range Plan for Library Service, 1990-1995," Mr. Gnat saw the need for a mission statement which incorporated the Library's future goals and objectives. To meet this need a "Speak Out For Libraries" survey was mailed to 309,000 households county-wide, with 28,000 surveys returned. In addition, public forums were held in all public service agencies, and a staff survey was conducted. The analysis of these surveys together with information garnered from the public forums resulted in the publication of a working document, "Long Range Plan for Library Services, 1990-1995," which is currently in the process of being implemented.

Raymond E. Gnat's tenure as Director of Public Libraries has been marked with years of record-setting growth for the Indianapolis-Marion County Public Library, both in new facilities and services added, and in their use by the public. His philosophy of service has proven to be an effective one, and holds the potential for continued future growth.

The Public Library reaches farther and touches more people than ever. Year after year the Library has enlarged its book collection, increased its readership, improved its buildings and modernized its services.

—Raymond E. Gnat.

The annex completed in 1975 added 40,000 square feet of service space to the Central Library.

Assistant Librarians and Associate Directors

Not all Directors of the Library have had assistants, but a list of those who have served in that capacity is included, for they too helped shape the policies of the Directors and frequently were responsible for translating those policies into action. It is also interesting to note that three of them moved to the top position when the director retired or resigned.

ELIZA GORDON BROWNING retired as Librarian in 1917 after serving in that position for twenty five years. She became assistant to Charles Rush, her successor, serving until her death in May, 1927.

AMY WINSLOW became assistant to Mr. Rush in July, 1927, having served as Head of the Technical Department. She served until 1932 during Luther Dickerson's administration and resigned to go to Baltimore, Maryland, to head the Enoch Pratt Library.

NANCY E. TODD was Head of the Technical Department, and although never formally appointed Assistant Librarian, she performed duties sometimes assigned to the position from 1933 to 1943.

MARIAN McFADDEN was appointed Assistant to Luther Dickerson in July, 1943, and served until his retirement, when she became Acting Librarian until her appointment as Librarian in 1945.

WILMA E. REEVE filled numerous staff positions during her career with the Library and was Head of the Circulation Department when she was appointed Assistant Librarian in 1945 under Marian McFadden. She served in that position until her retirement in 1956.

NEVIN RABER became Assistant Director under Harold Sander in 1956. He had been a librarian and then Head of the Business Library in Indianapolis from 1950 to 1956. He resigned in 1962 to become Head of the Business Library at Indiana University, Bloomington, Indiana.

RAYMOND E. GNAT was appointed Assistant Director by Harold Sander in 1963, serving in that capacity until the end of 1971. He was appointed Director of Public Libraries in January, 1972, upon Mr. Sander's resignation from the position.

MARILYN J. McCANON became Associate Director for Extension Services on October 1, 1973, having served the Library since December, 1948, including the positons of Head, Bookmobile Services and Supervisor of Extension

1917-1991

Eliza G. Browning, Assistant Librarian, 1917-1927.

Nevin Raber

Facing page — top left — Marilyn J. McCanon; top right — Lawrence J. Downey; bottom left — Laura G. Johnson; bottom right — M. Jaqueline Nytes.

Services. She served as Associate Director until her retirement on June 30, 1986. Upon her retirement the Staff Association established the Marilyn J. McCanon Scholarship Fund in her honor.

At Miss McCanon's retirement reception Mr. Gnat stated that "she was largely responsible for the location and opening of all the storefront branches, the subsequent location and purchase of permanent sites and the eventual building of the new library buildings. In addition to the phasing out of several agencies, Marilyn was responsible for the relocation, renovation and/or expansion of every library branch facility in the system. Quite a list of accomplishments for a gal that started out playing string bass in the MacMurray College dance band."

LAWRENCE J. DOWNEY was appointed Associate Director for Centralized Services on October 1, 1973, having served on the Library staff since March, 1951, in a variety of positions including clerical assistant in the Circulation Division, and Librarian and Manager in several branch libraries. Mr. Downey was Coordinator of Technical Services, 1963 to 1965, and Coordinator of Personnel Services, 1965 to 1973. His position title was changed to Associate Director for Management Services in July, 1986. He retired from the library staff December 27, 1988. An endowment fund for the Fine Arts was established in his honor by the Library Staff Association at the time of his retirement.

At Mr. Downey's retirement reception Mr. Gnat commented, "Larry had been appointed to more top-level administrative staff positions than anyone else in the library's history. In addition, he had major responsibility in the various Central Library space recapture/remodelling projects, especially the renovation-restoration of the Central Library Reading Rooms. All of this activity led another retiree, Dave Linder, to comment that 'the Central Library has been a construction zone for the 20 years he had worked at the Library.' Larry was responsible for shifting the entire Central Library collection at least five times during all the construction projects. Not bad for someone who started his library career as a part-time high school page responsible for shelving books."

LAURA G. JOHNSON became Associate Director for Public Services in June, 1986, upon the retirement of Marilyn McCanon, and the subsequent reorganization of the duties and responsibilities of the two Associate Director positions. She had previously served as Director of the Bedford, Indiana, Public Library, and as an assistant and then Head, Extension Division, Indiana State Library for ten years, prior to assuming her position with the Indianapolis-Marion County Public Library.

M. JACQUELINE NYTES joined the staff as Associate Director for Management Services in October, 1988 to succeed Lawrence Downey upon his retirement. She had been Director of the Carmel-Clay, Indiana, Public Library since 1981 and had held positions previously in the Appleton, Wisconsin, Public Library and the Rockford, Illinois, Public Library.

Raymond E. Gnat, Director of Public Libraries, and Marilyn McCanon, Associate Director, at the dedication of the new Broad Ripple Library, March, 1986.

Cerene Ohr, Supervisor of Branches, Marian McFadden, Library Director, and Wilma Reeve, Assistant Director, in 1948.

Formation of a New City-County Library System

The most significant events to impact the long history of the Library were the extension, in 1966, of free library services to over 200,000 residents of Marion County who were without them, and the subsequent creation of a county-wide library system in 1968. Both events necessitated major changes in the legal status of the Library and its long relationship with the Indianapolis Board of School Commissioners.

Public libraries in Indiana had for many years functioned under various laws. From 1873 until 1968 the Indianapolis Public Library was governed by the Indianapolis Board of School Commissioners under the provisions of the Indiana School Law passed by the General Assembly on March 3, 1871. Section 4, paragraph 3 of the law read, "To levy a tax each year of not exceeding one-fifth (of one mill) on each dollar of taxable property assessed for city taxes by the City Assessor for the support of free libraries in connection with the common schools of such city . . ."

In 1947 a bill sponsored by the Indiana Library Association was passed by the legislature which made it possible for public libraries to operate under a new law, although those governed by school boards could remain governed by them, or at any time could come under the new law.

Historically, as has been shown, the Indianapolis Public Library had been a department of the Indianapolis School System. The Library and the schools shared a Building and Grounds Department, and the School Business Office handled most of the Library's accounting and business routines.

While the Library staff prepared its own budget, it became a section of the entire School Board budget, and the money required for the Library's operation was part of the tax levied by the Indianapolis Board of School Commissioners. The Library provided library services for the city's schools as part of its responsibilities to the School Board.

During the 1950s and 1960s numerous demographic changes took place within Indianapolis. Population had grown rapidly during the post-war years and had expanded into the suburban areas of the county. Free library services to the residents of Marion County outside the city limits of Indianapolis now seemed warranted. The need had been observed and articulated by county residents as well as by Marian McFadden and her staff as far back as 1953. By 1958 there were over 200,000 people living in the towns and townships of Marion County who did not have free access to the services of the Indianapolis Library. Mr. Sander ultimately came to believe the time had come when the Library should sever its ties with the Indianapolis School System and form a separate entity with its own board controlling a tax-supported county library system.

On September 11, 1962, a report was made to the Board of School

Facing page — top photo — The first Marion County Library Board, 1966 — seated l. to r. — Albert H. Wood, John L. Gigerich, Doris Dorbecker. Standing l. to r. — Harold J. Sander, Gordon H. Thompson, Cathleen Mullin, Hortense Young, Monta Hale, Raymond E. Gnat.
Bottom photo — l. to r. — Harrison Eiteljorg, John L. Gigerich, Harold J. Sander involved in planning for the new Nora Library.

Gordon H. Thompson, President of the first Marion County Public Library Board.

Commissioners by an advisory committee appointed by Mrs. Ardath Burkhart, Chairperson of the Board's Library Committee. The advisory committee, composed of Carl R. Dortch, Chairperson, Mrs. Gertrude S. Appel, George H. Dirks, and Ralph Husted studied the methods of setting up county libraries, the laws, the costs, and the financing and budget procedures. They suggested "a proper financial relationship between the Indianapolis Board of School Commissioners and any authorized governmental agency outside of Indianapolis in the event a contractual arrangement for extended library services should be negotiated and executed."

The 1963 Indiana General Assembly clarified the authority of the School Board and legalized the Board's power to contract with a county library board, if and when such a board were created.

Several groups became involved—a new organization known as "Friends of the Library," the Chamber of Commerce, and the American Association of University Women. Their purpose was to lobby for the extension of library services to all residents of Marion County.

On May 20, 1965, a group of county residents formed the county agency necessary to interact with the city—the Marion County Public Library Association, with Mr. Albert H. Wood as chairperson. This organization became very active in holding meetings, getting publicity in the news media, sponsoring petitions, and pushing legislation to accomplish its goal of forming a Marion County Public Library.

The AAUW presented a petition to the Indianapolis Board of School Commissioners with the required number of signatures—20,000 registered voters—requesting the Board provide library services to residents outside the city limits.

The Marion County Commissioners were reluctant to approve the proposal which would tax residents of Marion County outside the City of Indianapolis for library service. It was not until March 14, 1966, that they, headed by Birney L. Weber, President of the County Commissioners, voted to establish a Marion County Public Library, and a tax-supported county system was finally established.

The members appointed to serve on the first Marion County Public Library Board were:

Gordon H. Thompson, President
John L. Gigerich, Vice President
Mrs. Doris Dorbecker, Secretary
Monta E. Hale, Treasurer
Mrs. Cathleen A. Mullin
Albert H. Wood
Mrs. Hortense Young

The two units were not as yet one; still, library service in the county did begin. Between 1966 and 1968 the Marion County Public Library Board contracted with the Indianapolis Public Library to provide library service to all those Marion County residents living outside the school-city limits. There were, however, jurisdictional problems, with the Director needing to work with two boards. The natural difficulties of being responsible to two "bosses" became apparent.

In 1967 and early 1968 the library administration and the attorneys for the School Board pursued legal methods for the establishment of a single county-wide public library under the provisions of the Public Library Law of 1947. The law permitted conversion of the Indianapolis Public Library to a Class I status, which in effect would create a "City Library Unit." This new unit could merge with the existing "County Library Unit" creating a new tax district.

On June 4, 1968, the Indianapolis Board of School Commissioners approved Resolution No. 5790 in which the Board: (1) converted its library operation to a Class I status, (2) divested itself of its responsibility for public library service, (3) created a new city library district under the terms of the Public Library Law of 1947, and (4) provided for the merger of the city and county library units. The city board and the county board adopted concurrent Resolutions of Merger, also in accordance with the Public Library Law of 1947. Following this action both boards resigned and a board was subsequently appointed for the new City-County Public Library District. The new district was effective July 1, 1968.

The Board was comprised of seven members serving four-year terms. Two were appointed by the Indianapolis Board of School Commissioners, three by the Circuit Court Judge, and two by the County Commissioners. This appointive procedure continued until 1984 when HB 1313 was passed by the General Assembly changing the appointing authorities for the Library Board. Under the provisions of the new act, two Board members were appointed by the Indianapolis Board of School Commissioners, three by the County Commissioners, and two by the City-County Council.

BOARDS OF TRUSTEES

The following individuals have served as members of the Library Board since the establishment of the newly created entity.

1971	Gordon H. Thompson, President
	L. Robert Mottern, Vice-President
	Mrs. Winifred E. Pettee, Secretary
	Monta E. Hale, Treasurer
	Mrs. Vivian Terry Moore (Resigned 1/71)
	Mrs. Cathleen A. Mullin
	Douglas L. Walker (Appointed 1/71)
	Miss Phyllis W. Waters (Appointed 3/71)
1972	Gordon H. Thompson, President
	Mrs. Winifred E. Pettee, Vice-President
	Miss Phyllis W. Waters, Secretary
	Monta E. Hale, Treasurer
	L. Robert Mottern
	Mrs. Cathleen A. Mullin (Term Expired 4/72)
	Mrs. Elizabeth M. Strain (Appointed 4/72)
	Douglas L. Walker
1973	Mrs. Winifred E. Pettee, President
	Douglas L. Walker, Vice-President
	Mrs. Elizabeth M. Strain, Secretary
	Monta E. Hale, Treasurer
	Arthur E. Ecklund (Appointed 5/73)
	L. Robert Mottern (Term Expired 5/73)
	Gordon H. Thompson
	Miss Phyllis W. Waters (Deceased 12/73)
1974	Mrs. Winifred E. Pettee, President
	Douglas L. Walker, Vice-President (Resigned 12/74)
	Mrs. Elizabeth M. Strain, Secretary
	Monta E. Hale, Treasurer
	Arthur E. Ecklund
	Mrs. Jessie H. Thomas (Appointed 2/74)
	Gordon H. Thompson
1975	Arthur E. Ecklund, President
	Mrs. Elizabeth M. Strain, Vice-President
	Mrs. Jessie H. Thomas, Secretary (Term Expired 4/75)
	Mrs. Winifred E. Pettee, Treasurer
	Edward M. Green (Term Expired 4/75)
	Monta E. Hale (Resigned 8/75)
	Roderick G. Macy (Appointed 8/75)
	Ms. Mildred E. Ryan (Appointed 4/75)
	Gordon H. Thompson
	Mrs. Kathleen P. White (Appointed 4/75)
1976	Arthur E. Ecklund, President
	Mrs. Elizabeth M. Strain, Vice-President (Term Expired 4/76)
	Ms. Mildred E. Ryan, Secretary
	Mrs. Winifred E. Pettee, Treasurer
	Mrs. Anna C. Dillon (Appointed 4/76)

Gordon H. Thompson
Mrs. Kathleen P. White

Roderick G. Macy, President
Mrs. Anna C. Dillon, Vice-President
Ms. Mildred E. Ryan, Secretary
Mrs. Winifred E. Pettee, Treasurer
Arthur E. Ecklund (Term Expired 5/77)
Ralph H. Furst (Appointed 5/77)
W. Rudolph Steckler (Appointed 4/77)
Gordon H. Thompson (Term Expired 4/77)
Kathleen P. White

Roderick G. Macy, President
Mrs. Anna C. Dillon, Vice-President
Mrs. Kathleen P. White, Secretary
Ms. Mildred E. Ryan, Treasurer
Wayne Moss (Appointed 6/78)
Mrs. Winifred E. Pettee (Term Expired 5/78)
W. Rudolph Steckler (Resigned 1/79)
Mrs. Catherine S. Wallace, (Appointed 5/78)

Mrs. Anna C. Dillon, President
Wayne Moss, Vice-President
Mrs. Kathleen P. White, Secretary (Term Expired 4/79)
Ms. Mildred E. Ryan, Treasurer (Term Expired 4/79)
Mrs. Marjorie Carter (Appointed 4/79)
Joe R. Corbett (Appointed 6/79)
Mrs. Ardella Donovan-Rinne (Appointed 1/79)
Mrs. Elizabeth M. Strain (Re-appointed 4/79)
Mrs. Catherine S. Wallace

Mrs. Anna C. Dillon, President
Wayne Moss, Vice-President
Mrs. Ardella Donovan-Rinne, Secretary
Mrs. Catherine S. Wallace, Treasurer
Mrs. Bobbie Beckwith (Appointed 3/80)
Mrs. Marjorie Carter (Appointed 4/79)
Joe R. Corbett
Mrs. Elizabeth M. Strain

Wayne Moss, President
Mrs. Catherine S. Wallace, Vice-President
Mrs. Ardella Donovan-Rinne, Secretary (Term Expired 4/81)
Mrs. Anna C. Dillon, Treasurer*
Mrs. Bobbie Beckwith
Joe R. Corbett
David F. McNamar (Appointed 7/81)
Mrs. Sarah W. Otte (Appointed 4/81)
Mrs. Elizabeth M. Strain

*The term of Mrs. Anna C. Dillon expired April, 1980, however she was not replaced until July, 1981

1977

1978

1979

1980

1981

1982	Wayne Moss, President
	Mrs. Catherine S. Wallace, Vice-President
	Joe R. Corbett, Secretary
	Mrs. Bobbie Beckwith
	David F. McNamar
	Mrs. Sarah W. Otte
	Mrs. Elizabeth M. Strain
1983 and *1984*	Mrs. Catherine S. Wallace, President
	Joe R. Corbett, Vice President
	Mrs. Sarah W. Otte, Secretary
	Mrs. Bobbie Beckwith
	David F. McNamar
	Wayne Moss
	Mrs. Elizabeth M. Strain
1985 and *1986*	Joe R. Corbett, President
	Mrs. Elizabeth M. Strain, Vice-President
	David F. McNamar, Secretary
	Mrs. Bobbie Beckwith
	Wayne Moss
	Mrs. Sarah W. Otte
	Mrs. Catherine S. Wallace
1987 and *1988*	Mrs. Elizabeth M. Strain, President
	David F. McNamar, Vice-President
	Mrs. Sarah W. Otte, Secretary
	Mrs. Bobbie Beckwith
	Joe R. Corbett (Deceased 1/88)
	Wayne Moss
	Mrs. Catherine S. Wallace
	Mrs. Jane Baldwin (Appointed 3/88)
1989 and *1990*	David F. McNamar, President
	Mrs. Sarah W. Otte, Vice-President
	Mrs. Bobbie Beckwith, Secretary
	Mrs. Jane Baldwin
	Mrs. Elizabeth (Strain) Gunn
	Wayne Moss
	Mrs. Catherine S. Wallace
1991	Mrs. Sarah W. Otte, President
	Mrs. Bobbie Beckwith, Vice-President
	Mrs. Jane Baldwin, Secretary
	Mrs. Elizabeth M. Gunn
	David F. McNamar
	Wayne Moss
	Mrs. Catherine S. Wallace

The first Indianapolis-Marion County Library Board, 1968. Seated, l. to r. — Vivian Terry Moore, Winifred E. Pettee, Cathleen A. Mullin. Standing l. to r. — L. Robert Mottern, Gordon H. Thompson, John L. Gigerich, and Monta E. Hale.

Mrs. Mottern looks on as Library Board President Winifred E. Pettee presents a Certificate of Appreciation to L. Robert Mottern upon his retirement from the Board in 1973.

87

The Library Mission

A Commitment to Service

The Public Library is a service organization which provides free information in various formats to residents of the library district. The purpose of the Public Library is to provide those library materials, information, programs and services which are most wanted by residents of the service area; to provide convenient access to needed materials and information; and to actively work to make community members and organizations aware of the resources and services provided by the Public Library.

Administrative Services

The library had opened in 1873 in just three rooms joined into one long one by a counter down the center, with shelves around the walls and presumably a few tables and chairs for the convenience of readers and students. One room in the upstairs of the building served as an office, and a small one back of the reading room provided space for behind-the-scenes work. What could be called rudimentary departmentalization was Charles Evans' idea of setting aside an area for the collection of Indiana historical material and separating shelving for reference volumes, which could be used only in the room. Primarily, however, the Library was a place where books "circulated" to the borrower and then came back again, the oldest public function of the library, surviving to this day.

As the years passed, the Library, like any business or public institution wishing to survive in a changing environment, had to absorb in an orderly fashion the tremendous increase of knowledge in all fields of human endeavor. It had to extend itself beyond its own walls to reach expanding boundaries and population. Slowly but inevitably, it had to pass from the age of counting beans with the attendant problem of rats, to more and more automation with its accompanying problems of "bugs."

The Central Library has always remained the nerve center of the entire library system, performing the necessary jobs common to all agencies and providing guidance and materials for those agencies. The number of departments has increased or decreased as circumstances or ideas of administrators have dictated, with the purpose always to bring a variety of functions into a cooperative and coordinated whole serving the public as efficiently as possible.

The Indianapolis-Marion County Public Library is under the jurisdiction of an appointed Board which, as a separate municipal corporation, is authorized to levy a library tax, issue bonds, outline policies, appoint a director and perform other duties set forth in the library law, subject to such limitations as are legally imposed.

The Director of Public Libraries in turn is responsible to the Board for the proper administration of all Library functions. Though the composition of the Board and the law under which it operates are relatively new, the basic nature of the organization has not changed since the Library was established over one hundred and eighteen years ago.

At first the Head Librarian did most of the work himself with a few untrained attendants to help. For many years after departmentalization took place, all department heads and supervisors reported directly to him or her.

A description of the Library's organization as it existed over the one hundred and eighteen years from its humble beginnings in 1873 to today can be of importance as both an historical record and also as a bird's eye view of its far-flung activities. Tomorrow's innovations and the organizational changes they will necessitate will be a part of its job in serving tomorrow's world.

ADMINISTRATIVE SERVICES

PUBLIC
RELATIONS
OFFICE

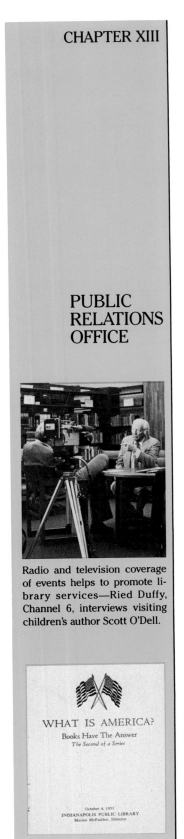

Radio and television coverage of events helps to promote library services—Ried Duffy, Channel 6, interviews visiting children's author Scott O'Dell.

WHAT IS AMERICA?
Books Have The Answer
The Second of a Series

October 4, 1951
INDIANAPOLIS PUBLIC LIBRARY
Marian McFadden, Director

Some still do. In 1968 when the Library was severed from the administration of the Indianapolis Public Schools, new responsibilities had to be assumed. As a result, two new administrative positions were established, as noted in an earlier chapter.

The position of Administrative Assistant, Finance, dealt with the Library's financial concerns and the supervision of the accounting assistant under the guidance of the Assistant Director. The Administrative Assistant, Buildings and Grounds, took over responsibility for the buildings and grounds administration, including supervision of janitorial staff, together with all maintenance, remodeling or building projects. A few other responsibilities were added to the position when it was established, including supplies and printing operations, formerly part of the duties of the office staff.

The Public Relations Office was under the immediate supervision of the Director until 1987, when it became the responsibility of the Associate Director for Management Services. As noted throughout this text, the Library has had its name mentioned in the newspapers from its beginning, most of the publicity favorable, some not. All administrators have emphasized that all staff members are public relations representatives in their every contact with the public. Branch librarians have usually had weekly columns in neighborhood newspapers, and various staff members have always been available for book talks and story telling.

As early as 1920 a staff member was placed in charge of staff publications; Amy Winslow was the first. Many delightful articles were written for the local newspapers during the middle 1920s and early 1930s by Mary Dyer Lemon and Edna Levey, who were successively editors of several staff publications during those years.

With the coming of radio, a new medium was available, and it was used to good effect. In 1939 Mr. Dickerson hired a publicity assistant to create library-orientated programs and to coordinate and help others on the staff in the work they were already doing in the field. From that time to the present, someone has been in charge of the ever increasing demands of effective library public relations.

One interesting project is well worth mentioning because of the national interest it aroused. Because so many books were being published which were hyper-critical of the American way of life, the library decided in 1950 to take a positive approach to the problem of loss of faith in America's mission. A series of annotated book lists in pamphlet form were prepared. The first two were entitled "What Made America?—Books Have The Answer," and "What Is America?" They were distributed to patrons and other libraries, including the Library of Congress, whose Librarian mentioned them in his Informational Bulletin. As a result requests for copies were received from the National Retail Book Sellers Association, which reprinted them, from the State Department, the Division of Overseas Information Centers, and the American University in Cairo, Egypt. Senator Homer Capehart wrote to Miss Dorothy Knisely, Public Relations Assistant at the time, "It should be a splendid contribution to one of the nation's greatest needs of the day: a rededication to the principles and philosophies which made America great."

The responsibilities of the Public Relations Office have now grown to include many of the activities of the whole library system. In addition to sending out news releases to the daily and weekly newspapers as well as the neighborhood papers, it handles requests from newspaper people who seek all kinds of information on every known subject and material for their "question and answer" columns.

Radio and television coverage for library activities has been excellent over the years. Weekly children's programs, story telling, book talks, book reviews, library activities, and other promotional programs have all been aired from time to time, and continue to be as time and interest are available from the various stations.

The Library distributes flyers, brochures, bookmarks, and booklets by the thousands, on every topic from "Choice Books for Pre-Schoolers" to "Famous Detectives and Their Creators." Subjects ranging from Afro-American books, to hobbies and crafts, history and science, are all covered. Although the individual departments, divisions or branches initiate these lists, it is normally the Public Relations Office that handles the proofreading, printing, and arrangements for the art work. If it is not done by a member of the staff, free-lance artists are employed. The distribution of all this material is also usually done by the Public Relations Office.

The Library's "Print Shop," under the supervision of the Public Relations Office, has been in existence for many years, using more sophisticated duplicating machines, printing presses and computers as they became available and affordable. Library publications, memoranda, printed forms, and even posters are produced. Today, three employees put out large quantities of printed material for internal library use and for distribution to the public for information and guidance.

One of the most interesting, eye-catching projects of the Public Relations Office is the constant change of exhibits in cases at Central Library. But the exhibits do not stop in the building itself; many appear in public locations such as the Home Show, Black Expo, and other large civic programs. In addition to the Public Relation Office, the Adult Services Office and the Children's Services Office also promote the Library at many of these programs.

Probably one of the most time-consuming projects of the Public Relations Office is the preparation of the twice-monthly library publication, *Reading in Indianapolis*, which will be discussed later in this text.

And finally, when new projects are planned for the Library, or new branches are opened, the Public Relations Office is always on hand to handle the essential publicity and to help with the programming of open houses or other festivities.

According to his first annual report in 1874, Charles Evans had four assistants, all women, and one night attendant, a man. Evidently it was believed it would be preferable to have a male to cope with the real or imagined dangers inherent in the hours of darkness. Just how much responsi-

For nearly fifty years the Library's Print Shop has turned out millions of flyers, brochures, bookmarks and other printed items annually for the use of staff and library users.

PERSONNEL
SERVICES OFFICE

bility was given the assistants is not known, but probably most of their tasks were of a clerical nature.

Eliza Browning, in her short history of the early years of the Library, speaks of Mr. Tyler, under whom she began her long career, ". . . he had library methods at his finger tips . . . He was our library school . . . ." She also worked under Mr. Evans when he returned for his second term of office in 1888. Of him she wrote, ". . . he taught his staff many things about library work from the book side of the question . . . this is a fountain of learning from which we must constantly drink. All the technical knowledge, all the modern and best methods are necessities but without a love for, and wide acquaintance with the books themselves, methods become mechanical . . . ."

Miss Browning put this philosophy into practice when she became Librarian in 1892 and required a four-hour examination on general literature as a pre-requisite to employment.

As mentioned earlier, Charles Rush instituted a training class in 1918 for prospective librarians who could be fed into the system, and the class became the chief method of recruiting from that time until 1941, with only a short break in its continuity.

The final decision to employ an applicant has always been the responsibility of the Head Librarian, subject to approval of the Board. Dismissals follow the same course, but non-probationary employees have the right to a Board hearing prior to a final decision.

As the number of employees increased, applicants were usually screened by others, usually supervisors or department heads, but final interviews continued to be held by the Head Librarian. Carrie Scott, Supervisor of Children's Work, and in charge of the Training Class, did a great deal of preliminary interviewing in the earlier years. Personnel files were kept in the Business Office, providing valuable information when staff members were being considered for a change of duty assignment, promotion, demotion or termination. The final decision and recommendation for these latter personnel changes were also made by the Librarian, but were subject to approval by the Board of School Commissioners, as was the appointment of all new employees to the staff.

With the coming of World War II, competition for labor was high in all fields including the professions. In 1943 Mr. Dickerson brought Marian McFadden into the office from her branch position to take over special assignments. Her first task was to analyze jobs to see how much work was being done by professional librarians which could be done more efficiently and at less expense by well trained clerical workers. At the same time, staff turnover was so great that Miss McFadden took over recruiting and interviewing applicants for clerical positions.

Following the end of World War II, the Library found itself catapulted into personnel practices already common to business and industry. Hours of work, pensions, "fringe benefits," and numerous other questions were stated as concerns of job applicants. In addition, a state law had become effective in 1942 requiring that librarians have certain professional training and experience to be certified for specific positions. Finally, the Public Employees Retirement Fund became a reality in 1946, tax deductions from pay checks

The library is often the setting for an intensive match between amateur chess enthusiasts, both children and adults.

were required, and numerous other personnel rules and regulations became effective.

To meet these increasing personnel services needs, Miss McFadden established the position of Supervisor of Personnel in 1947 to administer not only the interviewing and hiring of new employees, but also all other aspects of effective personnel management. The work load has expanded with the continuing growth of the staff, particularly following the Library's separation from the administration of the School Board in 1968, and the addition of custodial and maintenance staff to the work load of the Personnel Office. Orientation classes, job interviews, questions about the library profession, the preparation of increasingly complicated and computerized payrolls have carried the Personnel Services Office a great distance from the early years of just "hiring and firing."

As noted earlier in this text, the Personnel Services Office was placed under the supervision of the Associate Director for Management Services on July 1, 1986. Carolyn Wheeler, Administrative Assistant for Personnel Services, and her staff carry out all the functions of the office, under the guidance of the Associate Director.

ADULT SERVICES OFFICE

The Adult Services Office and the position of Coordinator of Adult Services have a relatively short history, having been created in 1957. However, many of their responsibilities date back to the very early years of the library system.

When Eliza Browning established the first branch libraries in the late 1890s, she appointed a Supervisor of Branches, whose duty it was to oversee and guide these neighborhood units of service. Many of these responsibilities were assigned to the newly created Coordinator of Adult Services in 1957. The position involves the planning and coordinating of services to adults in all library agencies including evaluating personnel, studying work loads, and assisting in training staff members who work with adults.

One of the chief responsibilities of the Coordinator of Adult Services is to oversee the selection of materials for the use of the public, the first and oldest function of the Library.

William Poole drew up the first list of book titles for the new Indianapolis Library in 1872. Eight thousand of these were purchased. Charles Evans believed the reading tastes of all people should be considered, but refused to buy fiction that was "vicious and immoral." Arthur Tyler, as a protection, submitted his selections to the Library Committee of the Board and to the Citizens Advisory Committee to prevent "unwholesome novels" from slipping into the collection. Lay library committees to help choose books seem to have existed off and on for some time, but finally the Head Librarian became the final arbiter of the Library's holdings.

Obviously, today it would be impossible for the Director, or any one person, to select all the books now printed in various specialized fields. Several plans have been used through the years to assure a good collection. Currently it is the duty of the professional staff in the Central adult divisions: Arts; Business, Science and Technology; and Social Science. Branches usually do not have titles not held in one of these divisions. Orders are sent to the Coordinator of Adult Services for approval. Some other titles may be suggested by the Coordinator, or some orders may be rejected in order that a proper balance may be obtained in the collection. It is also the responsibility of the Coordinator to decide if titles should be discarded or replaced.

Another important responsibility of the Adult Services Office is work with community groups. The office coordinates all work done with adult groups throughout the library system, consults with community leaders, and receives requests and assigns staff members for talks about books or library service to groups in the county.

Mr. Julius (Jack) Chitwood was the first staff member to be appointed to the newly created position of Coordinator of Adult Services. He served in that capacity from April, 1957, until his resignation October 10, 1961. He had been First Assistant in the Circulation Department at Central Library from January, 1954, until he was promoted to the Coordinator's position in 1957.

Miss Frances C. Stalker served as Coordinator from October, 1961, until her retirement on April 28, 1978. Miss Stalker had been a member of the staff since April 8, 1938, and held positions at the Rauh, South Grove, and Shelby Branch Libraries. She had been Head, Reference Department and Head Social Science Division prior to being promoted to Coordinator of Adult Services.

The current Coordinator, C. Catherine Gibson, has held the position since May, 1978. Before her promotion to the position she had been a librarian at Broad Ripple Branch Library and had been Manager of Brown Branch Library. She has been a member of the staff since January 27, 1969.

When the library was organized, little, if any, consideration was given to children and their book needs. Whether any children were among the first five hundred borrowers in 1873 is not known, but at a very early time there was a rule that no child under the age of ten could have a library card. Eliza Browning in her brief library history states, "Children were considered as necessary nuisances and in the way generally."

During William Hooper's administration a newspaper listed "urchins" among the patrons in the reading room, but to Hooper, a non-librarian, must

Story hours have never failed to attract hordes of youngsters to the wonderful world of books.

Carrie E. Scott—her life revolved around children and their books.

go the distinction of first recognizing the needs of young readers, for he published the first catalogue of books in the Library especially selected for young people.

In her history, Miss Browning continues, "When we built the library at Meridian and Ohio Streets in 1892, no provision was made for a Children's Room. Small tables were placed in the Reading Room, and juvenile books in closed stacks, but not a separate room. Few libraries had them.

"A wave of common sense awakening spread over this country and in 1899 we too opened a special corner for the children's use. We screened off from the big reading room a space 40 feet square."

Later, the School Offices moved from the building. Miss Browning comments, "Where the Board had had its offices we established the children's room—always inadequate, badly lighted by day and night and very cold in winter and hot and dusty in summer."

Not a very auspicious beginning, but at least the preamble of what was to become one of the most widespread and appreciated services the Library was to render.

As the first branch libraries were established prior to 1899, probably no specific provisions were made for children, but later the branches would have at least special sections where juvenile books were shelved and tables and chairs of the right size for the little ones, including "urchins."

When the Central Library moved to its new home in 1917, the Riley Room on the ground level was specifically planned for boys and girls. Since 1951, a portrait of James Whitcomb Riley by the noted artist Wayman Adams has hung in the room, a bequest of the author Booth Tarkington, and a continued reminder to young readers of the poet for whom the Library named this special room.

In 1917 Carrie E. Scott joined the staff, and her name became synonymous with work with children, not only locally but throughout the country. Though she also headed the training classes and performed many other duties, her life

Evelyn R. Sickles, noted story-teller and author, and the Library's Supervisor of work with children, 1943 to 1958.

revolved around children and their books. She knew most of the distinguished juvenile authors and illustrators of her time and brought many of them to Indianapolis to inspire the staff and to give children the opportunity of meeting "a real author."

Her administrative duties did not permit her time to be in the children's room often to suggest and hand out books, but some older adults today remember her telling them stories. She was very short and heavy-set, and her dark eyes shone from her kindly round face with a glow which came from the fire of imagination. It cannot really be said that she led children, but rather just joyfully went along with them into that eternally magic land of Once-Upon-A-Time. Miss Scott and Edna Johnson compiled the first edition of the *Anthology of Children's Literature*, published in 1935.

Evelyn R. Sickels, who succeeded as supervisor following Miss Scott's death in the summer of 1943, was also well known as a storyteller and author. Her *Pet Parade* was based on an actual event which took place in the Indianapolis Library. This was followed by *The Little Red School House* and *Here Comes Johnny*. She also was co-author of second, third and fourth editions of the Anthology, the last done after her retirement in 1958.

Mabel Leigh Hunt, a children's librarian and the first administrator of the Rauh Memorial Branch, also launched her career as a noted author of children's books while on the Library's staff. So successful was it that, she resigned her position and devoted the rest of her life to writing. *Lucinda, Little Girl With Seven Names*, and several others for younger children proved immensely popular. Two of her later books, *Have You Seen Tom Thumb* and *Better Known As Johnny Appleseed* were runners up for the American Library Association's Newbery Medal, awarded for the most distinguished children's book of the year. *Better Known As Johnny Appleseed* was chosen to be placed in the White House Library.

Due to the foresight of many people at the Central Library and in the branches working with children, and the wise direction of their supervisors, the Library has come a long way since the newspaper reported "a few urchins" usually looking at books "with a lot of pictures." Children's literature, of course, has also made great strides, with distinguished authors and illustrators contributing a flow of noteworthy books.

Rules have been changed to better fit the needs of children. No longer must they be ten years old to have a library card of their own, and even the pre-schooler can enjoy picture books or stories taken home by parents or older brothers and sisters. No longer are children restricted to borrowing just from the children's collection, but may borrow any book in the library's collection, adult or juvenile.

By 1880, or soon after, the policy of the Library's working closely with the schools was established. During Eliza Browning's administration collections were placed in all schools for the seventh and eighth grades, and a library assistant visited the schools once a week to help service the collection.

In 1917 a Schools Division Room was provided in the new Central Library building. It was combined with the Teacher's Room. In a survey of the Library, compiled by Mr. Rush for the years 1917 to 1922 it was stated, "This division has direct charge of work with grade schools—lending collections of books to any grade school room in the city." Although the Library was funded through the public school system, service was automatically extended to parochial or other private schools in the city.

Eventually deposit stations were placed in many large schools, and a librarian came once each week to circulate books. Other schools had collections in the classrooms under the direct supervision of the teacher. For many years the branch libraries provided the books to schools in their district, which were too far away for the children to come to the branch. They were also in charge of a few deposit stations. As the years passed, however, it became extremely difficult for the branches to spare the materials from their own shelves.

Faced with the tremendous growth of the school population in the 1950s, a change of policy was initiated. The deposit stations, all supervised by the School Services Division by that time, were closed, and the Division assumed the responsibility of sending collections to all class rooms if requested, unless the school was close to a branch library or to the Central Library. This resulted in a more equal distribution of books and services, with Division librarians assembling and changing the collections throughout the school year.

In 1967 the Indianapolis Public Schools began opening a library in each of its elementary schools. The School Services Division of the Public Library was abolished when the library separated from the school system in 1968.

Ruth Peaslee joined the staff in 1958, assuming the position of Supervisor of Work With Children following the retirement of Evelyn Sickels. Her title was subsequently changed to Coordinator of Children's Services. The duties of the Coordinator closely parallel those of the Adult Coordinator: the responsibility of planning and coordinating service to children in all agencies, interviewing, training and supervising personnel working under her direction, cooperating with community, school and other educational leaders and groups in the community, and most important of all, assuming ultimate responsibility for selection of materials for children.

The process of selecting juvenile books moves through several stages. Most books are read or examined before purchase as copies are received from the publishers. The responsibility for selection for the Central Library's Children's Division rests with the Manager of that division, subject to final approval of the Coordinator. The Manager assigns to staff members books in certain subject areas or for certain ages. Children's librarians in the branches are also involved in the process by reading review copies of books assigned to them, writing reviews, and recommending or rejecting for purchase. When a final list for purchase is prepared, the branches may choose those they wish to add to their collections.

The Riley Room for Young People, or Children's Division, is the center of activity for children at Central Library. Although there are few "neighborhood" children walking in now, many are brought in by parents and schools from all over the county. The pattern of service has changed in recent years, with many city and county school classes coming for scheduled visits, as well as scout, campfire, and other community groups. The emphasis has changed and is now placed on the many needs of children in culturally deprived areas,

Books provide a delightful fascination for even the youngest of toddlers.

The Golden Egg holds the attention of these three-year-olds at a preschool reading program.

Children often love best those books which are just sufficiently above their understanding to excite a wish to climb to their level.

—William deM. Hooper, 1883

on work with pre-school and toddler groups, and especially on providing programs of interest to the family as a reading group.

The library has an unusually fine staff of "storytellers," and the demand is great for their services, not only at schools, playgrounds, and community centers, but on radio and television.

All through the years there have been summer reading clubs, film programs, book talks, puppet shows, and other special programs to promote interest in reading, and each year librarians make thousands of visits to schools, both public and private, to create an interest in the library and what it has to offer. See Chapter XXI for further information on special programs for children.

One interesting statement concerning children and reading was made by Librarian William Hooper over 100 years ago, "Children often love best those books which are just sufficiently above their understanding to excite a wish to climb to their level." Those who have had the responsibility for choosing a wide variety of children's books for the Library have included "challenging" among their several criteria.

Commenting 100 years later Ruth Peaslee said, "Though patterns of service change, the goal remains steady: to provide each child the best for him in books and information and to aid each child to find and use those books."

Ruth Peaslee resigned as coordinator in August, 1973. She was succeeded by Evelyn Ann Strachan in February, 1974. Miss Strachan had been a children's librarian on the staff for many years serving at the Shelby, East Washington, and Brown Branch Libraries, and as Manager of the Children's Division. She retired from the staff on December 31, 1984. Her successor as Coordinator of Children's Services was Christine Cairo, who came to the Indianapolis library system from the Kokomo, Indiana, Public Library where she had been Head of the Children's Department. She had also held children's services positions with the Detroit, Michigan, Public Library, the Kent County Library System in Grand Rapids, Michigan, and had been Head of the Children's Department at the Grandville, Michigan, Public Library for several years.

Craft time at the Central Library.

The Central Services Department

When the Library was established in 1873, the public was served in one room. Reference books were separated from circulating books, but the special facilities which were set aside for children, opened in 1899, could be considered the first real department.

The planners for the new Central Library opened in 1917 envisioned further growth of specialized collections and specialized work in administration and book preparation. Beginning in 1918 several departments were established. Some were expanded, others combined or abolished, but the complete reorganization of Central Library public service agencies was not completed until 1960, during the administration of Harold J. Sander.

A feeling had been growing in the early 1950s that there should be a librarian of Central Library to better supervise and hold together these various units. To a limited degree this was done in 1958, but it was not until the major reorganization of 1960 that the Central Services Department was created.

Miss Pauline French was appointed as the first Supervisor of the Central Services Department on February 1, 1960, remaining in the position until her retirement December 31, 1975. She had been on the staff since February, 1941, and had served as a librarian at the Brightwood, Spades, Madison, and Broad Ripple Branch Libraries, as Adult Activities Librarian at Central Library from 1949 to 1957, and as Assistant to the Adult Services Coordinator and Head, General Adult Department from 1957 until her appointment as Supervisor in 1960.

The Supervisor administered the following Central Library agencies and services: Arts Division, Business Library, Children's Division, Circulation Control Center, Science & Technology Division, Circulation Division, Social Science Division, Film Division, Information Desk, and the Reader's Assistant.

The Social Science Division, one of the new agencies created in the 1960 Central Services Department reorganization.

Facing page — Main Reading Room, Central Library

CIRCULATION AND SOCIAL SCIENCE DIVISIONS

The Circulation Department occupied the stately Main Reading Room in 1917.

Because several of the divisions now under the department have long histories under other names, and because other organizational changes have been made since the reorganization of 1960, each division will be considered separately.

As the circulating of books was the first function of the Library, a Circulation Department was the first separate department established. The book checkout and return system was ponderous and time consuming, involving numerous slips of paper and much writing of numbers while the patron waited.

In 1892, as noted earlier in this text, Miss Browning changed to the much simpler "Newark System." In 1932 when business was reaching a peak never before experienced, Mr. Dickerson further speeded up the process by asking each borrower to write his or her number on the book card. After that, the attendant needed only to stamp the date and take the card. This "self service" was readily accepted by the public, and there were few errors.

When the first bookmobile went into service in 1952, a microfilm machine was used to check out books, and it proved to be accurate and efficient. This photocharging system, refined and expanded, was placed in use in all circulating agencies, and remained in use until the present automated circulation system was installed in all libraries between 1983 and 1985.

In the beginning most circulating books were shelved in the "stacks," closed to the public. The reader could only ask the attendant for a book, which was then brought to him or her. In 1892 the rule was relaxed somewhat, and a patron could enter book stack areas if granted permission; but by 1906 free access to the stacks was permitted.

Miss Browning tells of a "very short, rather stout lady who had clamored for years for open access to the books." Now she thought, this woman would be happy, but she continued to ask the attendant to get her books for her. Miss Browning finally asked her why she did this and the women confessed she could not reach the upper shelves, was too fat to stoop to the lower ones, and none of the books she liked were on the middle ones! Even as noble an institution as a public library cannot please all of the people all of the time.

The counting of the number of people entering the Library by using beans had ceased in 1880. For many years an attempt was made to keep some attendance figures by marking four lines on a sheet of paper and crossing them with a fifth, but at busy times this was a forgotten task. From time to time at Central Library a hand counter was also used. The first electric eye "people counter" was installed at Central Library in 1971, registering the number of people going to the adult divisions, and in 1972 a unit was installed for the Children's Division as well. Eventually such electric eye counters were installed in all public library buildings.

Regulations regarding the registration of those who wish library cards has changed little over the past 117 years, the only real requirement being the verification of the address. Any resident of the city, and since 1966, of the county (except the City of Beech Grove and the town of Speedway) is eligible. Out-of-county residents may purchase cards for a specified fee.

Eliza Browning in her history states that no child under ten could have a card, but an early report of Charles Evans states that the use of the library by children was determined only by their ability to print their names. However, the signature of the parent or guardian was and is required. Earlier, children were limited to the borrowing of juvenile books, but currently they may borrow any library materials. However, it is the responsibility of the parent or guardian to monitor what his or her child is reading.

The original 500 borrowers registered in 1873 had risen to over 42,000 by 1917, and at the end of 1990 the total reached 561,504, and continues to grow. The complete file of registered borrowers has now been computerized and is on-line in all agencies.

When the new Central Library opened in 1917, the honor of occupying the stately Main Room, which even during the busiest times manages to retain a serene dignity, went to the Circulation Department. A long-time member of the department once remarked, "You can't help feeling that you are a little better person because you have worked in such a beautiful place."

Known for many years as the "Delivery Room," the Main Room had a semi-circular desk opposite the front door in front of swinging doors which led to a passageway called "the bridge." Beyond were the book stacks, originally open to the public only on the first tier. Since the stack renovation project completed in 1973, three tiers of book stacks containing circulating books are open to the public. Originally these upper floors were for the use of bound magazines and reference and/or infrequently used materials.

The Main Room desk was truly the center of public-staff interaction, as it was here that all books were checked out and returned and patrons registered for library cards. Just as in the branches, there were regular borrowers who came week after week to their favorite librarians, and in turn many of the librarians knew the types of books their patrons wanted, often remembering better than the readers what they had already read.

Library Director Harold Sander confers with staff in the Circulation Department's returned book sorting area.

On the shelves near the desk were placed the "seven day" books and the "duplicate collection." These collections consisted of recent books of great popularity and a short lending period, and "duplicate," popular books which could be borrowed for a charge. The word "duplicate" was used because copies of all such titles were always available in the regular collection without charge if the borrower were willing to wait until the book became available.

Miss Browning initiated the duplicate collection with a charge of one cent a day per book, and when the book had paid for itself, it was transferred to the free collection. The continuing history of this collection is not fully known. It may have been dropped for a time, but Mr. Rush mentions the one-cent-a-day charge in 1921. Whether there was another hiatus or not, Mr. Dickerson continued or reinstated the collection by or prior to 1930 with the charge raised to two cents a day. In 1947 the collection was discontinued, and later the "seven day" books were also abandoned.

On the shelves around the lower level of the Circulation Department room was placed a collection known as the "Silver Star" books, a selection of outstanding titles in all classes under the jurisdiction of the Department. The collection was established in 1928, but in 1954 was changed to display a large number of books on subjects pertinent to changing interests of the time.

CHAPTER XIV

What in the world! This giant globe finds a welcome home in the Reference Department in 1946—the gift of L.S. Ayres and Co. James Haramy was the page.

For many years a Readers' Advisor's desk was located near the main entrance to the room. Here, from September, 1929, until her retirement in July, 1953, Mary Cain, better know to staff and patrons as "May," gave all kinds of information about books, coupled with personal interest, to all who needed assistance in selecting the appropriate book.

From her office just off the Delivery Room, Marcia Furnas, head of the Circulation Department from the time the building opened in 1917 until her death in 1941, supervised the busy scene at the Loan Desk. She was succeeded by Mary Wilson, who headed the Department until her retirement in 1957. Esther Thornton supervised the Department from 1957 until she retired in 1961.

The Department's name was changed in 1960 to Circulation Division. Harold Burton was Division Manager from September, 1961, until he retired from the staff in January, 1973. Rasheeda Randle was Manager of the Circulation Division from February, 1973, until August, 1987. The name of the division had been changed again in 1982 to Central Support Services, and in 1987 it came under the supervision of the newly created Central Services Division, an umbrella agency incorporating several Central Library operations. Stephanie Whitmore was appointed to the position of Manager, Central Support Services in October, 1987. Daniel Fast, a long time Central Library staff member, has been manager of Central Services Division since its formation in 1987.

The constant increase in business and the need for more and more space brought about some needed changes. These changes were inevitable and advantageous, but unfortunately marred somewhat the dignified serenity the room had provided for so many years.

The illumination from the great chandeliers was beautiful—but dim. There were spots where it was impossible to read book titles, and public and staff alike were observed, particularly after dark, using flashlights. In 1952-1953 new lighting was added in various departmental offices and stacks. In August, 1953, new lights were installed on the mezzanine, and in October, 1953, at last, the Main Room and its books could be seen. Lighting was again improved during the Central Library restoration project done in 1984-1987.

In 1960 the public catalog, which had been on the west balcony outside the Reference Room, was moved downstairs to the Main Room. Its location had been convenient for the Reference staff, but members of the Circulation Department, and especially the public, had to climb the stairs to reach it. The new arrangement was more convenient, but the broad expanse of the room had to yield to this convenience.

The moving of the catalog was part of the major reorganization of the department completed that year. In 1957 the routine duties of the desk—the loan and return of materials, collection of overdues fines, registration and the keeping of other records—were grouped into a new Circulation Section, while the responsibilities of the book collection and readers' assistance were grouped into a General Adult Department.

Then in 1960, as noted above, the name of the Circulation Department was changed to the "Circulation Division," and a new Circulation Control Center was created, where computers and other equipment performed many of the clerical routines pertaining to the circulation process, not only for the Central Library, but for the branch libraries also.

That same year the General Adult Department changed its name to the Social Science Division, retaining some of the original classes of material such as philosophy, religion, social sciences, travel, history and biography, which had been the responsibility of the old Circulation and General Adult Departments. The new Social Science Division also took on other duties previously carried by the Reference Department.

The first collection of books purchased for the library in 1873 had contained reference materials, and during the short regime of Albert Yohn a special alcove was set aside for the Indiana materials Mr. Evans had collected. The general reference collection was also strengthened. When the Central Library moved to its new home in 1917, the large west room on the second floor became the Reference Department, remaining and growing there until the reorganization of 1960.

When veterans were returning to school after World War II, the Purdue Extension, at that time located just a block from the library, was swamped with students. The school turned to the library for help, and the latter offered its facilities for study hall space. There was some fear upon the part of both institutions that discipline and disruption of normal services might be a problem. It never materialized. These were serious students, and they came between classes, filling every available chair, not only in the Reference Room but in all departments, impressing everyone with their dedication to learning.

Through the years the Reference Department helped many individuals find needed answers. It would be almost impossible for the public to realize the extent to which reference material has been used by students, authors, researchers, writers of club papers, and many others. Nor does the layman often comprehend the training and skill needed by the staff to make quick and efficient use of the thousands of books, clippings, pamphlets, government documents, bound or microfilmed newspapers and magazines, dictionaries, encyclopedias, indexes, histories, statistics, computerized database reference sources, and other materials.

The Pamphlet Division occupied the South Hall of Central Library from 1938 until 1952, when it was closed and its collection shelved with book materials on the same subjects.

The Information Desk—1960.

THE EAST
READING ROOM
AND ARTS
DIVISION

When the Reference Department was closed in 1960 and the room taken over fully by the Science & Technology Division, the reference materials were dispersed. The new subject divisions took over the responsibility for all reference materials covering the subjects under their jurisdiction, and the staff followed the materials into the new divisions.

The new Social Science Division, established in the Main Room on the first floor, absorbed the general reference collection, in addition to those reference materials falling into the subject classes the division covered. This included bound magazines and newspapers. This latter responsibility remained with the division until the new Newspaper and Periodical Division was formed in late 1981. Harriet Cohen has been Manager of this latter Division since its founding.

Irene Mischler was the administrator for the Social Science Division from October 16, 1961, until her retirement December 31, 1978. She was succeeded by Laura Bramble, who later resigned, and in October, 1981 Lois Laube became Division Manager, the position she currently holds.

As briefly mentioned earlier in this text, a pamphlet room had been set up in 1938 in the west corridor leading to the administrative offices. It contained ephemeral, inexpensive but valuable material on all subjects. In 1951 it was dismantled to make room for the new film collection, with the pamphlets going to the Circulation Department, and then in 1960 to the new Social Science Division together with the large collection inherited from the Reference Department.

The Information Desk had been placed in the Main Room under the direct control of the Supervisor of Central Services. At that time the Supervisor was responsible for the selection and maintenance of the informational files, using materials from all public service divisions. The desk provided answers for the simple sort of questions which required little or no research. As this desk was placed on the south side of the Main Room, most library users would stop there perhaps only for direction or referral information, but also for quick reference service.

In the space where the great Loan Desk had stood in the center of the Main Room, two smaller reference desks were placed, giving reference service and readers' assistance. A smaller checkout and return desk was placed on the southwest side of the room.

The large room on the east side of the second floor of Central Library was designated as the Reading Room in 1917. Here were kept all the current magazines and newspapers. The staff was responsible for caring for these materials, which were housed in the stacks until they were ready for permanent binding. All materials received in the room were checked in and dated on arrival and then placed on the shelves immediately.

At the south end of the East Reading Room one special section was set aside in 1917. It was stocked with low shelves and entered through swinging gates. Here was housed the Mears Medical library, used for reference by doctors, medical students, and other qualified personnel. The collection had been established in 1898 and had further developed with valuable gifts. More detailed information regarding the Mears Collection may be found in Chapter XXIII, *Special Gifts and Memorials.*

Also in the Reading Room in those early years was the small but useful genealogy collection which also was administered by the Reading Room staff. See Chapter XXIII, *Special Gifts and Memorials,* regarding the Darrach Memorial Library bequest.

The Library's materials in art and music were originally housed at the north end of the East Reading Room. In 1924 the Art and Music Department was established. It was the center of information in the fields of fine arts and music, including material on painting, sculpture, architecture, home-making and music for the amateur or the professional. To accomplish this the Art and Music Department maintained a vast assortment of books, pictures, pamphlets, clippings, music scores, phonodiscs and other materials, all of which have been augmented through the years by generous and outstanding gifts.

Elizabeth Ohr, Manager of the Department from 1928 until her retirement in 1958, once remarked, "We have a finger in almost every artistic pie that is made in Indianapolis," for into the room came many of the community's best known artists, painters, architects and musicians, some of them nationally known, besides a large segment of the public.

News of the day, from around the world! Current magazines and newspapers draw hundreds of readers to the East Reading Room daily.

As early as 1945 music lovers in the city, spearheaded by Leonard Strauss, began requesting that the Library provide recordings for lending purposes. With many generous gifts a record collection was started. The first record players were purchased in 1947; recordings could then be listened to in the library by individuals using ear phones. The new listening tables proved to be particularly popular with college students, who liked to listen to classical music while they studied. In 1948 the Library was able to purchase some recordings, and by March of that year there were enough recordings in the collection to begin lending them. This service has continued to grow and today is one of the most distinctive and popular services of the Library. Audiotapes were added to the collection in 1986, and compact discs will be added in the near future.

In the 1960 reorganization, the Art and Music Department was re-named the Arts Division. The real difference was the addition of the fields of fiction, general literature, drama, and language to the responsibility of the Division's staff. This seemed logical, as "Arts" could easily be expanded to include the "Humanities." One incongruity of this new subject arrangement, due to the inevitable peculiarities of the Dewey Decimal classification system, was the inclusion of materials on recreation, games, and sports under the Division's supervision; thus the football fan, golf addict, or chess buff, could find himself or herself seated next to a reader of Kafka or someone researching the architecture of ancient Rome.

Other Division administrators included Ruth Harry Hathaway from 1958 until her retirement in 1975. She was succeeded by Helen Barron from 1975 until her retirement in 1981. Both administrators had served on the staff for many years in several capacities before assuming the position of Manager, Arts Division. The current manager of the Division is Daniel Gann, who came to the staff from a position with the Memphis Public Library.

THE BUSINESS, SCIENCE AND TECHNOLOGY DIVISION

Central Library agencies answer over 400,000 inquiries by telephone each year.

It was in September, 1921, that the Technical Department began its existence. Mr. Rush described its purpose in these words, "(It) had for its aim the building up of a strong scientific and technical collection and the rendering of efficient reference and book service to the manufacturers, chemists, engineers and other scientific and industrial workers of this city."

The Department's collection was housed at the south end of the Reference Room, and there it remained until the reorganization in 1960. Its name was changed at that time to the Science and Technology Division, and with the demise of the Reference Department as such in that location, its collection and services took over the entire West Reading Room.

Mr. Rush had written that the collection had grown "appreciably" during 1921-1922. One had only to visualize the words "science" and "technology" to realize how their coverage was to extend from then until after World War II, and how it exploded in the years between 1950 and 1990.

Certainly, among its early holdings, the Library had books depicting a trip to the moon, a speedy journey around the world, and a voyage under the sea, and these Jules Verne classics would be followed by others telling of travels to other planets and the development of all kinds of improbable mechanical marvels. These books were not considered to be of technical importance. Instead they were classed as what came to be known as "science fiction." When science fiction fantasies became hard-rock reality, the new types of knowledge and theories poured into the Technical Department. The development of plastics, synthetics, the scientific penetration of space and the solar system; the studies in the field of aeronautics, the list could go on and on, and tomorrow technologies, sciences, words, and expressions unheard of today will have to be added to the collection.

From the very beginning it was the aim of the Science and Technology Department to maintain a close relationship with all research-oriented industries in the city. Through the years many of these developed their own private specialized technical libraries, but both Nancy Todd, long time head of the department, and Mary Jo Wood, her assistant, and later her successor, established a cooperative working arrangement with the librarians of Eli Lilly & Company, Naval Avionics, Allison Divison of General Motors and other specialized technical and scientific libraries. The various locations of material, expensive to duplicate, were known to all, and information was readily passed from one special library collection to the other. This cooperative working relationship with the special libraries in the city continues to be a priority of the Division today.

The Department had been renamed the Science and Technology Division in 1960. It was renamed the Business, Science and Technology Division in 1976 when the Business Library, located in the Board of Trade Building, was closed and its collection was moved to the Central Library and integrated with the business materials there.

Miss Todd served as Manager of the Department from 1923 until her retirement in April, 1948. She was succeeded by Miss Wood who headed the Department until her retirement on June 30, 1968. Miss Wood had been a member of the Library's staff since April, 1929. Barbara Frantz became Manager of the Division July 1, 1968, serving in that capacity until her retirement on June 30, 1982. Miss Frantz had been appointed to the staff on October 9, 1950, serving in several branch library positions prior to her appointment as Division Administrator. Her successor, Mark Leggitt, was appointed to the position on August 2, 1982. Mr. Leggitt had previously served in the Milwaukee, Wisconsin, and Knoxville, Tennessee, Public Libraries.

While this "division" was considered a part of the Central Services Department, it was unique in that it was not located at the Central Library until 1976.

The Business Library opened February 8, 1918 as has been said, in the old Central Library building at Ohio and Meridian Streets. Ethel Cleland was its founder and first administrator. Miss Cleland was a woman of outstanding ability who wrote numerous articles for library and business journals, did research work for the American Library Association and the Library of Congress, helped organize the Special Libraries Association, and for many years issued a weekly book list which was widely circulated. She served as Head of the Business Library until her retirement July 1, 1948.

The Library, as one of the first in the United States devoted entirely to business materials, was visited by librarians from many cities. Its holdings included an up-to-date collection of books on such topics as finance, accounting, marketing, and investments. Other business related subjects, government documents pertaining to business, city, telephone and business directories of many localities, house organs, clippings, pictures, and information of all kinds useful to the business community were also available.

From its opening until 1943 it had enjoyed a good location in the large south room of the building occupied also by the Teachers' Special Library and the offices of the Indianapolis Board of School Commissioners. In that year it was moved to the second floor of the building and was housed in the room directly above its original location. The new location created quite a public reaction because of the necessity for users to climb the steep stairs to reach the library; still, the Business Library continued to be part of downtown life.

The staff often commented that few Indianapolis business executives realized how important a part the Business Library was playing in their decision making. A president of a business would often tell his secretary to prepare statistical or other informational data for him. The secretary would call the library to obtain the desired facts or information and present it to her boss, who, in turn would congratulate himself for having such an efficient secretary. When Miss Cleland retired in 1948, the Chamber of Commerce gave a luncheon in her honor, attended not only by Mayor Philip Bayt, but also by many of those business executives whose secretaries had been so efficient.

On September 1, 1948, Miss Cleland was succeeded by Harold J. Sander, who headed the library until September, 1951, when he resigned to become head of the Roanoke, Virginia, Public Library.

Mr. Sander replaced the weekly book list with a newsletter titled "Your Cue To Business," which not only listed new business acquisitions of the library, but presented the information in a chatty, readable style. The clever comments it contained brought a request from *Readers Digest* to receive a

Ethel Cleland, founder and administrator of the Business Library, 1918 to 1948.

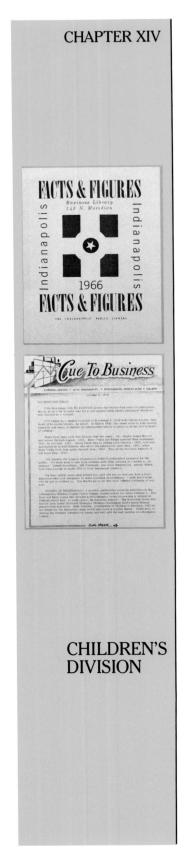

**CHILDREN'S
DIVISION**

copy and to be permitted to quote from it.

Another innovation of Mr. Sander's tenure was the addition of smoking privileges in the Business Library. Presumably, in the resulting haze, knotty business problems were better solved or just allowed to slip contentedly away.

Not only did the stairs the staff and public must climb present a problem, but the growth of the library's collection brought about desperately crowded conditions. A chance for expansion came on November 14, 1962, when the library moved across the street to quarters on the ground floor of the Board of Trade Building at 143 North Meridian Street. The open house for the new quarters was sponsored by the Better Business Bureau, the Chamber of Commerce, the Downtown Merchant Association, and the Board of School Commissioners.

A very useful booklet entitled "Indianapolis Facts and Figures" was compiled and prepared annually by the Business Library for several years, with financing made possible by an anonymous gift given in memory of Mary Wheeler Wells, one of the library's most able and admired librarians. The booklet was a statistical and governmental summary of Indianapolis and Marion County, and was of great value to anyone seeking brief, up-to-the-minute information.

Following Mr. Sander's resignation, Mrs. Wells was Acting Manager of the Business Library from September 19, 1951, until September 30, 1953, when Nevin Raber was appointed to the position. Mr. Raber administered the Business Library until his appointment as Assistant Director of the Library System in November, 1956. He was succeeded as manager of the Business Library by Ronald Roberts, who held the position from January 1, 1957 until his resignation on May 1, 1961. Mrs. Wells again served as the library's administrator until her death on May 31, 1964. Mr. Bruce Aldridge was appointed to the position July 1, 1964, serving until his death on April 29, 1975. No permanent successor was appointed, and the agency closed at its downtown location. Its collection was relocated to the Central Library on October 1, 1976.

The Riley Room for Young People housed the Children's Division of Central Library. The Riley Room of course, as we have noted, was named for the poet who gave the grounds upon which the room stood until 1975, when it was moved just a few feet to the new Central Library Annex. The Division's activities have been discussed earlier in the section devoted to the Children's Services Office.

In July, 1987, the Children's Division closed for a complete face-lifting. A room previously used primarily to house an historical collection of children's books was enlarged and converted into a story theatre with stair-step seating to accommodate sixty youngsters for a variety of multi-media program activities. Services and collections were completely rearranged when shelving and books were moved back. The project greatly enhanced the appearance and usability of the facility as well as adding to the delight of children able to browse through thousands of inviting books chosen es-

A group of children explore an early exhibit of books by Randolph Caldecott and Kate Greenaway.

Books, books everywhere!

pecially for them, or see puppet shows in a child-scaled setting.

When the new Central Library opened in 1917, Carrie Scott was appointed Manager of the Children's Department until she was made Supervisor of Work With Children on July 1, 1919, the position she held until her death on July 27, 1943. Zella Spence was Manager of the Riley Room from July 1, 1919 until her retirement June 1, 1949. She had been an assistant in the Children's Department since October, 1909. Kathryn Hodapp succeeded Miss Spence and was Department Manager until her death on October 28, 1958. Miss Hodapp was a member of the 1922-1923 Training Class, being appointed to the staff July 1, 1923, with subsequent assignments at Irvington, Broad Ripple and West Indianapolis Branches, and at the Teachers' Special Library and in the School Services Department.

Evelyn Ann Strachan was appointed to head the Riley Room on December 1, 1958, holding the position until February 4, 1974, when she was promoted to Coordinator of Children's Services. Since February 4, 1974, Margaret Barks has been Manager of the Children's Division at Central Library.

FILM DIVISION

From the standpoint of function, the Film Division is the youngest in the Library. Started less than fifty years ago, it has been moved from one home to another with relentless frequency. The reason, however, is quite legitimate; it just kept outgrowing its quarters.

The introduction of films and film services to the Library was discussed at length in the section of this text dealing with the administration of Marian McFadden. Those early government war films which brought about its birth were housed on a shelf in the office of the Supervisor of Branches. They were then moved to the Assistant Librarian's Office, where there was more shelf space available. The number of people coming to borrow them, however,

Over 5,000 art prints are borrowed from the Visual Arts Division annually. It's a new library service since 1979.

Film librarian Jacqueline Ek inspects one of the thousands of 16mm films borrowed each year from the Division.

disrupted the privacy often needed in an administrative office.

Films were first purchased with Library funds in 1952, and though the amount spent was only a little over $3,500, the public demand was phenomenal. That year the space vacated by the defunct Pamphlet Division in the west entrance corridor was turned over to films and the broader services provided by what soon became the position of Adult Activities Librarian. As business grew, Jacqueline Ek was appointed to the staff in July, 1953, to assist the Adult Activities Librarian administer film services to the public.

The next move took the film collection to the south end of the East Reading Room, where it became the Audio Visual Section of the newly formed Arts Division in 1960. As the collection grew, it was moved once again, this time to the space on the lower level near the Pennsylvania Street entrance. It occupied space which had been vacated by the Extension Division when that division moved to the library annex in 1967. That same year the Audio Visual Section became the Film Division. Miss Ek was appointed Manager of the new division and continued to serve in that capacity until February, 1990. In 1973 the Division moved one last time to the Library Service Center Building, 1435 North Illinois Street, which was also the new location of the Extension Services Division, the Library Print Shop, and the Library's Supply Center. Randall Starks became Division Manager in February, 1990, succeeding Miss Ek. Mr. Starks had served as audiovisual consultant for the Indiana State Library since 1983.

The use of the film collection by the public continued to grow until 1979, when 52,417 16mm and 8mm films were borrowed and shown to over 2,760,000 individuals. The number of loans began to decline in 1980, and has continued to do so, particularly since 1981, when videotape loan service was first introduced by the Division.

The loan of 8mm films was discontinued in 1986, due to lack of use. At the same time, the borrowing of videotapes increased faster than any new service offered by the Library, exceeding 611,000 loans in 1990. Although still a viable service, the use of 16mm films has continued to decline each year, as the use of videotapes by individuals, schools, and groups has increased.

The name of the Division was changed once again in 1988 to Visual Arts Division to better reflect the scope of its collections. It lends films, videotapes, and framed art prints to both groups and individuals, keeps up-to-date information where films and videotapes not in the collection may be obtained, and supplies both adult and children's films for the many film programs offered free-of-charge both at Central Library and many branch libraries.

The loan of videotapes from branch libraries began in September, 1990, when small rotating collections were placed in each branch agency and at Central Library. The collections are extremely popular with the public, and systemwide availability has been primarily responsible for the substantial increase in the use of this relatively new medium.

"Cropsey Auditorium" was the name given the large public meeting room when the new Central Library opened in 1917. There was nothing to mark its identity, however, and as the years passed the name meant less and less to those who used the room—that name remaining a puzzlement to many.

This disturbed Anna Brockhausen, a long-time teacher in the Indianapolis Public School system, who had known Nebraska Cropsey and felt that she should be specifically recognized for her pioneer work as the first Elementary School Supervisor in the Indianapolis system. As a result of Miss Brockhausen's interest, the Indianapolis Council of Parent-Teacher Associations in 1951 placed a plaque at the entrance of the auditorium which acknowledges Miss Cropsey's position and contributions. In recognition of Miss Brockhausen's interest the plaque was given in her honor.

Cropsey Auditorium has always been a popular meeting place. It is used for staff meetings and gatherings and for programs planned by the Library for the public. Many outside organizations and groups also use the room, subject to a few regulations, among them that no admittance fee may be charged and that programs are open to everyone.

The auditorium has been refurbished twice in recent years, most recently in 1982 when new vinyl wall coverings, softly colored carpeting, new seating and enhanced lighting were added to make the room more attractive and functional.

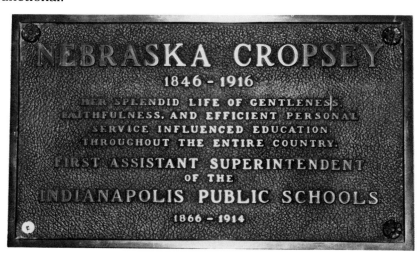

CHAPTER XIV

CROPSEY AUDITORIUM

Nebraska Cropsey.

Technical Services Department

The policies and divisions of responsibility for the selection of books and other library media were discussed earlier. However, selection is only the first of several processes necessary before Library materials are shelved and ready for public use.

The responsibilities of the Supervisor of Technical Services are to administer the purchasing and processing of all Library materials and to plan and coordinate the technical services in all agencies of the Library. Since 1980 it has also been the Supervisor's responsibility to supervise, coordinate, and implement the Library's computerization program and on-line book acquisition, circulation, and public access catalog system.

When the Central Library moved into its new home in 1917, Mr. Rush established three new departments—Order, Catalog, and Binding and Finishing. In 1947 Miss McFadden placed all three under the newly created position of Supervisor of Technical Processes. She reported, "It seemed advisable and economical to combine them under one head in order to facilitate the flow of work and obtain the maximum flexibility from the staff." Marjorie Bowers, who came to Indianapolis from the Gary, Indiana, Public Library, was appointed to the staff to fill this new position.

In later reorganizations the names were changed to Technical Services Department, Order Section, Catalog Section, and Processing Section. However, they have retained the same basic functions as when they were originally established in 1917.

In 1981 the Circulation Control Center, which had been established earlier as an entity of the Central Services Department, was transferred to the responsibility of the Technical Services Department. Its new function was to supervise the automation of computer-generated records relating to borrower card registration and delinquent material notices. Virginia Stroud supervised the Center and provided the initial routine circulation computer training for all new Library employees. She retired in 1989 and was succeeded by Ruth Smith, a member of the Circulation Control Center staff for many years, who currently supervises the operation and the training routines.

Mr. Evans, and probably his early successors, did the book and materials ordering themselves, but in 1917 the Order Department was established for this purpose. Its primary functions have never varied, although many routine changes have taken place. During the Dickerson administration a ruling of the Indiana Attorney General required that tax-supported libraries must annually prepare specifications and ask for bids for the purchase of books.

It was true that many titles of general up-to-date books could be

It seemed advisable and economical to combine [departments] under one head in order to facilitate the flow of work and obtain the maximum flexibility from the staff.

—Marian McFadden, 1947

ORDER SECTION

Facing page — Technical Services Department, 1959.

purchased from wholesale book jobbers, but the staff needed a wide knowledge of how to search bibliographical indexes for the obscure title or out-of-print material, and these had to be ordered from a wide variety of sources. Nevertheless, the State Library and the Public Library worked together to provide detailed but workable specifications.

As the Department was responsible for the expenditure of the entire book budget, it sometimes from necessity found itself engaging in book selection when funds were low, and a choice had to be made as to what would be purchased. By 1954 the Director and the Supervisor worked out a system by which each agency was allocated a portion of the budget, and the choice of what should be bought, or what could be eliminated, remained at the individual agency level.

Beginning in 1990 the Order Section was responsible only for the ordering and checking-in of materials when they are received. Approval of invoices, preparation of the claims for payments and the issuing of checks are the responsiblity of the Library's Business Office. The materials themselves are sent to the Processing Section.

When the Order Department was established in 1917, Jean Kerlin was appointed as its first Manager. However, she remained only one year and was succeeded by Ruth Wallace for a brief time. Grace Kerr held the position from 1920 until her retirement in 1947. She was succeeded by Isabel Russell who resigned the position in November, 1952. Her successor was Ethel Rush. Miss Rush headed the agency from October l, 1952, until her resignation on July 19, 1960. Marian Fay, a long-time staff member, succeeded Miss Rush, holding the position until her retirement in June, 1968. Ruby Suits, who had been an assistant in the Order Section for many years, became Section Manager July 1, 1968, serving until her retirement in May, 1981. Her successor, and current Manager of the Order Section is Arthella Hall, who also had worked in the section for many years prior to her appointment.

PROCESSING SECTION

In 1917 this section was called the Binding Department and Finishing Room, although it was generally referred to as the Binding Department. Like the Order Section, its basic function has remained much the same through the years. In 1960 the department was renamed the Mending and Finishing Division, and in 1968 the name was changed to Processing Section.

Much of the work of the section involves the physical preparation of books and other materials before they are sent on to the agency for circulation to the public. This involves adding the appropriate classification number to the item, applying a plastic dust jacket and book card pocket when required, and assigning the item to the ordering agency on the computer bibliographic record prior to forwarding the item on to the agency. A conveyor belt routes the materials to the appropriate processing station and greatly facilitates the handling of the over 250,000 new books and other materials received each year.

Although the processing of new materials represents the primary workload of the section, it also processes books for rebinding, as well as the mending and repair of older books for all Library agencies.

In the 1880s Mr. Hooper instituted the idea of hiring a professional binder with two assistants to work on premises, which proved to be much cheaper than having the work done by a commercial binder. However, in later years, with the expansion of the book collection and its increased use, books were once again sent to professional bookbinding companies for rebinding. Normally, binding specifications are prepared and the binding contract awarded to the lowest and best bidder.

Mr. Evans in an early report recommended, "as a precautionary measure against wear of books, and as a preventive against soiled and greasy covers, that the volumes in greater demand, namely fiction and juveniles, be covered."

For many years rows of dull brown or black books lined the Library's shelves. Eventually, with the introduction of new rebinding materials, the rebound book began to wear bright and inviting colors. In 1949 plastic covers were first used to cover the original book dust jackets. These not only protected the book, but also permitted the retention of the original attractive book cover. Currently most books, other than prebound juvenile titles, receive a plastic jacket when they are processed for circulation.

Finally, there are the "wounded" books sent to the section to be repaired and returned for further useful service. During Miss Browning's administration, it was reported that attendants repaired books "whenever time allowed,"

The department ordered, cataloged and processed over 250,000 new books in 1990.

117

Staff member repairs one of the library's "wounded" books.

CATALOG
SECTION

a policy followed in the branch libraries for many years. When the Binding Department was established in 1917, only Central Library books were mended, and the branch libraries, often desperate for books to fill the demand, especially for children, mended their own items. During the Depression years of the 1930s, when new books were scarce, Mr. Hooper's remark that the public "prefers a dirty copy of a book rather than to go without," was still applicable. During these same years WPA workers were taught to mend, which helped with the backlog. In the 1950s several staff were trained in the Binding Department and then sent to the branch libraries to do the mending and repair of books, moving from one branch to another as needed. This practice has been discontinued, and currently all books needing mending are sent to the Processing Section for repair.

Edna Kennedy headed the Department from April, 1923, until her retirement on August 17, 1950. Her successor was Ethel Weldon, a long-time member of the department staff. Mrs. Weldon held the position until her retirement June 30, 1968. She was succeeded by Marilyn Thiel, who is currently the administrator of the Processing Section.

All selection, ordering and physical preparation, important as these processes are, would have little meaning if the material were not finally organized in such a way that both public and staff could locate it as quickly as possible. Cataloging and classification of new materials is the function of the Catalog Section and, though its reason for being has remained constant for over one hundred years, no department of the Library has been subjected to so many mechanical and other procedural and automated changes in achieving its goal as has this section.

Charles Evans during his first years in Indianapolis explained to the Board that for economy and good working management, three types of catalogs were necessary, "the Accession catalogue, the Shelf catalogue, and the card catalogue which gives entries as the book may require under its author, title and subject."

In those early years, as new books arrived, they were listed in an Accession Book, each assigned a number, the first acquired being number l, with others following in sequence. This cumbersome method was employed for many years by libraries. The early accession volumes have been preserved, however, and from them the interested individual can find what the original holdings of the Indianapolis Public Library were.

The first author is described in the card cataloges

Allibone, Samuel Austin, 1816-1889. A Critical Dictionary of English literature and British and American authors, living and deceased, from the earliest accounts to the latter half of the nineteenth century.

There were three volumes listed in the shelf cataloges; the third volume at some time was marked "missing."

After the books had been accessioned, they were classified based on subject content. When the Indianapolis Library was established in 1873, the collection was so small some simple classification probably was in use; but

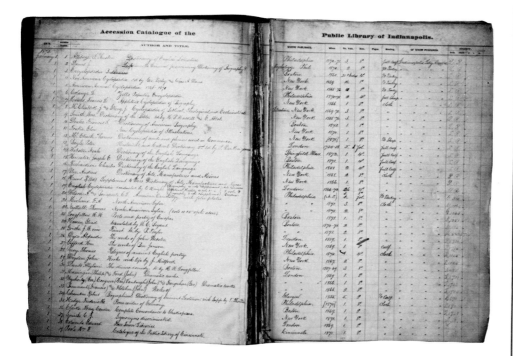

A Critical Dictionary of English Literature by Samuel Allibone is listed as the Library's first book in the Accession Catalogue of 1873.

there seems to be no clear record of what it was. When Mr. Evans returned for his second administration in 1888, the collection had grown to the point where a reclassification was necessary.

As we have indicated, Mr. Evans used the system devised by William Poole, one in use by many libraries at that time. The Poole classification placed books according to their subject matter into an alphabetical grouping, "A" being assigned to fiction, continuing on to "X" for periodicals, with a few letters not used. It will be remembered from earlier comments in this text that this change-over, with its attendant amount of work, was one of Mr. Evans' ideas that irritated the Board. Nevertheless, the new Poole classification system was implemented and was used from 1889 until December, 1917.

It was Charles Rush who decided to change to the Dewey Decimal Classification, a system devised by Melvil Dewey, one of the early giants in the library field. Mr. Rush, in his Five Year Survey, 1917-1922, writes: "The whole collection of books is being changed . . . to the Dewey decimal system, a system much better adapted to public library use, as it is more logical, consistent and comprehensible. All new books are classified by the Dewey numbers, and as rapidly as time and cataloging staff will permit the old books are being reclassified also." In 1922 he estimated that over 35 percent of the work had been done. However, in the 1930s books with the old Poole classification would still appear now and then.

Once books are classified the actual cataloging begins. In the early years there was a card index listing the Library's holdings, but it was for the use of the staff only. The public was never allowed to touch it, and according to Miss Browning, "the young and inexperienced attendants were never encouraged to meddle with it."

For public use most libraries once issued printed catalogs. Mr. Evans

CATALOGUE
OF THE
PUBLIC LIBRARY
OF
INDIANAPOLIS.
1873.

INDIANAPOLIS:
PRESS OF PRINTING AND PUBLISHING HOUSE,
1873.

issued the first for the Indianapolis Library on November 1, 1873, listing in dictionary form all the books the Library had received to that date, which was approximately 10,000 volumes. Copies of this first catalog were sold for $2.00 and some were sent to the principal libraries in the United States and Europe. As noted earlier, acquisition lists of new books were published every month in the newspapers in order to provide the public with up-to-date information. Later, supplements were printed. Mr. Tyler issued part of a second complete printed catalog, which Mr. Hooper finished in 1885. It contained entries by author, subject and title for all books purchased since November, 1873. Miss Browning refers to it as a "huge volume" and well it was. Several copies have been retained in the Library's archives for historical purposes.

Fortunately, the 1885 tome seems to have been the last complete book catalog published. A union catalog entered on cards, hand written, for all books in the system was provided in 1889, apparently under the supervision of Mr. Evans during his second term as Librarian. However, several "Finding Lists" were published between 1885 and 1904 for specific subjects, such as history, poetry, and biography. Copies of these have also been retained for the Library's historical archives and remain well preserved.

It was Miss Browning, that forward-looking, indefatigable woman, who decided to let into the Library a little fresh air of change. She writes in her manuscript history that from 1892 until 1907 the card catalog was used by the public upon request and "everyone who preferred to consult the books on the shelf had only to mention it and the permission was at once granted." Actually "open shelf" access to the books had started in 1906 and access to the catalog followed immediately.

The listing of so many books required systemized supervision. When Mr. Rush established the Catalog Department in 1917, Mary Johnson was appointed its first administrator. In 1919 Ruth Wallace took over the position which she held until her retirement in 1947. To Miss Wallace fell the responsibility for the reclassification of the collection to the new Dewey Decimal System. Mr. Rush's Five Year Survey shows that in 1917-1918, 14,252 books were cataloged. By 1921-1922 the figure had risen to over 52,000. No record was kept in 1917 of the number of cards required to provide the many entries for each book, but in 1921-1922 the number was 264,457.

Of course typewriters took over from the "library hand" for the preparation of these thousands of catalog cards. At the time the Department was created, the cataloging of branch library collections was added to its responsibilities, and the number of duplicate cards which had to be made increased substantially. Mr. Rush mentions that a multigraph machine had been purchased sometime between 1917 and 1922 to speed up the duplication process. When Miss Bowers became Supervisor, she introduced more time-saving office equipment.

With the advent of automation and the on-line public access catalog in the early 1980s, the card catalogs, which had been in existence almost since the Library's founding, were abandoned and eventually removed from all Library agencies. The new automated system provided instant and complete access to all the Library's holdings at any point in the Library System where a public terminal was located.

Administrative Staff, 1990
l. to r.— M. Jacqueline Nytes, Associate Director, Management Services; Susan Ebershoff-Coles, Technical Services Supervisor; Christine Cairo, Children's Services Coordinator; Laura G. Johnson, Associate Director, Public Services; C. Catherine Gibson, Adult Services Coordinator; and Raymond E. Gnat, Director of Public Libraries

Below—Among the over one hundred beautiful panels in the Central Library Main Reading Room Ceiling are thirty-two reproductions of colophons, or printer's devices. The word colophon is from the Greek word *kolophon*, for "finishing stroke."
The colophons, chosen by architect C. C. Zantzinger of Philadelphia, represent printers from the 15th through 19th centuries

Library Foundation Board Of Directors, 1990
l. to r.—Seated, Dr. Joseph T. Taylor, Raymond E. Gnat, Marjorie Tarplee, and Gordon H. Thompson; Standing, Robert E. Houk, Elizabeth M. Gunn, Winifred E. Pettee, H. Roll McLaughlin, and Joseph A. Rothbard

Fust and Schoeffer
Mainz, Germany 1457
(The Earliest Known
Printer's Mark)

Library Board Of Trustees, 1990
l. to r.—Sarah W. Otte, David F. McNamar, and Bobbie Beckwith; Standing, Catherine S. Wallace, Elizabeth M. Gunn, Wayne Moss, and Jane Baldwin.

Simon de Colines
Paris, France 1520-1546

Colard Mansion
Bruges (West Flanders)
1474-1484

Perrinus Lathomi
Jean Boniface
Jean de Vieilleville
Lyon, France 1493-1495

Antoine Verard, Paris,
France 1493-1494

Central Library—Main Reading Room

Right and facing
page: Two of a
series of twelve
bas-relief plaster
plaques depicting
the early history
of Indiana which
are found on the
Central Library's
Main Room
Ceiling

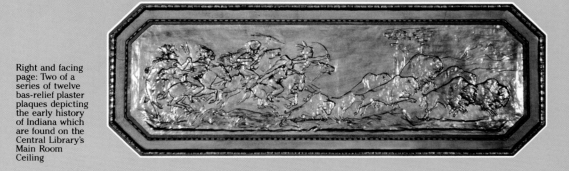

Central Library—South Mezzanine

Thomas de Blavis
(de Alexandria)
Venice, Italy, 1476-1488
Motto: "Thomas [de Blavis]
and Andreas [Torresanus]"

The Chiswick Press,
(Charles Whittingham, Founder)
London, England 1828

Robert Wyer
London, England 1529-1560

Jac Sacco, Sacon, Zachoni
of Romano (Piedmont)
Lyon, France 1498-1530
(Date of Colophon, 1512)

J.B. Lippincott & Co.,
New York, c. 1923
Motto: *Droit Et Avant*
"Right And Ahead"

Mathias de Hupfuff,
Strasbourg, France 1499-1520

Central Library—Newspaper and Periodical Division, East Reading Room.

The classically inspired Central Library designed by Paul Cret and opened in 1917

Gone forever was the tedious and time-consuming process of catalog card reproduction. Gone also was the need for a book accession number. In its place could be found a machine readable, bar-encoded label with a number unique to that particular bibliographical item. The world of computer technology had found a welcome home in the Technical Services Department.

Although items are constantly being withdrawn from the collection because they are out-of-date or worn out from use, thousands are added each year. At the end of 1990, the materials count was 1,646,018, a far cry from that approximate 10,000 volumes Mr. Evans first recorded in 1873. This 1990 count includes not only books, but also bound magazines, audio and video cassettes, films, recordings, and framed art prints.

As noted earlier Ruth Wallace headed the cataloging operation until 1947. Her successor was Verna Hankemeier, a long-time member of the cataloging staff, who held the position of Manager, Catalog Department, until her retirement in 1953. Thera Cavender held the position from 1953 until her resignation in 1956. Elsa Carlson was appointed to manage the agency on July 16, 1956, and continued in the position until September, 1965, at which time she was appointed Coordinator of Technical Services.

Other staff who supervised the cataloging functions as administrative assistants were Ruth Wilson from 1965 to 1968; Lola Carpenter, from 1968 until June, 1969; Nancy Stassus, from August, 1969 until January, 1971; Susan Ebershoff-Coles from January, 1971 until December, 1975.

Mrs. Ebershoff-Coles headed the Catalog Section while she was Assistant Supervisor. She was succeeded by Luana Stanley, who supervised the Section from December, 1975 until her resignation in August, 1980. She was succeeded by the current Manager of the Section, Charity Mitchell, who was appointed to the position August 25, 1980.

Due to an urgent need for additional space for ordering, cataloging and processing of the tens of thousands of books added to the Library's holdings as a result of the expansion of service to all of Marion County in 1966, in 1967 the Technical Services Department was moved from the Central Library building. The Department was relocated to the second floor of the building adjacent to the Central Library at 833-837 North Meridian Street. The Department was moved once again in 1975 to its current location at 815-817 North Pennsylvania Street, a building which was purchased and renovated to fill the Department's needs at that time. The Department will move to more spacious quarters in the new Library Service Center scheduled for completion in 1993.

Marjorie Bowers was the first Supervisor of Technical Processes from 1947 until her retirement in 1962. Lawrence Downey succeeded Miss Bowers, serving until 1965, when he became Coordinator of Personnel Services. Mr. Downey was succeeded as Coordinator of Technical Services by Elsa Carlson in September, 1965, until she resigned the position June 1,1969. Her successor was Lola Carpenter, who headed the Technical Services operation until her retirement on December 31, 1975. The current Supervisor of Technical Services is Susan Ebershoff-Coles, who was appointed to the position December 20, 1975. As noted, the title of the position has changed several times since its creation in 1947 as a result of reorganization of the Department's structure and operation.

Since the advent of the computer catalog, gone forever is the tedious and time-consumming process of catalog card reproduction.

On June 23, 1971, *Profiles of Excellence* by Martin McAuliffe became the one millionth volume added to the Library collection. It was the first publication of the University of Evansville Press, and the fact that Director Harold Sander was a graduate of that institution made the choice of this title interestingly coincidental.

Service To Community Neighborhoods

The mention of the word "library" to many people in Indianapolis and since 1966 to the residents of Marion County will not necessarily bring to mind the rather massive stone building downtown, but rather the building just down the street or around the corner. There they find the reading materials they want and have a friendly chat with the people who assist them and who know them well.

As noted earlier it was during Miss Browning's administration, in 1896, that the first community branch libraries were established. Actually the initiative came from some northside residents who found that transportation to the library by horse car or bicycle was most inconvenient.

A committee appointed by the Board to investigate the matter recommended that four branches be established, one each in the northwest, northeast, southeast and southwest segments of the city, and, that at other locations deposit stations be placed.

In her manuscript history Miss Browning wrote, "The Board agreed to this (undertaking) as it would provide shelf room for about 10,000 books still accessible and give the Main Library a chance, for some time to come, to house on its shelves a generous lot of new books. And also they thought patrons in the vicinity of the branches would find it more convenient to patronize the libraries nearer their homes. The result was that these extension enterprises advertised the Main Library so extensively that the congestion, instead of being relieved was doubled, and we had to increase our branches and stations beyond all expectations."

Thus it was discovered over ninety years ago that each geographic expansion of the Library, such as the addition of a new branch library in an area where there has been no library service, results in greater use, not only of the new facility, but also of the Main Library. This phenomenon remains true even today.

As the city of Indianapolis grew, it began to incorporate neighborhoods such as Haughville, Irvington and Broad Ripple, which were almost self-sustaining small communities in themselves. They often contained a majority of certain ethnic, religious, cultural or economic groups, and there was usually an active business district with stores owned and operated by local residents. Several churches were a part of the neighborhood, and nearly all the so-called villages became a parish of the Catholic church with its own parochial school. At least one public school would also be in the area. Settlement houses were established in some of them, and with the coming of the motion picture, there was usually a theater situated among the stores and shops. There was also a sense of collective pride among the inhabitants. For them the coming of "our own library" was another source of pride.

Early Developments

A van makes a delivery to the West Indianapolis Branch in 1921.

Students at School No. 67 select books from the library deposit collection.

Employees of the Diamond Chain Co. visited their library station, one of several at business and industrial locations provided by the Library's Extension Division.

Sometimes the branch librarian or members of the staff lived in the neighborhood, but wherever they lived, they were accepted, after a little cautious looking over, as full-fledged community members, and in the early, more leisurely years, the library was often a place not only to pick up books but to exchange some innocent gossip as well.

With the passage of time changes have come, some almost imperceptibly, others with startling rapidity. The so-called inner city has pushed outward, taking over the old, distinctive neighborhoods. Interstate and city highways have cut regions apart, and the old inhabitants have been replaced by a less stable population. Small stores have decreased and large shopping centers farther away from the neighborhoods have taken their places, and the inconvenience of the horse car and the bicycle have given way to the inconvenience of "no parking available."

Nowadays, newer branch libraries have required large lots to provide space for those who need to drive to reach them. They are more strategically located near or in shopping centers, and the clientele has been drawn from wider areas. Nevertheless, the sense of pride in one's branch and the feeling of intimacy have not been lost even though large, well-lighted, colorful buildings have replaced those early, humble, little stores or houses which for so long welcomed their neighbors to the books within.

At the Board meeting in September, 1896, it was reported that a storeroom on the northwest corner of Linden and Woodlawn Avenues could be leased for $12.50 a month, and that the second floor of a new building at the corner of Udell and Lulu Streets could be rented for $200 a year. By the end of 1896 two other locations were chosen, one at Brookside Avenue and East Tenth Street, and another at 548 South Meridian Street.

There was some discussion about naming the branches for some distinguished individual, but the final decision was to use numbers for those first branches.

In October, 1896, bids were received for the necessary furnishings for those four new branches. The items purchased from the W. L. Elder Company of Indianapolis and their 1896 cost were:

4 oak flat top desks	$39.20
16 large oak chairs	$22.40
192 small oak chairs	$84.00

Purchased from the Sander and Recker Company of Indianapolis, long noted for its fine furniture until it went out of business during the Depression years were:

16 green leather top tables	$128.00
4 swivel arm chairs	$17.00

Presumably these furnishings were for the first four branches, as the fifth, located in a building on West Morris Street, did not open until the following year. There is no record of how long the furniture was in use, but it is easy to surmise that it was solid enough to resist wear and tear for many years.

These first branches were modest little rooms, most of them "store fronts." Each had a good collection of books containing from 1,500 to 3,000 volumes. In addition, there were current copies of the popular magazines of the day; *Century, Harper's Monthly, Scribner's, Scientific American, St. Nicholas,* and *Youth's Companion.* Patrons could request books which were delivered semi-weekly from the Main Library.

The attendant in charge of the branch library was paid $25.00 a month, but by doing her own janitor work she could augment her pay by receiving the janitor's salary of $10.00. This required not only cleaning the room or rooms, but carrying in coal to stoke the pot-bellied stove which provided heat and carrying in water. There was no indoor plumbing.

It was necessary to provide some supervision for the branches to insure that their common needs were met, to select the staff to run them, and to help in scheduling their hours. Selecting, ordering and cataloging their books, work which had been done originally in each agency, needed to be standardized. Ella Saltmarsh first assumed these supervisory responsibilities, but she moved to overseeing the children's room in the Main Library in 1899. She was succeeded by Clara Dippel. It was not until the administration of Charles Rush that a full-time Supervisor of Branches was appointed. Cerene Ohr assumed this position in 1918, after having been in charge of the School Libraries division since 1915. She was to guide the branch libraries for over thirty years until her retirement in 1949.

CHAPTER XVI

Cerere Ohr, Branch Supervisor, 1918-1949.

Haughville Library overflowed when children from a neighborhood school visited the branch about 1920.

There were thirteen branches in 1917. During her administration Miss Ohr opened seven additional branches, moved several others into more modern and commodious quarters, and closed one branch. However, it was not until shortly before her retirement that she assisted in designing a new branch. This was the Broad Ripple Branch which opened on Guilford Avenue in 1949. Broad Ripple was the first new branch building since the Carnegie libraries built during the Browning administration in the early part of the century.

Mr. Rush, in his Five Year Survey, speaks of the phenomenal growth of the branch library book stock and circulation from 1917 to 1922.

The development of better adult collections made the patrons of the branches feel that they had book service almost as good as those who went to Central.

He continues,

During the last year (1922) the adult circulation was 49 percent of the total (system) circulation, (and) in seven branches (it exceeded) the juvenile circulation. A great deal of the credit for the recent development of the branch system is due Miss Cerene Ohr who has supervision of the work.

Through the year it was Miss Ohr's responsibility to be the "liaison" between each of the community branches and the Librarian, and to coordinate their work with all the divisions and departments at the Central Library, in order to facilitate a harmonious working relationship among all agencies. She had to be aware of all building and equipment needs and personnel requirements, as well as assisting staff members to carry out their goals and objectives for each branch. She assisted in maintaining an adequate, well-balanced book collection for each branch suitable for its specific needs, kept the statistical records of each branch which showed the accomplishments of the year, and encouraged displays, exhibits, and publicity.

Elizabeth Hesser was appointed Supervisor of Branches when Miss Ohr retired, holding the position until her resignation in 1957. During these years branch neighborhoods were rapidly changing and operating costs increasing, leading inevitably to the closing of several branches. Others were made sub-branches of a nearby larger branch library in order to provide more flexibility and economy in staffing. Experimental changes were made in hours of opening, and a careful study of the branch delivery truck route resulted in a revised delivery schedule which saved time and money.

Miss Hesser planned for the first bookmobile and organized its schedul-

A visit to a nearby branch library is often a family excursion.

ing. She also assisted in designing the new Hilton U. Brown Library in Irvington and arranged for the temporary remodeling of an old house which became the first home of the Emerson Branch.

Despite the increase of business and program planning, despite the expanded county areas to be covered, the number of branches has increased very little during the last seventy years, although the new county ones have added to the total. In 1991 there are twenty-one branch libraries, just eight more than in 1917 when Miss Ohr became the first Supervisor of Branches. However, more than eight new branches have opened since that time, because several of the early branches have been closed as demographic circumstances dictated.

To many people public libraries seem staid and remote institutions. They do, of course have a very pragmatic side. True, they are not concerned with the usual meaning of profit and loss, but libraries, like any retail or marketing business, must locate where customers will be attracted to them, and they too make surveys of potential locations. In recent years the tendency has been to move from small neighborhoods with restricted facilities to larger buildings with greater service areas. With increased space and larger book collections libraries are usually able to give their users the materials they want and need.

Staffing responsibilities have a certain similarity also, although there have been changes. In the early years the branch staff consisted of an attendant and the janitor. As late as the 1950s there were never more than four persons in the busiest branches, in addition to part-time pages. Until centralized automation took over, most clerical work was done by the branch staff.

Many staff members preferred working in the branches, while others preferred the more specialized duties at Central Library. Now relieved of some of the clerical work and with larger staffs and larger buildings with auditoriums, branch libraries have more opportunity to make their facilities real gathering places for the community.

Story hours, visits by school classes, magic shows, puppet plays, and other activities for children make use of the trained talents of the staff. Nor are adults neglected. Film programs, travel talks, concerts, book talks, and programs on all kinds of hobbies and special interests bring them into the library often, along with their children. Meeting rooms are sometimes filled to capacity with audiences ranging from preschoolers to grandparents.

One enthusiastic branch worker has summed it up: "Even though trying at times, the rough and tumble of branch work is a satisfying experience, and we make every effort to give good service and offer materials which we think are needed."

This library agency was designated as the Extension Department until the reorganization in 1973, when the name was changed to Extension Division. It had been located at the Central Library until 1973 when it was relocated in the then newly-acquired Library Service Center, 1435 North Illinois Street. The Division is currently responsible for providing bookmobile, stations, and collection services.

EXTENSION
SERVICES
DIVISION

In January, 1897, after Miss Browning had surveyed what was being done in other cities, as an experiment she started opening what were then known as delivery stations. These were small collections where the general public could obtain books and were set up in fire stations for use of the firemen, and in drug stores. Ninety-two years later the "experiment" is still going on, a healthy, vital part of the library system.

It is uncertain at just what date a special department was established to supervise this work, but it probably was in 1917, when the Central Library moved into its new building. Mr. Rush, in his Survey Report covering the years 1917 to 1922, differentiates the types of collections, "Delivery" being those where requested books were picked up and delivered to the station the next week; "Deposit" stations were comprised of collections which could be borrowed by the public, with the collections being changed at intervals for variety. At some time the delivery stations were dropped, but when the Central Library relocated in 1917 there was a room used by "stations," and evidently it acquired the status of a department at that time.

In his 1922 Survey Mr. Rush lists three delivery stations and many deposit stations in industrial plants, department stores, settlement and community houses, fire stations, and hospitals. The list does not include any schools, whose stations were supplied and staffed by either a branch library or the School Services Department.

The Stations Department had direct responsibility for most of these stations, although some were under the supervision of neighborhood branches. Department staff members were sent to the stations to actually check books in and out and to take requests for books to be delivered the next week.

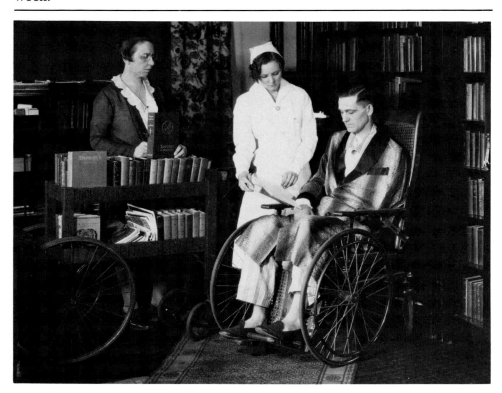

Library service to patients at several of the city's hospitals began in 1921. Librarian Alice Griffin at Methodist Hospital in 1931.

Hospitals were also served by a member of the Department staff who took a cart of books directly to the wards and rooms, from which the patients could select an inviting title. Service was begun in 1921 at City, Long, Methodist and Coleman Hospitals. This program in later years was confined to Wishard (General) Hospital, but was discontinued in 1986 at the request of the hospital administration. From February, 1973, until its closing the hospital library was the Hospital Branch Library with the same administrative status as the other neighborhood branch libraries. Mrs. Mary Burns served as hospital librarian and Hospital Branch Manager from February, 1953 until her retirement on December 31, 1984.

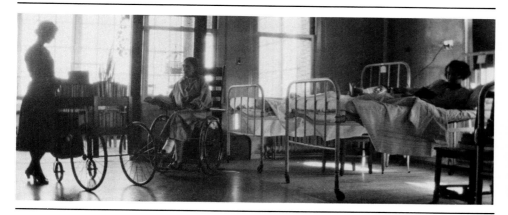

Librarian visits the Women's Surgical Ward at Long Hospital.

In 1940 a separate Extension Department was established. It was partially an outgrowth of the old "Out-of-School Division" created in 1924. This Division had also supervised the setting up of very small stations in stores during the Depression years using WPA staffing. The new Extension Department took over the work of the Stations Department, which continued the important duty of working with the branch libraries. It handled book and reference requests, the packing of new books, periodicals and supplies, and whatever other materials requests the branches made or Central Library wished delivered. Packed in boxes, individually marked for each branch, the books and other materials were sent by truck, which visited each branch every other day. The deliveries, now daily Monday to Friday, were, and are still a vital link between the Central Library and the branch libraries.

In 1946 Stations as a separate department ceased to exist. Its last function, work with the branches, was placed under the direct supervision of the Supervisor of Branches. Then in 1957 Catherine Bailey, who had been Head, Extension Department, became Supervisor of Extension Services, taking over all the duties of the Supervisor of Branches. As a result, all public service agencies outside of the Central Library, except School Services, were under the supervision of one administrator. Under Miss Bailey's supervision, the new Broadway Branch Library was planned and built in 1957-1958. When she retired in 1960, Miss Bailey was succeeded by Marilyn McCanon.

Miss Browning many years ago believed a library should reach out and serve the whole community. One must wonder whether, even with her keen vision of the future, she could have foreseen just how far that reach would need to be.

The Branch Libraries And Other Extension Agencies

Though all the branch libraries have had much in common, all have their own individual traditions and styles of service. Some have grown and expanded through the years, and are still providing service to the public. Others served their time and place and then faded away, but all contributed their share of legends and stories to the annals of the Indianapolis-Marion County Public Library. The branches are described chronologically by the date of their opening.

The oldest branch library building in the city and one of the four first established, Riverside Park, opened in December, 1896, above Grould's drugstore at Udell and Clifton (then called Lulu) Streets. After one year, Belle Abrams turned over the running of the library to Harriet Manning, who remained as librarian for more than thirty-three years. Although it was only one room, "it was made cheery with potted plants growing in the windows."

The branch had an air of sociability, for Miss Manning and her sister Ella Hazelrigg, who had started working at the library without pay just because she liked to help her sister, soon knew all the people of the community and could call most by name. The city grew up around their family home, so the interests of the neighborhood were their interests.

After it outgrew the one-room site, the branch was moved to a one-story building nearby which the Board of School Commissioners rented for five years at $15 a month. It moved again in 1906 to its own building. This Carnegie-style building, designed by Robert Daggett, who was also to be the architect for the new West Indianapolis Branch in 1911, was built at a cost of

RIVERSIDE PARK BRANCH LIBRARY

Facing page — The North Indianapolis Club gathers at the Illinois Branch in 1914 to hear Rev. Mr. Phillpott.

131

CHAPTER XVII

Ella Hazelrigg and Harriet Manning.

Riverside Branch Managers
Belle Abrams, 1896-1898
Harriet Manning, 1898-1926
Irene Smith, July 1927-March, 1928
Louise Hodapp, March, 1928-September 1, 1934
Opal Foxworthy, 1934-1935
Melbourne Davidson, 1935-1944
Leila Marquis, 1944-1950
Lyndell Martling, 1950-1951 (with South Grove)
Catherine Sullivan, 1951-1959 (with East Washington, 1955-1959)
Betsie Collins, 1959-1961 (with Rauh)
Georgia Lewis, 1961-1967
Annetta Boone, January-June, 1968
Betsie Collins, 1968-1971 (with Rauh)
Lilla Adams, 1971-August 31, 1971

$4,000. It was erected on land already owned by the Board at 3101 Clifton Street, one of the busiest areas on the northside of Indianapolis, and it had the distinction of being the first building to be constructed explicitly as a branch library.

Early statistics show Riverside Park was always a busy branch. It became an integral and important part of nearby School No. 41, the largest grade school in the state at that time and consequently was an active center of activities for the children of the neighborhood. The first year's circulation of 5,598 books doubled by its tenth year, and in 1929 the library loaned over ninety-two thousand books.

One of its unique services was a reading club for the blind, most of whom were students in the Indiana School for the Blind employed in a nearby broom factory.

Not long after Miss Manning resigned as head of the branch in 1926, she returned part time to assist Louise Hodapp, the new librarian. When Miss Manning retired at age 88, the entire staff of the Public Library honored her and her sister with a garden party at the Rauh Branch Library. As one of her patrons described her, "She was an institution, and to find her gone is like finding the building missing." By the time she retired, she could count among her library patrons the grandchildren of some of her early borrowers of that grand old neighborhood of early Indianapolis.

The years of the Depression brought increased business to the Riverside Branch, as it did to most other library agencies. The friendly, book-filled walls of the library meant a great deal to the many readers who were out of work and turned to it for escape reading or for job training materials.

During World War II a prominent Indianapolis banker was asked to head a war bond drive sponsored by the Indiana Library Association. His first thought, due to the pressure of business, was to decline, and then he remembered how good Miss Manning had been to him when he was a youngster. With this in mind he said, "I knew I could never turn down a request from librarians."

When World War II ended, the use of the branch by students from Butler University increased substantially. Many were returning veterans studying on the GI Bill of Rights. The branch became a beehive of activity, with patrons reading for a purpose and requiring a great deal of research and reference work, especially in business and technical subjects.

For many years it was a very busy branch, the staff working under more and more crowded conditions. The growth of the affluent Golden Hill area to the north brought many avid new readers, and there were still scores of the faithful old neighborhood users. In the 1940s there was considerable discussion of how the building might be enlarged.

Then in the 1950s the demographics of the surrounding district began to change rapidly. Plans for highway construction resulted in demolition of homes, and long-time residents began moving out. The branch began to have trouble with gangs and rowdies, so much so that for awhile the police escorted staff members to the bus stop at closing time.

By 1965 the circulation was dropping at an alarming rate, due not only to population shifts within the community, but also because the interstate highway just to the north had cut off the library from many of its faithful users. In 1929, 92,209 books had been circulated. By 1970 circulation had decreased to 15,453. The branch had the lowest circulation of any branch in the library system when, after nearly seventy-five years of service, it closed its doors for the last time on August 31, 1971.

The second of the four original branches opened in December of 1896 in a small frame building occupied by a Gospel Rescue Mission at the corner of Brookside Avenue and Tenth Street. Just why it did not remain in that location is uncertain, but in less than a year it was moved from the east to the west side of town. It may have been because early in 1897 the village known as Haughville became a part of the city and soon afterwards the residents petitioned for a library in line with, "the early recognition on the part of the town fathers of Haughville that education and culture were as much a necessity in their daily life as streets and sidewalks."

Branch No. 2 was moved to the westside and opened its doors in October, 1897, at 2523 West Walnut in a small frame building in the yard of School No. 52. In 1901 it moved again to rented quarters in the former Town Hall on Germania Avenue, later renamed Belleview Place. In this storefront building the library was expanded three times from a small, one-room library to the entire first floor. Its shiny, dark wood paneling and old pendulum school clock, hanging on a children-adult book divider in the center of the room gave it a warm, friendly atmosphere. In 1904 the library was partially destroyed by fire. Much of the furniture was lost, along with more than four hundred books. However, it was able to reopen a little later and it remained at this location until 1972.

CHAPTER XVII

HAUGHVILLE BRANCH LIBRARY

The Haughville Library today—a storefront facility located in the Michigan Plaza Shopping Center.

The branch was located at 519 North Belleview Place from 1901 to 1972.

133

A young reader gives her book report for the Summer Reading Club—always a popular branch activity.

Originally the Haughville neighborhood was mostly foreign- born. In the early 1900s the residents were chiefly German, Irish, and English. By 1915 the iron foundry of Ketcham and Haugh, the neighborhood's chief industry, needed more labor. Many immigrants came from southeastern Europe and settled in the community. During World War I, when more laborers were needed, many blacks came from the deep south.

By 1929 there were twenty-nine nationalities in the Haughville area and the branch provided books, newspapers and magazines in fourteen languages: Arabic, Bulgarian, Croatian, Danish, Dutch, French, German, Greek, Hungarian, Italian, Polish, Romanian, Slovak, and Slovenian.

Haughville Branch became the interpreter of American life to the community, specializing in easy reading books written in English, material on how to become a citizen, and answers to all kinds of questions about government, history, and customs of daily life in a new country. It provided classes in English, citizenship, and home economics, had story hours, and sponsored a variety of reading clubs. Haughville, like Riverside Branch, had a reading club for the blind. The librarians visited neighborhood meetings and tried by letters and calls to bring the people to the library.

During the Depression years people turned more and more to their library for recreation and escape. One branch annual report stated, "The people were proud and wouldn't take relief. They'd sell their furniture, mortgage their homes. Some almost starved." Still, they did have more free hours and seemed determined to pass them decently. As the library assumed an important place in their lives, book circulation soared. Haughville Branch was usually first and never lower than second in circulation among all the branch libraries. The peak came in 1933 with 182,733 books loaned by only four staff members.

It seemed as if the library should be called appropriately the "Court of human relations." People turned to it for all kinds of help—from finding a job to having a letter written. A boy was recommended for special eyesight classes, and at least three boys, who were constant library users, in later years became well-known political figures in city and state government. The library and the neighborhood were close friends, and librarians served on committees advancing the welfare of the community. Outside organizations such as the Chamber of Commerce, Travelers Aid and the American Legion began to depend on the branch when translators were needed.

The staff showed ingenuity in the varieties of programs planned to create interest in the library, such as an open house with pretty young hostesses from the neighborhood dressed in their native costumes, and a lecture by Louis Adamic presented to more than one hundred Americanized Yugoslavs.

As the area gradually began to change and to become more industrialized, the library successfully changed with the times. Although the needs of a non-English speaking clientele were no longer so pressing, it was still an integrated community of white and black and of people with foreign background. The old residents still centered their lives in their homes and maintained a pride in their history and in the achievements of their neighbors, and they valued their branch library and the resources it provided.

Perhaps none had more influence than Margaret O'Connor Cobb, who

Children of many nationalities and ethnic backgrounds found a welcome home at the Haughville Library in the 1920s.

was librarian over a span of thirty-three years from 1929 to 1962, with only a three year intermission in the 1940s to serve in the Women's Army Corps. While she was away a group of young girls started a club in the library calling it "The Margaret O'Connor Bookworm Club" in her honor.

Other neighborhood attractions—a bowling alley, a park, and a swimming pool—began to take away many of the library's users, but while book lending declined, reference work continued to grow. Yet in spite of the efforts of the staff, the discouraging years of decreases in use statistics had come. Mrs. Cobb described her feelings in a poem:

> The time has come, it seems, to mull
> Over a year that was excessively dull
> Ideas and service that come out of reading
> Haughville grownups just weren't needing
> The kids read enough to make up for their seniors
> That helped brighten the look of all our demeanors
> If the kids had been snooty we all would be grievin'
> Thanks to the young ones we are going to break even.

By 1971 a new city park was being planned in the neighborhood, and the ground upon which the library stood was supposedly to be purchased for that purpose. It had for several years been the desire of the administration to relocate the branch, as the building was very old and had endured long years of hard wear. After much searching they located a vacant store building to rent at 3815 West Michigan Street in the Michigan Plaza Shopping Center. So, at last Haughville closed its doors upon its long, colorful career in the old town hall building it had rented and occupied since 1901.

It began a new life just fourteen blocks to the west. The branch continues to provide full library services at this new location, and with the demise of the Riverside Branch Library in 1971, Haughville became the oldest city branch library still open for service.

Haughville Branch Managers
Mary Algire, 1896-1902
Frances Elliott, 1902-1903
Margaret Carlisle, 1903-1905
Eva Hutchinson, 1905-1912
Margaret Wahl, 1913-1917
Rose Thienes Kane, 1918-1921
Catherine Bailey, 1921-1922
Vera Morgan, 1922-1929
Margaret O'Connor Cobb, 1929-1943; 1946-1962
Harriett Barkalow Golay, 1943-1946
Lawrence Downey, 1962 (four months)
Jacquelyn Harris, 1963-1964
Margaret Barks, 1964 (three months)
Inez Babb, 1964-1971
Betsie Collins, 1972 (nine months)
Nancy Endsley, 1972-1978
Ann Herber Jarboe, 1978-to date

From 1906 to 1941 this small frame building at 1913 Prospect Street served near Southside residents.

PROSPECT BRANCH LIBRARY

Prospect was the third of the first four branch libraries, opening December 9, 1896. It was located at Woodlawn Avenue and Linden Street, on the near southside of the city and moved several times, first to State and Prospect Streets, then to 823 State Street, and to other temporary quarters nearby. Finally in 1906 it was moved to 1913 Prospect Street where it remained for thirty-five years. At this time the facility became known as the Prospect Branch Library.

In 1941 Prospect Branch moved again into a building which had formerly been occupied by School No. 20 at 1125 Spruce Street. Remodeled and refurnished, it was light and airy and had space for an auditorium. It was the first library in the city to have flourescent lighting. The upper floor was used for storage of old volumes from the Central Library.

Prospect was a busy branch, including in its service district thirteen schools and an orphanage, and providing service to the whole Fountain Square area. Its early years at its new location were the years of World War II. Gas rationing was strict and there was little opportunity for the residents to seek recreation which was not close by, so the librarian, Millie Drane, started a program to help build up morale in the neighborhood. Many lectures and concerts held in the auditorium attracted Fountain Square area folks to the library and at the same time helped them pass wartime hours.

Louise Hodapp, who succeeded Mrs. Drane as librarian, found that the hard working people were proud of "being Southsiders." The library was a focal point in the neighborhood, not only as a source for information, but also a place to which people could bring their problems, show off a new baby, or meet friends and neighbors. The library worked with the churches and their ministers, and one especially interesting group was the displaced persons who arrived from Europe after World War II. When the branch needed redecorating, "even some of the patrons pitched in," in appreciation of the help given them by the library, Miss Hodapp recalled.

By the 1950s old Fountain Square area families were starting to move out, to be replaced by poorer white and black families from Kentucky and Tennessee. Most of the adults showed a pitiful lack of reading interest, but the children needed the library's help. The showing of films always brought a good audience and provided incentive for the staff, because the programs provided films that the people might not otherwise see. The branch also gave Christmas parties and other seasonal or theme parties which the children eagerly attended in droves.

In the 1960s and 1970s the Prospect librarians worked with retarded children, talked to mothers at the well-baby clinic, and went into the community to extend library services. Ruth Peaslee, then Coordinator of Children's Services for the library system, gave programs for the Childrens' Protestant Orphanage which helped to create a continuing interest in the library for the orphanage children. When Beverly Salzman, librarian from 1967 to 1970, left the branch, more than two hundred children attended a party given in her honor, indicating the importance of the librarian in their lives.

In April, 1969, another era began when the Madison and Prospect libraries were merged in a new building at 1831 Prospect Street, its current location. Opening day was a gala occasion with a sixty-piece band from Manual Training High School on the lawn and a forty-five-voice glee club on the inside celebrating the branch's expansion and new location.

Although the use of this facility has remained relatively stable at this location during the past twenty years, the administration has been seeking a more suitable location further west on Prospect Street, in the heart of the revitalized Fountain Square business district. The 1990s may bring a relocation of the facility to this area, if a suitable building can be found to lease or land can be located on which to build. The branch continues to be a vital part of the community after nearly ninety-five years of service to this near southside segment of Indianapolis. In 1990 it was loaning approximately 50,000 items each year to community residents and ranks well among the library system's neighborhood branches.

On December 10, 1896, the last of the first four branch libraries, No.4, opened with a book stock of only 1,000 volumes in a small grocery store at 548 South Meridian Street, with Gustav Jose as its first librarian. It was later to become the Madison Avenue Branch.

Above the library on the second floor were rooms occupied in turn by a prize fighter and then a ballet dancer, both of whom did not help the plaster on the ceiling below. Later, a washer woman who moved in emptied her wash tubs on the floor, and although she swept some of the water out onto the little upstairs porch, a large part of it dripped through the holes in the ceiling into the library below.

The library was finally forced to move to the old Lyra Hall, opposite the Oriental Theatre across the street. In 1906, this building had a bad fire; however, the library escaped damage. In 1912 the library moved into a cottage on South Alabama Street, then finally on April 26, 1914, into its new Carnegie building at Madison Avenue and Colburn Streets. Colburn was later to be

Prospect Branch Managers
  Alma Wilson, 1896-1908
  Nora Kirkland, 1909-1917
  Millie Drane, 1917-1922
  Catherine Bailey, 1923-1924
  Millie Drane, 1925-1945
  Louise Hodapp, 1945-1959
    (with Madison)
  Catherine Sullivan,
    1959-1962
  Mary Alice Brown,
    1962-1967
  Beverly Salzman, 1967-1970
    (with Madison 1967-1968)
  James Clark, 1971-1974
  Sharon Baumgartner,
    1974-1976
  Carol Blake-Hinshaw, 1976
  Marian Rees, 1977-1978
  Charles Ransom, 1979
  Laurence Whitmore,
    1980-1983
  Sharon Bernhardt,
    1984-1986
  Jo Ellen Klemme, 1987-1989
  Cheryl McCulley, 1989-date

MADISON AVENUE BRANCH LIBRARY

CHAPTER XVII

Madison Avenue Branch Library—one of five Carnegie Libraries built between 1910 and 1914.

Madison Avenue Branch Managers:

Gustav C. Jose, 1896-1902
Mary Algire, 1902-1903
Marie Lockwood, 1904-1918
Jeannette Mathews, 1918
Lucille Wright, 1918-1922
Gertrude Due, 1923
Grace Wilson, 1924-1927
Edna Bernstein
   Moment, 1927-1929
Berniece Kiefer, 1929-1939
Louise Hodapp, 1939-1945
Nina Keppel, 1945-1947
Pauline French, 1947-1948
Catherine Sullivan,
   1948-1949
Louise Hodapp, 1950-1959
   (with Prospect)
Catherine Sullivan,
   1959-1961
Inez Babb, 1961-1964
Margaret Cobb, 1964-1965
   (with Shelby)
Beverly Salzman, 1965-1967
Mary Alice Brown, 1967
   (6 mos.)
Carolyn McGinty, 1967
   (3 mos.)
Beverly Salzman, 1967-1968
   (with Prospect)

named Prospect Street. The new building, designed by E.G. Graves, was completed by Robert Daggett and was located at the north end of Noble Park.

According to a history of the branch compiled in 1942 by Louise Hodapp, its librarian at that time, the site of Noble Park was supposedly part of a land grant given to the state by Governor Noah Noble in the 1840s. However, investigation of deeds showed that the land had been sold rather than given and was city property. William Hamilton Lazarus Noble seems to have been the owner in earlier times; his home was built there and his son in 1857 sold the ground which became "Noble Park."

The new library became a real community center in a neighborhood which was composed of a large Jewish population as well as Italians, Germans, Austrians, Hungarians and Swiss. The people turned to the library for every kind of help and guidance as they struggled to become adjusted to the ways of a strange, new country. The branch was the meeting place for all kinds of groups and clubs, such as the Brighter Prospect Club, the Stitch and Chatter Club, and the Southside Original Women's Club.

During its long years of leadership in the community, the branch served eight elementary schools, both public and parochial, and in later years the students from Indiana Central College. The branch staff worked closely with several nearby community centers. Between the year 1929 and 1945 it reached its peak years of service.

Life at the Madison Avenue Branch was always interesting. One year a canning festival was held jointly with the Prospect and Shelby branches in the Prospect auditorium. A home economist from the Citizens Gas Company gave a lecture. The library furnished books, pamphlets, and even recipe cards. While the mothers learned the art of canning, the children were being entertained with story hours by the children's librarians. The climax came in the fall with an exhibit of canned fruits, vegetables, jellies and relishes.

Another time a children's spring festival was held when neighborhood children exhibited everything from a circus parade illustrating *Toby Tyler*, to a scene from *Rackety Packety House* or *March the Windy Month*, complete with kites, tulips, and airplanes.

138

In 1945 the branch celebrated its thirty-first anniversary in its Carnegie building with Miss McFadden, the Librarian, and Miss Ohr, the Supervisor of Branches, as special guests. The party featured a large birthday cake with thirty-one candles.

As years passed, this old residential neighborhood became industrial and commercial. Big business bought and demolished many of the homes. In 1950 Madison became a sub-branch of Prospect, but in 1961 it regained its individual status. The projected inner loop for the interstate highway spelled doom for the old library, however, making it virtually an island. The book circulation, which had totalled 136,822 in 1933 dropped to 17,636 in 1967. The building was finally sold for $55,000 in 1968 to the State Highway Commission to make way for Interstate 70.

The Madison Avenue Branch library had provided community library service for seventy-two years, and although its demise had been foreseen for a long time, old and faithful friends regretted its closing on November 29, 1968. Its book collection was merged with that of the Prospect Branch when it moved to its new location at 1831 Prospect. It continued to serve at that location the few remaining patrons of the old Madison Avenue Branch.

In 1897 when West Indianapolis was annexed to the city, the Librarian, Eliza Browning, and the Superintendent of Schools organized a little library which became the fifth branch in the public library system, opening in April, 1897. First located "in the valley" on a low lot endangered by floods from the White River, it was soon moved to a little one story building on higher ground in the yard of School No.46 on Howard Street.

On January 12, 1912, a new building was dedicated at 1926 West Morris Street. It was designed by architect Robert Daggett and built with funds from the Carnegie grant of 1909. The new library was proudly received by the community.

There is an often retold story about the West Indianapolis Library which illustrates both the vitality of the library system and Miss Browning's extraordinary interest in all her agencies. Hearing that the new branch was threatened in the great flood of 1913, she took her field glasses and went to the top of the Soldiers and Sailors Monument on downtown Monument Circle, from which she could see that the branch was almost surrounded by water. Making the trip by bicycle and by boat, she arrived in time to help move the books. It has been reported that water came within a half inch of the shelves where the books were stored.

West Indianapolis was, and still is, an industrial area ringed by railroad tracks. Its residents were mostly from the south, Kentucky and Tennessee, people who had moved north to find work. Because of their long working hours and the little education they had received, they were not accustomed to frequenting libraries. It has always been necessary for the staff to "sell" their services to many of their potential readers. Fortunately, it was able to reach the children through the six public schools and one parochial school in the area. Through story hours, school visits, as well as constant programs for adults, the library finally became important to its neighbors.

CHAPTER XVII

WEST INDIANAPOLIS BRANCH

CHAPTER XVII

This handsome Carnegie Library served the residents of West Indianapolis from 1912 to 1986.

West Indianapolis Branch Managers
Gertrude Hilligoss, 1897-1904
Margaret Carlisle, 1905
Anna Guenther, 1906-1913
Jeannette Mathews, 1914
Effie Barnes, 1915
Lucille Nordyke, 1915-1918
Mary J. Cain, 1919-1929
Nina Keppel, 1929-1945
Lyndell Martling, 1946-1950
Emilouise Statz, 1951-1956 (with Shelby)
Margaret Cobb, 1956-1962 (with Haughville)
Alice Carr, 1962-1965
Esther Cauble, 1965-1971
Ann Herber Jarboe, 1971-1978
Nancy Endsley, 1979-1984
Beverly Salzman, 1984-date

In later years large industries moved into the area, taking over acres of ground, tearing down houses, forcing the owners to move elsewhere. The building of Interstate highway 70 in the 1970s just north of the library, with one of its primary interchanges at Harding Street, just east of the branch, caused further shrinking of the community served by the branch library.

During the Depression years, there was, as elsewhere, an upturn in the use of the West Indianapolis library. With unemployment growing, more people turned to the library to read, for whatever purpose. As Nina Keppel, the branch librarian during that period, said, "They had nothing else to do." However, some came to learn new skills and to prepare themselves for a better future.

Then the war came. Jobs were plentiful, the new-found patrons had no time to read, and circulation declined. During the period 1951 to 1962, the West Indianapolis Library was supervised jointly first with the Shelby Branch, and then Haughville Library, becoming an independent agency once again in 1962.

The type of borrower has constantly changed as the area has become more and more occupied by transients, but librarian Esther Cauble, herself a West Indianapolis resident, helped to create a warm and welcome atmosphere for community residents. Later librarians, seeking new ways to attract the public, old and young, began to work with the nearby Mary Rigg Community Center in order to create new interest in the library among the residents of the community.

In 1981 the administration began plans for the purchase of land owned by and adjacent to the Mary Rigg Center just across Morris Street from the old Carnegie branch opened in 1912. The land was subsequently purchased, but it was not until 1986 that plans were completed and construction began on a new West Indianapolis Branch Library at the corner of Morris and Kappes Streets.

This new 5,000 square foot building was opened and dedicated on November 15, 1986. It had been built at a cost of $575,437 and paid for from the 1981 sale of bonds. The building houses 22,000 volumes, has a fifty-six-seat meeting room, a twenty-car parking lot, and is accessible to the handicapped. The new building is a vast improvement over the 1912 facility and will continue to provide quality service to the residents of West Indianapolis well into the next century.

BRIGHTWOOD BRANCH LIBRARY

Readers come in all sizes.

An overgrown village, Brightwood had been annexed by the city of Indianapolis in 1897. Its original access to the city was what became known as Roosevelt Avenue. It had often been said a satanic cow laid out that winding path, and to find Brightwood was quite a chore. When Mr. Rush became Librarian in 1917, Miss Ohr was asked to take him around town to visit all of the branches. She started out quite competently, but Roosevelt Avenue defeated her. On that first trip she never got her new boss to Brightwood.

In the first years after annexation, the city's energies were focused on providing Brightwood with water, gas, sidewalks, and a new school. Brightwood, with its foundry, its roundhouse and railroad yards, did not feel as yet the urgent need for the amenities of culture, such as a library. Those interested in reading could get their books from the deposit station which brought books to the neighborhood drugstore once a week. However, an area library committee was formed and stressed the need for a community library.

Finally, on June 6, 1901, branch library No. 6 of the Indianapolis Public Library opened in rented quarters in a small gray house at 2456 Station Street. The one-room library was bright and sunny and in winter was heated by two little stoves. The librarian, Sarah Swain, carried in buckets of coal from the woodshed in the rear and did her own sweeping and dusting. Library staff members considered it "a nice little place," even though there was no indoor plumbing.

The Brightwood Library opened in 1901 in a small house at 2456 Station Street, remaining there until 1922.

CHAPTER XVII

A discussion of the civil rights movement by Dwayne Brown highlighted the 1991 branch celebration of Dr. Martin Luther King, Jr. Day.

Brightwood Branch Managers
Sarah Swain, 1901-1916
Mary Black, 1916-1919
Augusta Yakey, 1919-1923
Sarah Walker, 1923-1924
Jeannette Williamson, 1924-1926
Mary Welborn, 1926
Lucille Nordyke, 1926
Nina Keppel, 1926-1929
Jeannette Mathews, 1929-1933
Gertrude Rhoades, 1933-1936
Marian McFadden, 1936-1942
Gertrude Rhoades, 1942-1952
Lyndell Martling, 1952-1961
Lawrence Downey, 1961-1962
Barbara Felton, 1962-1964
Bonnie DeCoito, 1964-1968
Glida Bothwell, 1968-1969
James Leachman, 1969-1971
Inez Babb, 1971-1974
Mary Ann Parks, 1975
Charles Ransom, 1976-1978
Alice Greenburg, 1979-1980
Millicent Jackson, 1981-1983
Laurence Whitmore, 1984-1985
Nancy Endsley, 1986-1987
Ruby Anderson, 1988-date

Ruth Metcalf Johnson, a long-time resident of Brightwood, and for many years a page in the library, recalls how stern the librarian was. The library, relates Mrs. Johnson, was a place of QUIET, and it was the librarian's clear duty to chastise any offender who broke the peace. Her public was afraid of Miss Swain's austere manner, which perhaps is the reason that the daily circulation usually totaled no more than twenty-five to fifty books during those early years. Miss Swain was the librarian until 1916.

However, times changed with the coming of new, young, and enthusiastic librarians who made it their business to advertise the library. But in spite of all efforts, it was not until 1919, when Mrs. Augusta Yakey became librarian, that Brightwood Library began to grow. There were only 250 adult borrowers in a community of 12,000 people. The numbers of registered borrowers began to increase as well as did the circulation, as she made her neighbors "library conscious."

By 1922 the library had long outgrown the little house and was moved to the Roesch Building at the corner of Station Street and Roosevelt Avenue. Circulation began to grow, and even though Mrs. Yakey had been transferred to Shelby Branch Library, the new librarians at Brightwood continued the planned reading courses and the neighborhood visiting. They organized clubs, had story hours and contests for the children, and even gave a big Christmas party.

Meanwhile, the library was moved once again, this time across from the Town Hall to the Yankuner Building at 2346 Station Street, in the center of the business district. The building itself was no showplace: a long, narrow storefront with only small, high windows along one wall, and two showcase windows facing on Station Street. In 1936 when Marian McFadden became its librarian, she compared it on a hot summer evening to Dante's Inferno.

Even though there was indoor plumbing, the washroom had no heat. The soft wood floors had become termite-infested, making it necessary to treat them heavily with creosote. The first act of a staff member upon arrival was to change shoes to a creosote-soaked pair, but by the day's end, even the staff member's clothing was permeated by the "Brightwood odor." Even books loaned by Brightwood to another library agency carried with them the ominous, easily identifiable smell.

The library finally had won an important place in the Brightwood community and became involved in many of its activities. Brightwood residents were a well-knit group of middle class citizens. With their mutual concern for each other, the staff and readers formed genuine friendships. During the 1930s the Depression hit the area very hard. In fact, the neighborhood was such a sensitive economic barometer that when, after a better year in 1936, when recession returned in 1937, the library staff sensed it before it became a newsworthy item. The reason was that suddenly there was an influx of men during the afternoon who inevitably said that they wanted something to read because they had been "laid off."

All branch staff members during the 1930s had to endure the sight of underfed children and depressed, often embittered adults. Brightwood witnessed another facet of those years. The New York Central Railroad shops and yards were nearby. Many men, most of them young, seeking work anywhere, dropped off freight cars arriving at the nearby railyards. Coming to Station Street, the busiest around, they discovered the library and came in to seek help. Many a bus token passed from the librarian's hands to those of a nameless man, along with instructions as to how to reach the Wheeler Mission or the Salvation Army for food and shelter.

During the war years Brightwood experienced a boom in circulation. People flocked to the library for training materials for defense jobs and for materials about the war. During the 1950s and 1960s circulation grew rapidly, as the branch began to serve the residents of the fast-growing neighborhoods to the north and east of the branch above 38th Street and east of Emerson Avenue.

Until 1957, when Emerson Branch opened at 37th and Emerson Avenue, the circulation of materials from the Brightwood Branch usually ranked second or third among all the branches of the library system. However, with the opening of the Emerson Branch, and subsequently the Northeast, Warren and Lawrence branches further to the north and east, the use of the Brightwood Library declined significantly. Demographic changes in the neighborhood and the intrusion of the interstate highway to the south also had their effects on the use of the agency.

After approximately forty years in the same location on Station Street, the branch was moved on April 4, 1971, to the Brightwood Plaza Shopping Center, 2435 North Sherman Drive, built on the site of the former roundhouse and railyard. In these spacious new quarters with room for over 20,000 volumes and for separate reading areas for children and adults, the staff continues to provide service to the residents of the immediate community. Although not as busy as in some prior years, the branch still loans approximately 50,000 items annually.

Library Board member Winifred Pettee and Librarian Charles Ransom helped celebrate the Brightwood Library's 75th anniversary in 1976.

HILTON U. BROWN BRANCH LIBRARY (IRVINGTON)

A pretty, tree-lined section of winding streets bearing such names as Lowell, Whittier, Audubon, and Hawthorne, Irvington was incorporated as a town in 1873, the same year in which the Indianapolis Public Library was established. One of its important cultural influences was Butler College, originally the Northwestern Christian University, which had opened there in 1855. Into the story of this little village of Irvington, named for Washington Irving, has been interwoven for years the story of the public library's service on the eastside of Indianapolis. Irvington was a proud community of families who perhaps held themselves a bit aloof. It was always made clear that Irvingtonites were interested in things educational, which, of course, included libraries.

On December 20, 1903, the Bona Thompson library was given to the college by Mr. and Mrs. Edward Thompson in memory of their daughter, who had graduated in 1897 and had died two years later. Its entrance, with Ionic columns, was a copy of the Erechtheum at Athens. Called "a specimen of modern classic architecture," its vestibule was marble with a mosaic tile floor, and its windows were of leaded prism glass.

In 1902 Irvington was annexed by the City of Indianapolis and therefore was eligible for library service. Immediately after the Thompson Library was

Bona Thompson Library.

143

A rented storefront at 5518 East Washington Street became the branch's new home in 1914.

"It takes only three pairs of little feet to start the floor a-wiggling"—Irvington's library 1921 to 1956.

given to the Butler College in 1903, the college entered into an agreement with the Board of School Commissioners for the Thompson Library to become a branch of the Public Library. According to a document attributable to Miss Browning, the branch was to occupy the building "rent free," and as late as 1914 she refers to the hours of the Bona Thompson Library, which served the college students as well as the public.

Apparently this agreement with the college was in effect until 1914, when what was then known as the Irvington Branch Library opened in a rented store room at 5518 East Washington Street. In September, 1921, it moved into a small, two-story house, owned by the School Board, at 5427 East Washington Street, at which address it has remained to this day.

From the first there was not enough space for all the materials, and in 1926 the upstairs was converted into a children's room. Although the expansion was a great help, the Children's Librarian, Hortense Kelly, commented—"It takes only three pairs of little feet to start the floor a-wiggling." Although an additional wooden stairway was added outside the house, there was a real traffic problem when school classes visited or a story hour was scheduled. The narrow steps caused Mrs. Kelly to warn the children, "Watch your step—all seventeen of them."

In the adult section the shelves were so crowded that books were piled on top of each other. Pamphlets and pictures were filed in the kitchen, and seating space was so scarce that readers had to take turns using the few chairs. The whole building became more and more of a fire trap. Library officials shuddered at the thought of a roomful of children on the second floor, with only a narrow inner stairway and wooden steps outside.

Inadequate as the building was throughout the years, it always was one of the busiest branches in the library system. As Indianapolis grew eastward, it served this expanded area, including sections as far east as Cumberland, as far north as Windsor Village at 21st and Arlington Avenue, and as far south as the city limits along English Avenue. During these early years it also served the students from four high schools and five elementary schools.

As early as 1947 the neighborhood began to change, and librarians reported that the many long-time residents of the community began to move away, only to be replaced by newcomers who moved into the area to work at the factories which began to appear on the outskirts of the community. Nonetheless, many of the "old timers" remained loyal to the library. It is interesting to note that even under the precarious physical conditions of this frame structure, in 1951 the staff pioneered a pre-school story hour, now an integral part of children's work in all library agencies.

Several petitions were sent to the Board of School Commissioners requesting a much-needed new building. These petitions had been strongly backed by the library administration. However, it was not until 1955 that planning began. The old house sat far back from the street, allowing sufficient space for the new structure to be built in front of it, so business continued, although inconveniently, while the new building was being completed.

When the library moved into the new building in 1956, the old house was torn down to provide space for parking. In 1971 additional parking space was added when land west of the library was purchased. In 1988 two small structures on this land were demolished, the entrance to the parking lot relocated, and additional parking spaces provided.

A request had been made to the Board that the new library be named in honor of Irvington's most distinguished citizen, Hilton U. Brown, editor of the *Indianapolis News* and vice president of Indianapolis Newspapers Inc., whose home and family had become a part of Irvington lore. The Board had a policy at that time that no school or library could be named for a living individual, but by unanimous vote the policy was abrogated in this instance.

On the day of opening, July 18, 1956, the 97-year-old Mr. Brown was the honored guest. The Irvington Historical Society later gave to the branch a photograph of Mr. Brown, and has installed on loan files of records of Irvington history, so that they may be used by the public as well as members of the Society. In front of the branch the Society has placed a plaque designating the location of Irvington's historic buildings. In recent years a small room in the basement of the library has become the repository of records pertaining to the history of Irvington, and the walls of the stairwell and lower corridors are lined with photographs that are historically significant to the Irvington community.

CHAPTER XVII

Hilton U. Brown Branch Managers
Retta Barnhill, 1904-1905
Margaret Carlisle, 1905-1912
Charlotte Ferguson, 1913-1914
Alice Branham, 1915
Edith Gwartney, 1916-1920
Louise Hughel Payne, 1920
Lucille Nordyke Wright, 1921-1922
Beatrice Geddes, 1922-1938
Frances Killen, 1939-1944
Hortense Kelly, 1944-1962
Catherine Sullivan, 1962-1966
Barbara Felton, 1966-1971
Mary Miles, 1971-1972
C. Catherine Gibson, 1973-1977
Lois Leamon, 1978-date

The Hilton U. Brown Library today.

When Hortense Kelly, who had been branch librarian since 1944, retired in 1962, she summed up Irvington as she had known it. She had seen it change from "a tight little village proud of its history and traditions and fighting to the finish to maintain its independence and its quiet residential atmosphere, into just another part of the big city . . . . To the new people moving in with the factories, Irvington is not a place. It is just a name for the East end of Indianapolis."

The fight was by no means to the finish. More historical homes in the area are being preserved, due to the work of the Irvington Historical Landmarks Foundation. Interest in the past is still being rekindled, and the library should continue to be a part of Irvington's past and its future for many years to come.

Irvington's Hilton U. Brown Library has continued to be a center of activity for the community. It currently houses over 33,000 volumes and circulates over 215,000 items annually, usually ranking eighth or ninth among the system's twenty-one branch libraries.

McCARTY BRANCH LIBRARY

The McCarty Branch varied from the pattern of most libraries, for it was housed in a church. For years the Union Mission Sunday School had met there, until 1905, when F.A.W. Davis and the other workers of the Sunday School gave the building to the School Board to be used as a branch library. The only string attached to the gift was an agreement that the School Board should pay $150 a year to the Teachers' Pension Fund. The church, with its gray brick walls and belfry tower stood at 415 West McCarty Street in the middle of the neighborhood of factories and factory workers' unpretentious dwellings.

Part of the building was used for the manual training department of a nearby school. Most of the children who came to the branch were foreign born, or their parents were foreign born, primarily Irish, German, and Romanian, together with a large Russian, Polish, Austrian and Sephardic

In a church-like atmosphere, the McCarty Branch provided library service to a near South-side neighborhood for twenty-five years.

146

Jewish settlement. The children were the real customers, as many of the parents did not read English well enough to be patrons of the library. However, the library belonged to the people. They had a keen feeling of ownership, and here people of many nations met on common ground—the library as a veritable melting pot.

During the first years the circulation remained static, but by 1920, in spite of special efforts on the part of the library to encourage its use, statistics began to decrease. Mr. Rush, the Librarian, met with the school authorities to discuss closing the branch. The school officials felt that the library was a more important factor in the community than the statistics indicated, and the decision was to keep the branch open.

As one of its efforts to attract young readers, the library decided to try a story hour as an experiment. Four hundred children came to a room that would accommodate only forty. The library took over an extra room used by the school. Mr. Rush, in his Five Year Survey, writes in 1922 that the branch had shown a phenomenal growth, concluding, "The large increase in library activities has required the addition of an extra assistant."

In subsequent years this phenomenal growth began to decrease, and again the statistics declined. Low figures where not the only trouble. In its last years the branch became a victim of neighborhood discipline problems. Apparently the church-like atmosphere was not conducive to good behavior, although fortunately most of the mischief occurred outside the library. Stories of staff fears and annoyances were widespread and included the slashing of tires on cars belonging to staff members.

A final attempt to keep the branch open on a part-time basis was tried in 1926, but the branch was finally closed on October 1, 1930.

In February, 1899, a petition was presented to the Board from the citizens in the vicinty of Illinois and 30th Streets asking that a branch library be established in their neighborhood. The decision was subsequently made to establish a library station in the drug store at 30th and Illinois.

In March, 1908, a small branch was opened in the basement of School No. 60 at Pennsylvania and Thirty-Third Streets, primarily for work with children. It was soon realized that the library was inadequate to meet the needs of all the community residents, and a storeroom was rented at 3355 North Illinois Street. When that, too, became too small, a third location was found two blocks south in a storeroom at 3209 North Illinois Street, adjoining the branch post office. Here the Illinois Branch library remained until 1929, when it became the Rauh Memorial Library and moved over to Meridian Street.

In May, 1929 the beautiful home of Mr. and Mrs. Samuel E. Rauh at 3024 North Meridian Street was given to the Board of School Commissioners for use as a branch library. This very generous gift was the result of Mr. Rauh's expressed desire that he might partially repay the city of Indianapolis for the many opportunities that it had afforded him, and at the same time give the friends and neighbors of the locality that he loved a chance to enjoy his lovely residence and garden.

The house provided a large general reading room, a browsing room with

McCarty Branch Managers
Nora Kirkland, 1907-1908
Effie Barnes, 1909-1914
Nina Keppel, 1915-1922
Edna Bernstein Moment, 1922-1927
Opal Foxworthy, 1928-1930

RAUH MEMORIAL BRANCH LIBRARY (ILLINOIS BRANCH LIBRARY)

CHAPTER XVII

One of the early locations of the Library—near 34th and Illinois Streets.

a large Rookwood fireplace, dark panelled woodwork and Tiffany glass doors. Also on the first floor were a book stack room, a work room, a big room for little children and another for older boys and girls. A broad, sweeping stairway led to a room upstairs large enough to be used as an auditorium. There was a room, too, for a staff lounge and several meeting rooms. Living quarters on the second floor were provided for the custodian. Illinois Branch, always hampered by inadequate space, had now become the most spacious and attractive branch in the city.

At the formal dedication, Charles W. Kern, President of the Board of School Commissioners, presided, and addresses were given by Meredith Nicholson and Rabbi Morris Feuerlicht. The building was formally presented by Mr. Rauh and accepted by Librarian Luther L. Dickerson. In a gala atmosphere of orchestral music, flowers, and refreshments, came the high note. Bronze portrait busts of Mr. and Mrs. Rauh by local sculptor Robert Davidson were unveiled by the Rauh grandchildren, Estelle Burpee and Jane Weil.

The library soon became heavily used, serving a densely populated apartment district. Rauh, Irvington, and Broad Ripple branches usually ranked at the top of annual circulation statistics for the library system.

Meeting rooms were also heavily used. Programs for adults, although not numerous, were very successful. During the summer, concerts were held in the garden, and one year a series of musical events, "Symphony at Sunset," attracted over 3,000 people.

There were no adjacent or nearby schools, so the branch did not become an adjunct to the school system. This, however, by no means lessened the work with children; it merely kept it in better balance with the service given to its adult users. However, since eventually its next door neighbor to the south was the Children's Museum, together the two facilities provided a real cultural center for the young.

In the 1950s and 1960s, many avid adult readers moved away, and gradually more work was done with children than with older adults. With the discontinuance of the Crispus Attucks High School Library as a public library agency in 1959, the Rauh Memorial Library became a cultural center for the black population of the city, a function which the Attucks Branch Library had performed since it was established in 1929.

In 1970 a Festival of Negro History, planned by Betsie Collins, the branch librarian, enjoyed wide publicity and success. Utilizing art, music, story hours, films and other media the staff worked to make the branch an active cultural center in the community.

The building served for many years as a gracious home, and then for over forty years as a library and community and cultural center. The wear and tear to which the building had been subjected over these many years resulted in higher and higher maintenance cost. Circulation and use of the facility had continued to decline during the 1960s and 1970s.

When in 1973 the Children's Museum expressed interest in the property for expansion of the museum, the decision was made to close the library. Its last month of service was August, 1973. According to the terms of the 1929 agreement, the property would revert to the Rauh heirs if the house were no longer used for library purposes. The property was returned to the Rauh family, and they subsequently gave it to the Children's Museum. The house was eventually demolished to make way for the new museum, which was to become the largest Children's Museum in the world.

The stately Rauh home became a branch library in 1929, serving the community until 1973.

Author Aileen Paul and Ann Strachan, Coordinator of Children's Services, visited the East Washington Library.

A group of students from School No. 3 utilize the library with their teacher in 1948.

EAST WASHINGTON BRANCH LIBRARY

This branch, located at 2822 East Washington Street, was the first to be built with funds from the $120,000 grant received from the Andrew Carnegie Foundation. Construction started in 1909, with the dedication on November 14, 1911. One local newspaper enthusiastically described it: "The design in a general way follows that of a Carnegie library in Albany, New York, reputed to be the finest building of its kind from an artistic viewpoint in the United States. The exterior of the building shows a handsome design in brick and stone work."

The basement was to be used as an assembly room for neighborhood meetings. The main floor followed the usual rectangular pattern, with the circulation desk in the center, the adult room on one side and the juvenile on the other. The branch was located in a business area of small shops, a drug store, a laundry, and doctors' offices.

The residents of the area in those early years were mostly middle class, and many owned their homes. It was not and is not today an affluent or "club" neighborhood, but is composed of stable, middle class people. In later years many of the homes were occupied by renters, and the population became more transient. The two large plants in the area, P.R. Mallory and RCA, had their own libraries, and had little real need for the branch. With four elementary public schools, two parochial schools, and three high schools to serve, the library became a center of activity for school age clientele, but it never became one of the busiest. In the 1950s the area became even more of a business center, when more stores and shops developed along East Washington Street. The branch received new fluorescent lighting; new books were made attractive with plastikleer covers; and teenagers became "Young Moderns." Although business did pick up during this decade, the branch was never considered to be in a prosperous or growing community.

When Marian Dunlap came to the East Washington Library in 1959 as librarian, she found the corner of Rural and Washington Streets deserted, as the drugstore, restaurant, and hardware store were closed and empty. However, through the persistent efforts of the staff, providing a wide variety of program activities such as films, story hours, seasonal celebrations, and the establishment of a retirees' group, the Pioneers of the 70s, the circulation has remained relatively steady through these past thirty years.

A complete renovation of the branch was begun in the Fall of 1977, at a cost of $194,605. Service was provided by a bookmobile placed in the parking lot until the branch reopened on July 30, 1978. In 1990 the branch circulated over 69,000 items and ranked 18th among all the branch libraries.

The Hawthorne Branch Library, located at Mount and Ohio Streets, was the second of the Carnegie-funded buildings. It was dedicated on November 18, 1911, just four days following the opening of the East Washington Branch. It stood on property donated by Lem Trotter and Andrew Henry, and its name came from the nearby Nathaniel Hawthorne school. Built during a period of serious labor troubles, the building was bombed during its construction, but when finally completed, it was considered a model community library.

The library did not serve a large area, because it was cut off both north and south by railroads; the neighborhood was sparsely settled on the west, so most of its users came from east of the branch. There were no big factories to bring in new residents, but there were many schools to serve. Until the neighborhood Community House was built in 1924, all community activities took place in the library, including church social gatherings, PTA meetings, plays, and even basketball games.

The Hawthorne Branch had its busy days in its early years, and its proximity to two other branches, West Indianapolis and Haughville, eventually caused a serious decline in its use. It came to serve more and more as a school library for the adjoining Hawthorne school. In the early 1950s it was kept operating in conjunction with Haughville. In 1952 its hours were radically reduced, but due to insistent neighborhood requests, in 1954 it was opened again five days a week. However, the Board closed the library on September 1,

East Washington Branch Managers
    Grace Walker, 1910-1919
    Gertrude Ryan, 1919-1924
        ? 1924-1925
    Grace Wilson, 1926-1951
    Lyndell Martling, 1952-1955
        (with Brightwood & Dunbar)
    Catherine Sullivan, 1955-1958 (with Riverside)
    Marian Dunlap, 1959-1971
    Joyce Karns, 1972-1973
    Joan Switzer, 1974-1975
    Beverly Salzman, 1976-1984
    Marcia Capron, 1985-date

HAWTHORNE BRANCH LIBRARY

Hawthorne Branch Managers
    Eva Hutchinson, 1913
    Ruth Copeland, 1914-1919
    Margaret Black, 1920-1921
    Jessie Logan, 1921-1922
    Jeannette Mathews, 1922-1929
    Helen Miller, 1929-1934
    Louise Hodapp, 1934-1939
    Isabel Garrison, 1939-1941
    Edith Griffin, 1941
    Helen Thompson, 1941-1943
    Marian Dunlap, 1943-1951
    Margaret Cobb, 1952-1955
        (with Haughville)

Hawthorne Branch—the second of the Carnegie-funded library buildings—opened in 1911. It was closed in 1955.

1955, in spite of pleas and protests of the neighborhood. One Board member described it as having "gathered more dust than patrons." Statistics had not proven its need, as it had shown the lowest circulation of any branch for the three years prior to its closing. Following its closing the neighborhood continued to be served with school collections and bookmobile service, although the latter for awhile was literally boycotted by the residents of the area to protest the closing of the branch.

SPADES PARK BRANCH LIBRARY

The Spades Park Library was built in 1912 at the west end of Brookside Park on the corner of Commerce Street and Nowland Avenue on property given by Michael H. Spades, who also gave the land for the park across from the branch library. The new Carnegie library was built in Italian style of oriental brick and terra cotta with a red tile roof. The second floor was designed as a meeting room. At the opening dedication on March 22, 1912, Joseph McGowan, chairman of the School Board, presided. Speakers were Demarchus Brown, State Librarian, and Carl Milam, Secretary of the Indiana Library Commission.

The branch was located in a quiet middle class area with no business district in the immediate vicinity, and although a change in the character of the neighborhood came in later years, the circulation and use of the library remained relatively stable, neither spectacularly high nor dismally low.

When the branch first opened, it served the historic old neighborhood of Woodruff Place, a section of fashionable homes occupied by families who were avid readers. In the 1950s and 1960s many of these homes were turned into small apartments or rooming houses. However, today many of the fine older homes are being restored, and the library continues to have patrons.

Although several of the public and parochial schools in the area have closed in recent years, Arsenal Technical High School is within easy walking distance as are School No. 101, the James E. Roberts School for Crippled

The Spades Park Branch, another built with funds from Andrew Carnegie, opened in 1912. Below, a photo taken in 1915 shows youngsters enjoying a quiet visit.

Spades Park Branch Managers
  Frieda Woerner, 1913-1921
  Corinne Metz, 1921-1922
  Jessie Logan, 1922-1932
  Vera Morgan, 1932-1933
  Jeannette Mathews,
    1933-1945
  Millie Drane, 1945-1954
  Hortense Kelly, 1954-1955
    (with Irvington)
  Lyndell Martling, 1955-1961
    (with Brightwood &
    Dunbar)
  Lawrence Downey,
    1961-1962
  Emilouise Statz, 1962-1966
  Mamie Beamon, 1966-1968
  Bonnie DeCoito, 1968-1978
  Ann Brady, 1979
  William Liles, 1980-1984
  Carol Schlake, 1985-date

Children, and the Theodore Potter School. As demographics have changed the area, there has been less interest in reading and consequently a decline in circulation and usage. However, the branch has retained a small core of good readers and an interested public who truly love the branch. The staff has keep quite busy with reference work, especially with the school-age patrons. The branch has taken joy in giving to a smaller group of eager, intelligent readers the very best possible service.

Badly in need of repairs, the branch was closed November 15, 1986, for a major renovation, and did not reopen until October 24, 1987, due to the delay in the delivery of new furnishings and shelving. The renovation, costing $610,407 included replacement of the roof and sidewalks, new heating, air conditioning and lighting, and all new carpet, shelving and furnishings. In addition, an elevator was installed which now makes the reading rooms and the auditorium accessible to the elderly and the handicapped. Currently circulating nearly 80,000 items annually, the branch should be able to provide effective service to the community well into the next century.

CHAPTER XVII

SHELBY BRANCH LIBRARY

In the days when it was still surrounded by farmland in 1918, a small library was opened in the old, frame District School No. 34, located at 2359 Shelby Street. The first librarian, Lillie Wilson, was a woman of abundant energy and a great deal of civic pride who contributed books of her own and begged donations of books from neighbors and friends to make the library a success.

When the Indianapolis Public Library took over the building to make it a branch of the library system, Mrs. Wilson continued as librarian. It opened for business as the Shelby Branch Library on September 9, 1918. There were only two rooms, one used for the library and the other as a kindergarten, another of Mrs. Wilson's projects. However, the library soon became so overcrowded that it was necessary to use the second room, redecorating it for use as a children's room.

For years the Shelby neighborhood was predominantly Catholic, although there were fourteen small churches of other denominations in the vicinity. This interest in religious activity allowed the staff to do a great deal of work with church groups. It was primarily a neighborhood of middle class working people who took pride in their homes and gardens.

By the 1940s some industries had settled in the area, including two steel mills, a bag company, and a creamery. In the 1950s and 1960s the development of the neighborhood was so rapid that it brought several shopping centers into the area. South of the library today is a diversified suburban district of attractive homes that reaches all the way to the county line and beyond. This area was served by the Shelby Library until November, 1967, when the new Southport Branch Library was opened in the Madison Square Shopping Center at 6840 South Madison Avenue.

The Shelby Library remained in its first, overcrowded home until the site was purchased in 1964 by the Indiana National Bank. The library opened in temporary quarters at 2041 Shelby Street while a new building was under construction at 2502 Shelby Street adjacent to Garfield Park.

The library opened in its new quarters on November 8, 1965. It is a one-story building with a street level entrance, surrounded by trees and built to be compatible with the park site. The walls are of natural rubble stone laid in an irregular pattern, and are accented with narrow, vertical windows.

The interior provides an atmosphere of warmth and charm, and the 6,500 square feet provide a feeling of spaciousness, giving adequate room for work with both children and adults. Its attractive wood-paneled meeting room, which will seat approximately seventy-five persons, provides space for community meetings, library film programs, story hours, and other library-related activities.

The library has a capacity for 30,000 books and provides seating for sixty-seven in the reading rooms. The building is electrically heated and air-conditioned. Parking is provided on a paved lot to the north of the building.

The gala grand opening of Shelby Branch was planned with the combined assistance of a committee of neighbors, the School Board, the Staff Association and the branch staff. Although the gala was planned for five hundred, over seven hundred enthusiastic patrons and friends came. The program included a flag-raising by the area Boy Scouts, an invocation by Dr. J. Lynd Isch,

The old, frame District School No. 34 became the Shelby Branch Library in 1918. Below, the present library, located at 2502 Shelby Street adjacent to Garfield Park, opened in 1965.

President of Indiana Central College (now University of Indianapolis); remarks by Harold Sander and Mr. Harry McGuff, President of the Board of School Commissioners. Also featured were a presentation of a plaque in honor of Mr. Wallace Sims, former member and President of the Board; a history of the branch by Margaret Cobb, its librarian; and benediction by Reverend Walter Laetsch, Pastor Emeritus of the Garfield Park Baptist church.

The first year in its new home the Shelby branch recorded a seventy percent increase in circulation, and usage continued to climb until 1972, when it began to note a gradual decline in usage as a direct result of the opening of the Southport Library. However, the branch has continued to be heavily used by the immediate community, with circulation currently in excess of 155,000 each year.

CHAPTER XVII

A small house owned by the School Board served as the South Grove Library for over thirty years. It closed in 1955.

SOUTH GROVE BRANCH LIBRARY

South Grove Branch Managers
Nina Keppel, 1922-1925
Louise Hodapp, 1925-1928
Lucille Dichmann, 1928-1939
Emilouise Statz, 1939-1943
Melbourne Davidson, 1944
  (with Riverside)
Leila Marquis, 1944-1950
  (with Riverside)
Lyndell Martling, 1950-1951
  (with Riverside)
Catherine Sullivan,
  1951-1955 (with
  Riverside)

DUNBAR BRANCH LIBRARY

The South Grove Branch opened on May 11, 1922, at 2003 Sugar Grove Avenue, housed in a small home owned by the School Board adjacent to School No. 44 on the west side of the city. The branch was named for a grove of sugar maple trees behind Riverside Park on land that had once been used as a shooting grounds. South Grove served a rather small area of population cut off by Riverside Park on the west, Fall Creek on the south, and the canal and a railroad on the northeast.

Because of the very definite boundaries of its district, South Grove had always been one of the smaller branches, and by 1929 its circulation was declining at such an alarming rate that an appeal had to be issued to the community to make use of their branch. In 1930 the School Board suggested moving the branch to another location.

Beginning in January, 1932, the branch was open to the public just three days each week, and by 1944 it had become almost exclusively a school library serving only the one school, No. 44. From 1944 until 1955 it was a sub-branch of the Riverside Branch Library, open to the public just thirteen and a half hours a week.

South Grove Branch was closed permanently on September 1, 1955, because its low circulation did not justify its continuance. School No. 44 continued to be provided service by the Library's School Services Division. The Bookmobile was scheduled to stop at 16th Street and Harding and at 16th and Medford to provide service to area residents. This service was eventually discontinued also because of low usage.

The Paul Laurence Dunbar Branch Library opened on May 16, 1922, in School No. 26, located at 16th Street and Columbia Avenue. It was situated in the thickly populated, near-eastside area made up primarily of neighborhoods with large families. Its boundaries to the west and south were restricted by a railroad and an industrial district. The greatest growth in the area in the library district's early years was to the north and northeast, making the branch located in the south end of a long narrow tract.

156

Librarian Charles Rush stated at the time of its opening that it was "the first branch library for colored people in Indianapolis". This might have given a very false impression, although Mr. Rush obviously did not intend to do so. All residents of the city, and now the county, have always been welcome to any public library. Since its founding in 1873 the library's philosophy of "open to all" has not changed. However, the public schools at that time were still segregated, and School No. 26 was an all-black school in a solidly black populated area, and the branch library was used primarily by those who lived conveniently near.

The branch, situated at a corner of the school building, was small, slightly below ground level, with its entrance some distance from the sidewalk and not readily seen from the street. As a result, from its beginning it was more a school than a public library. In addition, the percent of illiteracy among the adults in the community was very high in those early years. In 1950 when the school was enlarged, the library was moved to more commodious and pleasant quarters with an attractive, easily seen entrance facing Columbia Avenue.

Providing service to the community was always a challenge to the library staff. There was extreme poverty in the neighborhood, especially during the Depression years. Many of the people were new to the city, and the library, as well as the school, had much social service work to do in the broader concept of education.

Wyetta Gilmore, who had worked at the branch for many years, once said that it was a discouraging assignment. Many of the area's residents did raise themselves economically and moved to more attractive neighborhoods, leaving their housing to a new group of the poor. Thus the process of "education" began all over again.

In time, as the more stable families left the community, it became a neighborhood of transients with a high rate of unemployment, juvenile delinquency and crime. The many children living in the area received little encouragement from their parents to read.

Even following its move to more attractive and visible quarters, the branch continued to be used less and less by the adults of the community. In an effort to revive its sagging circulation, the staff conducted a house-to-house survey, visited the pastors of the area's churches, and contacted the school's parent-teacher organization. As Olivia Anderson, Dunbar's librarian from 1962 to 1967, stated, "The staff of this branch will always have to encourage and encourage and encourage and never let up."

The branch sponsored many library programs and activities such as hobby clubs, a Booklovers Club, a play entitled "The Wonderful World of Books," garden shows, a kite contest, and a Ladies' Night Out Club. Young people in the neighborhood were taken on tours, such as to the Powerama Show, to make them realize that just finishing grade school was not enough, and to help them understand the importance of study and initiative if they wished to get ahead in the world.

Although the branch had well served its school clientele, the library was finally closed as a branch of the public library in June, 1967, because of little use by the adult residents. The library's room ultimately became the school

A group of students enjoy a library program on the lawn outside School No. 26, home of the Dunbar Branch Library.

Dunbar Branch Managers
Lillian Hall, 1922-1927
Ruth Coleman, 1928-1934
Effie Stroud, 1934-1944 (?)
Wyetta Gilmore, 1944-1950
Lillian Hall, 1950-1954
    (with Attucks)
Lyndell Martling, 1954-1961
    (with Brightwood &
    Spades)
*Olivia Anderson, 1962-1967

*Mrs Anderson remained with the Indianapolis Public Schools and became the school librarian at Dunbar Library, School No. 26

library. The Spades Park Library, less than a mile to the south and west, began to serve those from Dunbar's neighborhood who needed and wanted library service.

The Broadway Branch Library opened on June 1, 1925, in a small frame house at 615 East 42nd Street which had been purchased by the School Board as a temporary location for the new branch. It opened with only 1,472 books, and yet the circulation its first month open was 3,445, or more than two circulations per book.

Its neighborhood during those early years was made up largely of business and professional people and housewives who had leisure time for reading. There were several elementary schools in the area, so work with children, too, was important. Although there were no big shopping centers, a small but active business community was located just one block to the east at 42nd Street and College Avenue.

Until the Broad Ripple Library opened in 1930, the Broadway Library was the farthest northside branch, serving a large area of the city which showed phenomenal population growth between 1920 and 1930. It had one of the most popular residential areas of the city, extending to Indianapolis' northern outskirts, and was populated not only with large, beautiful homes, but many apartment buildings. Usage of the branch was also affected by the move of Butler University from its eastside location in Irvington to the Fairview Park area near 46th Street and Boulevard Place, just to the north and west of the Broadway Library.

This large, old house became the branch's "temporary" home, serving the library needs of this thriving Northside neighborhood from 1925 until 1958.

158

The library was soon overcrowded. Books were piled on top of each other, and shelves were built in every tucked-away corner or closet. In spite of physical handicaps, the amount of service to the neighborhood was overwhelming. Story hours and reading clubs flourished, but in spite of the heavy demand, staff were unable to accommodate all of the wanted activities because of lack of space. By 1939 circulation reached 95,345. As the bedlam grew, Lois Zimmerman, librarian for many years, emphasized the desperate need for more space. As one patron succinctly expressed it, "This isn't a branch. It's a twig." The staff and public patiently waited, and waited, to replace the down-at-the-heels branch.

Finally, after thirty-four years in its temporary quarters, several petitions to the School Board, and many committee studies, a beautiful new building was constructed at 4186 North Broadway Avenue, adjacent to the old house, opening on October 11, 1958.

The new 6,500 square foot building was light, colorful, and inviting. At the formal opening, Miss Ohr, who had been Supervisor of Branches for thirty-nine years, was honored. She had retired in 1949.

At last there was room for the long-desired programs, which could be held in the branch's meeting room, and ample space for shelving the books, so they could be more advantageously and invitingly exhibited. The old house was finally torn down and the space used as a parking lot. Business grew, and in the first year circulation increased over fifty-nine percent.

Circulation topped out at over 114,000 in 1960-1961, but it was in 1961 that changes in the neighborhood and in the schools began to affect usage of the branch. Many stores at 42nd Street and College Avenue closed, as did the Uptown Theatre. The more affluent families were moving to the suburbs, a factor affecting the usage of several branches. However, there continued to be some stability in the deteriorating neighborhood: some of the "old timers"

Moving day—October 4, 1958.

Broadway Branch Managers
Edna Johnson, 1925-1929
Marian Saylor (Masarchia)
1929-1938 (?)
Lois Zimmerman, 1938-1966
Catherine Sullivan,
1966-1971
Harold J. Sander, 1972-1973
Betsie Collins, 1973-1978
Marian Crawley, 1979-1981
Bernice Peters, 1982-1983
Millicent Jackson, 1984-date

A new and inviting building—a welcome addition to the community.

159

CRISPUS
ATTUCKS
BRANCH
LIBRARY

continued to use the agency, as did students from Butler University, nearby St. Joan of Arc school, and the Indiana School for the Deaf. The branch's most popular activity continued to be pre-school programs.

Although usage has declined in the past twenty-five years, annual circulation has continued in the 60,000 to 80,000 range during this period, placing the branch as one of the busier inner-city neighborhood agencies.

The Crispus Attucks Branch Library was opened on September 18, 1927, in a large attractive room on the first floor of Crispus Attucks High School, located at 1140 North West Street, less than one mile west of the Central Library.

Primarily planned as a school library to serve the high school students, and those of two elementary schools, No. 23 at 13th Street and Missouri Street and No. 40 at 702 North Senate Avenue, the library was intended also as a neighborhood branch, having its own separate entrance. It soon became an important part of the community, although it was used mostly by students, largely because the adults in the neighborhood felt timid about using a branch library located in a school building.

Located in a busy residential and business area, it served the general public as well as day and night school students, the YMCA, YWCA, Flanner House, and many neighborhood churches. It became a meeting place for social, civic, and religious organizations, such as YWCA Board, Alpha Home Board for Aged Negroes, the Book Lovers Club, Flanner House Neighborhood Committee, the State Baptist Sunday School Association and several garden clubs. In addition, the librarian served on various boards and committees in the neighborhood.

The library emphasized a collection of literature written by and about negroes as it served an old, established black area of the city. It promoted a Life Career Club helping students in vocational guidance, participated with the high school in a program for Developmental Reading and provided a variety of activites during the annual Black History Week.

In later years usage by the adults in the community declined drastically, and in 1959 the Board of School Commissioners approved the transfer of the Attucks Branch Library from the Public Library to the high school, effective July 1, 1959. Its adult collection remained as the core for the high school library and the children's materials were transferred to the Bookmobile collection.

Betsie Collins commented in her final annual report: "Community wise, Attucks Branch Library did not become the integral part of the community that I hoped it would . . . For 31 years, 9 months, and 12 days it functioned as a public library serving a high school. In its last years Attucks Branch Library's public was very small, and it was mainly a high school library."

The Broad Ripple Library opened on December 15, 1930, in a store building located at 910-912 East Sixty-Third Street near the center of the Broad Ripple community. Broad Ripple itself had been annexed to the city of

Indianapolis on October 4, 1922, and there had been repeated requests from area residents for a public library branch. Reports of librarians from the start tell of "a responsive, reading public," and it immediately became one of the busiest, most active branches in the library system.

In the fall of 1938 it moved into the first floor of the Masonic Lodge Building at 6235 Bellefontaine Street, which was later to be renamed Guilford Avenue. The area to the east of the library was one of the fastest growing in the city. The vicinity directly north of the library was originally developed as a summer cottage neighborhood, but an increasingly large number of people were making their year-round homes there. A study completed by the WPA in the early 1930s indicated that also in the area were the developments of Meridian Highlands, Shooters Hill, Spring Hill, Rocky Ripple, Crow's Nest, Woodstock, and High Woods.

The library soon became overcrowded and the Lodge needed the rooms it occupied, so plans were begun to construct a new branch building, just south of the Lodge, on ground owned by the School Board at 6219 Guilford Avenue, adjacent to school No. 80.

Although the library system had seen a great deal of expansion in the previous forty-five years, the new Broad Ripple Branch Library, which opened on March 28, 1949, was the first new branch building to be constructed since 1914, when the last branch was built from the Carnegie Corporation grant.

The attractive L-shaped brick building, built at a cost of $250,000, was considered the "latest" in library design and equipment. It featured recessed lighting, floor-to-ceiling picture windows, noise-proof floor and wall coverings, and an open-air patio. The lower level provided space for a 150-seat auditorium, kitchen and restroom facilities, and a stack room for 30,000 books.

The new branch soon became the busiest in the library system, with annual circulation exceeding 250,000 in those early years. Even with the opening of the new Nora Library in 1971, usage remained high. It was customary for families to come together to the branch, which caused reading statistics to be fairly well divided between adults and children. Librarian Leila Marquis commented, "There is no problem of dusting (the books). The public

CHAPTER XVII

BROAD RIPPLE LIBRARY

The Broad Ripple Library, opened in 1949, was the first new branch building to be constructed since 1914. It soon became the busiest in the library system.

takes care of that, as there is constant use of virtually everything." Within five years after the opening, it was necessary to convert the auditorium into a children's room.

The need for a larger facility in Broad Ripple became apparent in the early 1980s as use continued high and the collection outgrew the thirty-year-old building. An attempt was made by the Library Board to acquire by right of eminent domain the adjacent, and vacant, School No. 80 building to renovate as a new Broad Ripple Library, but the building was already scheduled to be converted to condominiums.

On March 17, 1983, the Library Board adopted a resolution offering to acquire a two-acre site in Broad Ripple Park from the Indianapolis Board of Parks and Recreation. The Park Board declared a tract of land west of the park entrance off Broad Ripple Avenue "surplus" property and it was sold to the Library Board for $45,000.

Ed Gibson and Associates, Incorporated, was selected as architect for the new 11,100-square-foot building. However, construction contracts totaling $896,784 were not awarded until July 9, 1984. Federal Library Services and Construction Act Title II funds of $254,962 were received to aid in the cost.

The new library was designed to accommodate 58,000 volumes, 20,000 more than in the old building, and would incorporate a seventy-two seat meeting room and provide a sixty-one car parking lot. Construction on the new library, located at 1550 Broad Ripple Avenue, was delayed because of the electrical contractor's financial problems, and the completion, scheduled for August, 1985, did not take place until March, 1986, with the opening and dedication on March 22.

There has been an increase in use of the new facility far in excess of expectations, and shelves are often depleted, particularly of picture books and popular fiction. A whole new clientele seems to have discovered the Broad Ripple Library, even though it had relocated less than a mile from its previous location. Its high visibility on Broad Ripple Avenue may have contributed to this new-found success. Circulation now exceeds 485,000 annually, and is far in excess of the branch's busiest years at its old location.

The old building on Guilford Avenue has continued to be used as a staging center for the library's discarded and gift book operation. It also serves as the site for the Library Foundation's book sales held several times throughout the year.

GEORGE WASHINGTON CARVER LIBRARY

A new branch library, located in Public School No. 87, 2411 Indianapolis Avenue, was opened on October 7, 1937. Luther Dickerson, Head Librarian, at that time commented in a memo to the Board of School Commissioners, "It is our intention to have this branch provide library service for Schools Nos. 87 and 42 and give an opportunity for colored high school students and adults in the general vicinity of School No. 87 to obtain library service at a convenient location. The book collection ready for installation consists of 3,500 volumes. The principal part of this collection consists of reference and other books which are required by those of school age in the preparation of their lessons. Included, however, is an excellent collection of general literature of interest to adult readers."

On November 9, 1944, the Board of School Commissioners officially renamed both the school and the branch for George Washington Carver, the famed negro scientist.

The library staff emphasized reference work with children, and the librarian, Edna Howard, commented in 1944, "The reference work is heavy. Study groups from Attucks are lovely to work with . . . the club work and recreational reading give play and fun for the younger children . . . Open house in the fall, and the meeting of the PTA in the library are looked upon as great events in the library year."

It soon became evident that the adults were reluctant to use a public library facility located in a school building, as had also been true of the Crispus Attucks and Dunbar branches. In addition, staff time had to be spent working with the students and providing programs and activities for the children.

Adult usage continued to decline over the years. For example, between 1942 and 1949, overall circulation dropped 44.8 percent. From 1943 to 1949 adult circulation declined from 27,849 to 15,559, and for the eleven months of the 1950 school year declined even further to just 9,013.

Much to the regret of the neighborhood and the school the Board of School Commissioners decided, upon the recommendation of the Library administration, to close the library as a branch of the public library system effective June 30, 1950.

The location was within one mile of the Riverside and Rauh libraries, and only one-and-one-half miles from the Attucks library to the South. These factors, coupled with the expense of maintaining the facility, led to its closing. A deposit station was provided to the school by the School Services Division. Its collection was distributed to other Library agencies.

In 1946 Miss Clara E. Holladay, a retired teacher, willed her home at 5549 North College Avenue to be used as a library. There was considerable discussion between the Library administration and the School Board whether to accept the gift. It was too close to Broad Ripple Library on the north, and Broadway Library to the south, to warrant placing another branch library there, and although both of these two established branches were desperately in need of new quarters, neither the house nor its location was suitable. Following much deliberation it was decided to develop it into a special library for teenagers.

There was some neighborhood objection regarding boys and girls invading a quiet, residential area. The city's Zoning Board granted the right to establish the library, and during its short but successful life it caused no difficulties.

After a great deal of planning and some remodeling, the Holladay Memorial Library opened September 17, 1949. Board members, schools, librarians, and especially the young people themselves greeted with enthusiasm the attractively decorated library with it bright, new collection of books arranged on the shelves by "reader's interest." A basement room was made into a model social center.

Borrowers were from all high schools—public, private and parochial.

Mrs. Edna Howard served as Carver Branch Manager throughout its history.

HOLLADAY MEMORIAL LIBRARY FOR YOUNG PEOPLE

The home of Clara E. Holladay opened in 1949 as the Holladay Memorial Library for Young People.

Guided by Dorothy Lawson, the branch's activities ranged from social clubs to discussion groups on foreign affairs, special interests, hobbies, a Great Books course, a drama club, a creative writing group which published "Pan-O-Rama," a collection of the best selections from the classics, and a monthly paper titled "Holladay Headlines." Special groups like French or Spanish clubs invited native guest speakers who discussed individual countries and their customs, followed by question and answer periods.

At the time the branch opened it filled a real need, but its location prevented it from being a central point in such a far-flung community. The branch was closed February 1, 1958, and the collection became the nucleus of the new Young Adult Department at the Central Library. As the nature of school assignments changed, work with young adults was absorbed more and more by the adult departments. The Young Adult Department was closed on March 15, 1960, and Miss Lawson, the Young Adult Librarian, was assigned to the Central Services Department. The collection was recataloged, dispersed, and shelved with the adult books. Miss Lawson was made Young Adult Consultant July 1, 1963. That position was eliminated September 1, 1965, and she was made administrator of the Emerson Branch Library. Miss Lawson had been the only librarian to head the Holladay Memorial Library. The Holladay property is still owned by the Indianapolis Board of School Commissioners and used for one of their departmental functions.

EMERSON BRANCH LIBRARY

The Emerson Branch Library opened on October 7, 1957, in a temporary location at 37th Street and Emerson Avenue—a house purchased by the School Board, and reputed to be one hundred years old. Following conversion of the house into a library, Miss Gertrude Rhoades, the librarian, described it as more substantial than a new crackerbox. It had adequate space for offices, storage space upstairs, and plenty of shelves. By June of 1958, the branch ranked third in circulation, behind Broad Ripple and Brown Branches.

The branch had been established in a growing and intellectually curious community, so the early years became a challenge for the staff. Statistics revealed constant growth in circulation and use, and in 1961-1962 the Emerson Branch Library exceeded 200,000 loans, leading all other branch agencies, except the Broad Ripple Library. This phenomenal growth, coupled with crowded conditions in the old house, necessitated the need for a new home.

On March 29, 1962, just four and one-half years after its first opening, the branch moved. It relocated in a new, modern building constructed adjacent to its original home, at 3642 North Emerson Avenue, a beautiful, one-story brick trimmed with Indiana limestone. The well planned spacious interior with 7,500 square feet was bright and attractive, with pastel colored walls, colorful tile floors, and streamlined equipment.

The consistent, steady growth of public interest in the library was proof of the drawing power of its convenient location and pleasant residential surroundings, and in 1963-1964 the branch made 295,404 loans, exceeding all other branch agencies.

By 1965, when Miss Rhoades retired, the community had begun to change, and by 1970 the new librarian, Dorothy Lawson, was describing the community as "unstable" because of the high incidence of residents moving in and out, and with neighborhood children being bused to three elementary schools outside the neighborhood. A branch report at that time read, "The social and economic character surrounding Emerson has changed faster perhaps than any other community in the city." Circulation by 1970 had dropped to less than 182,000.

The cross section of cultures brought a wide variety of experiences to the library and to its staff. A "teen club" was promoted, and a "Paint-In" to paint the fence surrounding the property brought an unexpected number of young people to the library, which helped to create friendly feelings among the youngsters of widely varied backgrounds. The "Paint-In" was publicized in the *Indianapolis Star* of June 6, 1969, as one of a "series of programs to attract book-weary pupils to the summer library activities." One librarian commented in the *Star* article that "there are white and black teen-agers from all economic levels in the program. If they reap no benefit other than the experience of working together, we will consider it a success."

Emerson Avenue, between 34th and 38th Streets, was closed from March to December, 1972, for widening. This resulted in decreased use of the library during this period. A portion of the library property on the East was required for the widening, necessitating several architectural changes to the building, particularly the closing and relocation of the meeting room entrance which had been located on the Emerson Avenue side of the building.

Even though the circulation at Emerson Library has continued to decrease dramatically during the 1970s and 1980s, loans still are approximately 120,000 annually, a most respectable figure. The branch's helpfulness, importance, and place in the neighborhood has not diminished. The community surrounding the neighborhood has changed, but it still is challenging and remains a viable library service area.

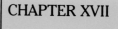

A house reputed to be one hundred years old opened in 1957 as the Emerson Branch Library.

A new modern building replaced the old house in 1962.

Emerson Branch Manager
Gertrude Rhoades,
1957-1965
Dorothy Lawson, 1965-1973
Marie Wright, 1974-1979
Charles Ransom, 1980
Alice Greenburg, 1981-date

165

EAGLE BRANCH LIBRARY

The Eagle Library opened in this small storefront located in the Safeway Shopping Center.

A pet show — one of the branch library's many fun activities.

Library service in the Eagledale area on the westside of Indianapolis began in the 1950s with visits from the bookmobile. This service, soon well appreciated in a community that liked to read, proved that the people cheerfully stood shoulder to shoulder for the pleasure of choosing something more varied than the high-art paperback of the drugstore, as one early report commented.

In response to a petition from the residents of the Eagledale neighborhood, the School Board authorized the Library administration to start planning for a permanent branch library facility. A storeroom was leased in the Safeway Shopping Center at 2707 N. Tibbs Avenue, located at the hub of two heavily traveled roads. The new library was to serve a large, heavily populated area more than two miles from the nearest branch library.

The small library, with just 1,350 square feet of space, opened on December 9, 1960. Eagle's patrons proved to be a variety of people with a variety of vocations—executives, office workers, industrial workers, and homemakers, mostly young to middle age. There were many children, also, with one nearby block housing 125 of them.

The library's collection contained nearly 5,000 volumes, 2,000 of which came from the Book Fair, sponsored jointly by the *Indianapolis News* and the Indianapolis Public Library. This event was held in October, 1960, at the World War Memorial.

Eagle patrons were responsive and appreciative, and by 1962 the annual circulation exceeded 100,000. A wide variety of books was needed for tastes which ranged from Faulkner to the lightest love story. The children came from homes where the parents were convinced of the value of reading, and the children's collection grew rapidly, too.

Only a few years had passed before the branch found it difficult to provide service in such a small area. In each monthly report the librarian stressed the need for space for books, for people, and for service. An adjoining room was added, which helped temporarily, but it too was soon outgrown. The bookstock had reached 12,000 in just five years. The area was constantly expanding with new schools, new businesses and new homes. Larger quarters were now imperative.

Construction began on a new, larger Eagle Library on land purchased at 3325 Lowry Road, just east of Georgetown Road in Eagledale. On March 16, 1970, the newly completed building was opened to the public, with an open house celebration scheduled on April 12th.

When the Eagle Library first opened in 1960, it had the distinction of being the first branch in the Indianapolis Public Library system to be placed in a shopping center. When the new building opened on Lowry Road almost ten years later, it had the distinction of being the largest branch in the system at that time, with 12,000 square feet of space on one floor, a startling contrast to the old store-front facility—with six times more space.

The new buff brick building provides a spacious, well-lighted, cheerful interior with a comfortably furnished adult reading lounge in one corner. An inviting section of the children's room provides a carpeted setting for picture book browsing. The community room has seating for 100 persons, and the building provides a well-lighted parking lot which accommodates forty cars.

The new Eagle Library, built in 1970 was the largest branch in the library system at the time— 12,000 square feet.

The total cost of the air-conditioned building, the site, and outside improvements was $318,612.70, of which $107,417.00 came from a federal Library Services and Construction Act grant, provided through the Indiana State Library. The branch was built for a capacity of 50,000 books, and opened in 1970 with 26,000. Their current holdings exceed 65,000 volumes of which over 27,000 are children's books.

Neighborhood response to the new building was tremendous and 2,900 books were borrowed the first day the branch was open. Soon monthly circulation averaged 21,000, twice that of the original Eagle Library. By the end of its second full year in its new building, 1972, circulation had reached 257,873, the second highest of the library system's twenty-one branch libraries, in which the Nora Library was the highest circulation agency.

Eagle Branch is no longer "new," but in spite of the many demographic changes in the area, still serves a growing community with a diverse and interested reading public. Service and circulation statistics have continued to grow these past twenty years since the new building opened. In 1980 the circulation of books exceeded 300,000, and by 1990 it had grown to over 390,000 annually.

Eagle Branch Managers
Barbara Frantz, 1960-1968
Lillian Ryan, 1968-1978
Beverly Martin, 1979-1987
Carol Blake-Hinshaw, 1987-1990
Sharon Bernhardt. 1990-date

NORTHEAST BRANCH LIBRARY

The Northeastwood community, located on the northeast edge of the city at 38th Street and Post Road, was a new and active one in 1964, made up primarily of young families grouped in many apartment and cooperative developments in a densely populated area. It was a reading community with varied reading interests, The area was delighted when the Northeast Branch Library opened on October 2, 1964. The new branch was situated in the Northeastwood Shopping Center, 8939 East 38th Street, located in a constantly changing area of new streets and new homes.

The first full year of operation saw the circulation climb to 97,111. The library's immediate popularity soon brought the need to expand the small 2,400 square foot store-front facility. By 1968 the circulation had reached 145,000, and the library acquired the whole back half of the building, which allowed it to expand to 3,725 square feet. One of its great assets, an advantage of being located in a shopping center, was the almost unlimited parking space.

The branch served eight public schools and more than a dozen parochial and county schools. The children in the area were described as readers who read to learn, and the staff were always challenged by their many questions.

The Northeast Library became the pioneer for the Library system in 1965 when the changeover was made to the Recordak microfilm photocharging

Branch Manager Beverly Salzman shares a picture book with a young reader.

Northeast Branch Managers
  Barbara Felton, 1964-1966
  Emilouise Statz, 1966-1968
  Bernice Peters, 1968-1970
  Beverly Salzman, 1970-1973
  Barney McEwen, 1974
  Laura Bramble, 1975
  Sherrill Franklin, 1976-1982

DECATUR BRANCH LIBRARY (MARWOOD BRANCH LIBRARY)

system for the checkout of books. IBM punched cards became the standard for record keeping.

The Northeast Library continued to be heavily used by area residents, reaching its peak in 1973, when circulation topped 254,000, ranking second among all the branch libraries in the loan of materials for home use. However, the opening of the Warren Library in 1974 had a dramatic effect on the public's use of the branch library. Warren Library, located at 9701 East 21st Street, was just one and one-half miles south of the Northeast Library; and many library users preferred the newer, much larger regional facility.

Usage of the Northeast Library continued to decline rapidly, and by 1981, its last full year of operation, the circulation had dropped to 116,780. The Library administration recommended that the branch be closed when its lease expired in October, 1982.

Raymond Gnat, the Director of Libraries, commented, "When the Warren site was acquired in 1973 and the new Lawrence site was purchased in 1974, the concept was to build large, library-owned buildings in areas of potential growth and to close the two small rental libraries of Lawrence and Northeast . . . with new library facilities providing a full range of services. That is, larger book collections, specialized staff to serve adults and juveniles, and adequate facilities and meeting rooms to provide a variety of programs planned for adults and children throughout the year."

In spite of approximately thirty letters and telephone calls from residents opposed to closing the branch, and a delegation of more than 100 persons attending the Library Board meeting in June, 1982, the Board voted to close the branch effective October 9, 1982.

Bookmobiles continued to provide service in the 38th Street and Post Road area for those who did not find it convenient to travel to the new Warren Library.

In 1966 the Indianapolis Public Library began the long anticipated extension of library services to the residents of Marion County. The first visible results came quickly with the opening of seven new library facilities in Marion County between 1967 and 1971.

The Marwood Branch Library has the distinction of being the first county branch, opening August 9, 1967, in the Marwood Shopping Center located at 3373 Kentucky Avenue in the neighborhoods of Mars Hill and Maywood. When it opened the branch served a nearby community made up largely of residents with minimal formal education who came from Kentucky, Tennessee and West Virginia, but its service area also extended southwest to the rural areas which include Camby, Valley Mills and West Newton. In the immediate area of the branch are many small, owner occupied homes and numerous large and small industries and trucking firms. Its chief barrier to service was Highway 67, which cut off housing and trailer parks to the northwest.

The branch opened with a collection of 5,500 books in just 2,400 square feet, the smallest of all the branch libraries. However, circulation remained steady, reaching a peak of 101,000 in 1975, and averaging 80,000 to 90,000 each year.

A great deal of the branch's early success was due to librarians Mary Miles and Anna Jane Stiles, who worked constantly with visits to schools, invited speakers, and encouraged class visits to the library from the kindergartens and schools of the area.

A potentially dangerous incident occurred on July 28, 1972, when there was a major fire in the Marwood Shopping Center. The library was separated from the center of the blaze by only one store. Fortunately, the library suffered only minor smoke damage. Still the fire pointed out the inadequacy of the facility.

Feeling the need for a larger permanent facility in Decatur Township, the only township without a library-owned building, the Library Board purchased land in 1988 from the Metropolitan School District of Decatur Township adjacent to its high school at 5301 Kentucky Avenue. The new township library which opened July 2, 1990, replaced the small shopping center rental facility and is two miles southwest of the rental unit. Built on a beautiful, three-acre wooded site, the $1,300,000 building contains 11,300 square feet. It was designed by the Cooler Group to house an integrated adult and children's non-fiction collection and was funded by a 1989 bond issue.

The reading rooms, which will eventually house 60,000 volumes, have seating for eighty persons and feature several window seats. The building incorporates a sixty-five-seat public meeting room and is served by a seventy-car parking lot. It is completely handicapped accessible.

The new, larger branch will be able to provide a much larger book collection and considerably more programs and services than were able to be offered in the smaller rental unit. It is anticipated that usage of the new facility will far exceed the old with annual circulation of materials well in excess of 100,000. Circulation reached 105,000 in 1990, the branch's first year in its new modern facility.

CHAPTER XVII

The first county branch library opened August 9, 1967, in the Marwood Shopping Center.

Decatur (Marwood) Branch Managers
   Mary Miles, 1967-1968
   Gladys Baker, 1968-1969
   Anna Jane Stiles, 1969-1978
   B. Kay Record, 1979-date

The Decatur Branch, a new, large permanent facility, replaced the Marwood storefront library in 1990.

PIKE BRANCH LIBRARY (WESTLANE BRANCH LIBRARY)

Young readers flocked to the Westlane Library when it opened in 1967. The Westlane Shopping Center location was the system's smallest branch at the time—1,500 square feet.

The Westlane Library was replaced in 1986 by the spacious new facility built near Pike High School.

Westlane Branch Library became the second county branch library. It was located in the Westlane Shopping Center on the far northwest side of the county at 7141 North Michigan Road in Pike Township. The very small, storefront facility opened on August 14, 1967, with just over 3,000 volumes in only 1,500 square feet of space. It was the system's smallest branch. Circulation exceeded 80,000 in its first year of operation. Need for additional space immediately became apparent, and in October, 1969, its size was increased to 3,300 with the leasing of 1,800 square feet of adjacent storefront space.

The Westlane Library was located in a growing area of apartment complexes and single residences, creating a potential need for service. The library reached its peak circulation of 145,202 in 1971. However the opening of the new Nora Branch Library that same year soon eroded its usage and circulation considerably.

As the Westlane Branch Library was located on the eastern border of Pike Township, there was considerable interest by the residents of the township for a larger library-owned facility more centrally located in the township. A petition for a new library building signed by 3,800 township residents was presented at the August 18, 1983, Library Board meeting. The Library Board had already purchased a 2.76 acre site at 6700 Zionsville Road in July, 1974, from the Metropolitan School District of Pike Township for $27,600. It had been anticipated that a new branch would be built on the site as soon as funds became available.

Construction contracts were awarded December 10, 1984. The 13,000 square foot building, designed by the McGuire and Shook Corporation, was completed in 1986. The old Westlane Library was closed on April 5, 1986, and its collection of books and materials moved to the new Pike Library, which was dedicated and opened on May 3rd, with hardly a break in service.

The library was designed to be compatible with its Pike High School site and the predominantly residential character of the surrounding area. The building will ultimately house 70,000 volumes, 40,000 more than the old Westlane storefront location, housed in separate adult and children's wings.

The interior of the fully carpeted building is centered around the circulation desk. The main reading area provides the reader with abundant seating, study and lounge space, and browsing and reference sections. Structural trusses of laminated wood, combined with natural wood and bright color accents, lend warmth to the relaxing interior atmosphere.

A spacious and fully equipped auditorium with seating for eighty-five persons is available for community use, as well as library-sponsored programs. A well lighted parking lot for sixty-nine cars is adjacent to the public entrance and auditorium, and complete handicapped access and facilities are provided throughout the building. The total cost of the project was $1,180,884.

While the circulation of books at the old Westlane location had decreased to 111,910 its last full year of operation, circulation reached 155,000 its first full year at the new Pike Branch location. The branch has been well received in the community, and service and circulation have continued to increase each year, and are currently well in excess of 245,000 loans annually.

Arrangements were made to retain limited service in the area of the old location at the Westlane Shopping Center. On November 15, 1985, the Extension Division opened a new library station at the Crooked Creek Community Center, 6844 Township Line Road, to serve the elderly, the handicapped, and latch-key children. Annual circulation at this station is approximately 2,000. In addition, several bookmobile stops are scheduled in the old area.

The Lawrence Branch Library opened on September 5, 1967, at 4419 North Franklin Road, a storefront building previously occupied by the Lawrence Post Office. It was the first branch library opened in Marion County in an incorporated town. Completely redecorated and enlarged, it was equipped with modern and attractive furniture. Its 3,000 square feet of space contained about 6,000 books on opening day, with an eventual capacity at that location of approximately 13,000 volumes.

Its first year of operation, over 53,000 books circulated. As the population grew, the book stock increased, as did the use of the library for study, research and recreation. Circulation between 1970 and 1975 was well in excess of 100,000 annually, with a peak of 111,403 in 1973. However, between 1976 and 1982 there was a slight decline in the loan of books for home use, with an average of only 90,000 annually during those final years at the branch's storefront location.

As was the case with other new county branches, the Library administration felt the need for a larger, permanent library facility in Lawrence Township. On February 1, 1974, a 3.44 acre site was purchased at 7800 North Hague Road from the Metropolitan School District of Lawrence Township for $12,451.72, but it was not until April 5, 1982, that construction contracts were awarded for the new Lawrence Branch Library. In the intervening eight years there had been tremendous residential and commercial growth in the North Hague Road area of the county and the potential for future library use was excellent.

The new Lawrence Library was a "twin" of the new Wayne Library to be built at 200 South Girls School Road. The firm of Brandt, Delap and Nice, Inc., was selected as the architect for both library projects. Groundbreaking ceremonies for the Lawrence Branch were May 10, 1982. The rental unit on Franklin Road was closed on April 18, 1983. Books were moved to the new building, and the library opened for service on May 16, 1983, with an open house following on June 18th. The total cost of the project was $1,061,629.82.

The new 13,500-square-foot building was designed to eventually hold

Westlane/Pike Branch Managers
Mary Alice Brown, 1967-1983
Bernice Peters, 1984-1988
Joan Everett Emmert, 1989-date

LAWRENCE BRANCH LIBRARY

Branch Manager Jacquelyn Harris assists a young patron at the Check-Out desk.

The new 13,500 square foot Lawrence Branch was built in 1983 to replace the rental unit opened in 1967 in the old Lawrence Post Office.

Lawrence Branch Managers
Jacquelyn Harris, 1967-1978
Charlotte Evans, 1979-1990
Carol Blake-Hinshaw, 1990-date

SOUTHPORT BRANCH LIBRARY

70,000 volumes in separate adult's and children's wings. A spacious auditorium, seating 100 persons, with a fully equipped kichenette, is provided for community as well as library-sponsored programs. The building also provides a paved parking lot accommodating eighty-four cars. The building is gas heated, fully air-conditioned, with handicapped access and facilities throughout the building.

As with the other new branches, the interior of the spacious, fully-carpeted building is centered around the circulation desk. This area is lighted with a luminous ceiling; the location allows the librarian to view the entire library from the combined charging and return desk. Separate adults' and children's wings provide the reader with abundant seating, study areas, lounge areas and browsing and reference sections. Each wing is decorated with colorful vinyl wallcoverings, complemented by comfortable, coordinated oak furnishings. Sloping wooden ceilings, along with clerestory windows and large floor to ceiling windows providing natural light, combine to make a spacious and warm atmosphere. Continuous perimeter lights illuminate all wall shelving, and rows of pendant-mounted fixtures provide ample light for browsing and reading.

Use of the library increased substantially following the move to the new building. Circulation its first full year of operation at its new location exceeded 237,000, and by 1990 the loan of books was exceeding 542,000 annually, ranking third in circulation among all the system's branches.

The Southport Branch Library opened its doors for service on November 6, 1967, at 6840 South Madison Avenue in the Madison Square Shopping Center. It offered a collection of about 8,200 books housed in the small 2,750 square foot storefront facility. The library was located in a growing and prosperous residential community of attractive homes and apartment complexes.

Citizens of the area had been asking for a county library since the 1950s, and community representatives had several meetings with the Library administration. Local residents had considered organizing a separate library for the town of Southport. Their persistence and patience were rewarded without the necessity of having to take that step when in 1966 the agreement was reached establishing the county library, with the city system providing service.

Within three months of its opening, the new Southport Library ranked fifth in circulation among all the branch libraries. "The amazing success of the branch proves that residents of the area were eagerly awaiting library service," said Library Director Harold Sander. During its first year, having been open just eight months, the library had statistics to indicate that over 89,000 items were borrowed. By 1971 the circulation had reached 203,314. There also had been a fantastic growth in the number of newly registered borrowers, and almost from the beginning, more space was needed.

In line with the Library's policy of establishing permanent, larger, library-owned facilities, a building site for a new, permanent Southport Library was purchased on October 22, 1971. It was located on the north side of Stop 11 Road, just east of Madison Avenue, two miles south of its first location in the Madison Square Shopping Center. The cost of the site was $50,000.

The firm of Brandt, DeLap and Nice, Inc., was chosen as architect for two identical or "twin" buildings to be built in Perry and Warren Townships. Ground was broken for the new south-side building on May 3, 1973, and the new Southport Library was completed in March, 1974. The small rental facility was closed on March 18th, and its collection of books and other library materials was moved to the new building, which opened for service on April 1, 1974.

On opening day the new library had nearly 40,000 volumes, with an eventual capacity of 70,000. However, even before the move to the new facility, a group of Perry Township citizens, headed by Mrs. Leland Richards, organized a campaign to raise funds to purchase additional books for the new library. More than $5,000 was raised in the "Bucks for Books" project, which was tangible evidence of the high regard which the residents of the community hold for the library.

The new Southport Library is of red brick construction and has a street-level entrance. The electrically heated and fully air-conditioned building was built at a cost of $637,779, including furniture, equipment and building site.

Its narrow smoked glass windows at floor level provide maximum wall space for library materials. The interior of the fully-carpeted building is a splash of color with vinyl walls and bright furnishings. Alcoves on three sides of the main room have brick walls, clerestory windows for natural light, sloped wood ceilings, and chandelier light fixtures.

Special features of the 15,000 square foot building include a 125-seat auditorium with adjoining, fully-equipped kitchenette. To reduce noise and confusion within the library proper, the circulation area is completely separate, within an enclosed lobby. A lighted, paved parking lot for seventy-seven cars, and an after-hours book depository are also provided.

As the township grew, so did use of the library, with service and circulation statistics exceeding all expectations. A new record was set during

CHAPTER XVII

The spacious, well lighted reading room invites young and old alike.

Mickey Mouse welcomes a toddler to a Southport Library story hour.

the library's first week of service, April 1-6, 1974, when 11,458 books, recordings and periodicals were borrowed. Circulation by the end of the branch's first full year of service in the new building, 1975, was 318,722. Each succeeding year usage continued to climb dramatically. In 1990 when borrowing topped 571,000 items, Southport Branch Library ranked first among all the system's twenty-one branch libraries in the number of items loaned, with no change anticipated in this growth pattern in the near future.

WANAMAKER BRANCH LIBRARY

One of the library system's smallest branches, with 2,560 square feet, the Wanamaker Library, opened in leased quarters on April 14, 1969, at 8822 Southeastern Avenue in Franklin Township. It was the fifth of the libraries to open in the county, following the expansion of service to county residents in 1966.

The opening represented the culmination of the efforts of many local residents to bring library service to Franklin Township, and particularly to Wanamaker. As early as 1943, Mrs. Ethel Belton and other women had formed a reading club and later unsuccessfully petitioned the Indianapolis Public Library for materials to begin a staffed-by-volunteers library in the empty Catholic Church building in Acton. In 1965 an association was formed to petition the County Commissioners for library service throughout Marion County. Franklin Township residents responded with great enthusiasm to this effort and were gratified to finally see county library service begin in 1966.

In November, 1966, bookmobile service was begun in the township, first in Acton, and then in Wanamaker. Public response to these stops was among the best in the county, and soon planning began for a permanent branch library.

The leased building, occupied since 1969, was purchased by the Library Board on December 8, 1978, for $73,572. A new roof was added in April, 1979, and remodeling of the interior began on September 28, 1979. This renovation included an expansion of the library to include space at the rear of the building previously occupied by a beauty shop and was completed in 1980. Cost of the new roof and remodeling project was $43,755. In 1983 the exterior of the building was re-faced with a special decorative insulating material, DRYVIT, at a cost of $32,000.

Wanamaker Library—serving the residents of Franklin Township since 1969.

Wanamaker Branch Managers
B. Kay Record, 1969-1978
James Simon, 1979-1984
Carol Blake-Hinshaw,
1985-1986
Sharon Bernhardt,
1987-1990
Ruth Hans, 1990-date

During these past years there has been constant public interest and gratitude for the services the library has provided. No great population surge has occurred in the township, but rather there has been a steady growth in the area. Use of the library has also been steady and consistent, with circulation its first full year of operation in 1970 reaching 72,000. Annual circulation during the last twenty years has been in the 70,000 to 100,000 range with no particular pattern of growth or decline. The agency's peak year came in 1990 when the loan of materials exceeded 115,000.

There has been considerable residential growth on the township's western edge in recent years, and the potential for increased use of the library could see the circulation well exceed the peak year of 1990.

WAYNE BRANCH LIBRARY

The Wayne Branch Library became the sixth of the seven new branch libraries to open in the county between 1967 and 1971. It opened just before Christmas—December 15, 1969—in the newly built shopping center at 7341 Rockville Road on the county's far west side.

This new, storefront facility opened with slightly more than 13,300 books housed in just 2,907 square feet of space. In its first year of operation, the circulation reached 116,000, and continued to climb steadily each succeeding year.

The area, formerly served by visits from the Bookmobile, was a large and growing community in 1969. It was composed mostly of home owners who drove to the library and usually came in family units. The residents were, for the most part, professional people with young children and a wide range of reading interests. Although the libraries in the Wayne Township schools were good, the children were always eager to use the public library as well. Programming for pre-school children and scouts was heavy in those early days of the new branch, and juvenile activities were always well attended.

As had been quickly proven in several of the earlier county storefront branches, the eager patrons soon swelled the demand for more space. Thus it was for the Wayne Library. By 1973 the book collection had reached 23,232 volumes and the annual circulation had grown to 123,687.

Wayne Branch Library—its first location in a newly built shopping center at 7341 Rockville Road.

175

The new Wayne Library, a "twin" of the Lawrence Branch, was built in 1983.

Wayne Branch Manager Sherrill Franklin admires a quilt on display in the library.

The branch was enlarged in March, 1973, to 3,413 square feet, but remodeling was not fully completed until early 1974. The necessity for the acquisition of a site for a permanent, larger, library-owned branch became apparent as development in residential and commercial areas rapidly increased in the late 1970s.

A 3.3 acre site at 198 South Girls School Road was purchased from Mr. Kurt Mahrdt, Jr., in 1979 for $60,000. Mr. Mahrdt made a gift to the Indianapolis-Marion County Public Library of a twenty foot strip of adjacent land immediately north of the original site. In addition, Mr. John B. Urbahns and Mr. Raymond O. Lee made a gift to the Library of a parcel of land located immediately west of and adjacent to the newly acquired property. These gifts increased the library site to 4.12 acres.

The sale of the Public Library Bonds in 1981 provided the necessary funds for the construction of several new permanent branch facilities, including the Wayne and Lawrence Branches. As noted earlier, the firm of Brandt, DeLap and Nice, Inc., was selected by the Library Board as the architect for both buildings to be built as "twin" facilities, as had been done earlier with the Warren and Southport Branches.

The Wayne and Lawrence buildings were bid together and built simultaneously, with basic differences in exterior brick color and interior color selections. Fee savings were realized by using the same basic architectural plan for each of the two different sites.

Construction contracts for the two branches were awarded on April 5, 1982, with clearing of the sites beginning the first week of May. The Wayne Library was completed in February, 1983. The rental unit on Rockville Road closed on February 12th, and its collection of books and other library materials was moved to the new building, which opened for service on March 21, 1983. The formal dedication and Open House were held on April 9th. Its "twin," the Lawrence Branch, opened just a few weeks later on May 16th.

The new 13,500 square foot building will ultimately house 70,000 books in separate adult and children's wings, controlled by a centrally-located circulation desk. A spacious auditorium, seating 100 persons, contains a fully-equipped kitchenette, a projection screen, chalkboards and tackboards, and a controlled lighting system.

The interior architectural features of the new Wayne Branch are the same as those described earlier for the new Lawrence Library. Only the colors used for carpeting, vinyl wallcovers and upholstering distinguish the unique interior decor of these twin buildings.

A well-lighted and paved parking lot accommodating eighty-three cars is immediately adjacent to the main entrance and auditorium. A secondary entrance to the parking area is provided from the Rockville Plaza Shopping Center. Construction cost of the facility was $996,397; furniture and equipment cost was $94,074; architect's fees were $87,000; and the cost of the site was $60,000, for a total of $1,237,471.

Use of the new Wayne Library increased substantially, which has been true of most new or newly-built library facilities. By the end of 1984, the new branch's first full year of operation in the present building, circulation had reached 210,513, with steady and continuous increases noted each year since. In 1990 circulation topped 334,000 and the branch ranked 7th among the library system's 21 agencies. By 1990 its book collection exceeded 58,000 volumes.

At the time the Indianapolis-Marion County Public Library was formed in 1968, a large area of Washington Township was within the city limits, being served by two existing branch agencies, Broadway and Broad Ripple, and eight bookmobile stops. The township was the third most populated in the county, following Center and Wayne Townships, with approximately 100,000 population and a projection of over 200,000 by the late 1980s.

The area was dominated by low-density, single-family housing north of White River. Apartment complexes were being built at a rapid rate in the northwest section of the township; still, over eighty percent of all the housing was owner-occupied. The largest single construction program launched in 1968 was the College Park complex, now over twenty years old, built on a 612-acre site at West 86th Street and Michigan Road.

There was very little open space in the township, as the majority of land use was, and still is, in residential homes. The largest commercial centers in 1968 were the Glendale Shopping Center near Broad Ripple and the Nora Plaza Shopping Center on 86th Street. Other community shopping centers in the township were the Meadows on 38th Street, Town and Country and Keystone Plaza on Keystone Avenue, Emerson Way Plaza, the 86th and Ditch Road area, and at 62nd Street and Allisonville Road. The Castleton area was yet to be developed. Little land space in Washington Township was devoted to industrial or agricultural use.

A new branch library was badly needed to serve this rapidly expanding area of suburban Washington Township. The Library administration had been seeking an appropriate site when, on September 17, 1968, they were informed that Mr. and Mrs. Harrison Eiteljorg were giving a 2.56 acre lot located at 86th Street and Guilford Avenue, in Nora, as a site for a branch library. James and Associates was selected by the Board to be the architect for what was to be the largest branch library in the county system at that time.

The new branch library opened on July 1, 1971. The one-story building

Wayne Branch Managers
Sherrill Franklin, 1969-1974
Joyce Karns, 1975-date

NORA BRANCH LIBRARY

The 15,000 square foot Nora Library was built in 1971 on land donated by Mr. and Mrs. Harrison Eiteljorg.

combines a contemporary and traditional architectural style, with colonial red brick walls accented by sun screen fins and a roof-line overhang of white marble chips. In the design the architect made every effort to retain the texture, scale and rhythm of the surrounding residential neighborhood, as the library serves as a buffer between a residential area and a major commercial center. Interior walls are also of colonial red brick, with large window walls in the adult reading lounge and in the children's area. The 15,000 square foot building was designed to house 70,000 volumes and opened with 26,800 circulating and reference books. By 1990 the collection exceeded 95,000 volumes.

The branch's auditorium, which seats 120, was named in honor of Harrison Eiteljorg, the Indianapolis businessman and philanthropist who had donated the site on which the building is built. It has its own separate entrance and an adjacent kitchen and rest rooms. The fully carpeted and air conditioned library had an adjacent, seventy-four car parking lot on the north side of the building. The total cost of the original structure, including furniture and equipment, was $599,225.42. At the time of the branch's opening Mr. Sander said, "Completion of the Nora Branch Library building brings to a realization the dreams of far northsiders for a library branch of their own."

The building's original design included two sheltered alcoves outside the large window walls in the adult and children's lounge areas. These were to provide space for future expansion; the alcoves were to be brought inside the building by adding the exterior walls. This expansion was completed as originally conceived when a major renovation and expansion project was begun in 1989, adding 2,500 square feet to the building's original 15,000, making the Nora Branch Library once again the largest branch in the library system. The roof and the mechanical systems were replaced, and the parking lot was expanded to accommodate an additional fifty cars. The total cost of the 1989-1990 renovation and expansion project was $675,000.

Use of the Nora Library has continued to increase dramatically from the first day of its opening. In 1972, its first full year of service, 287,143 items were borrowed. By 1979 circulation exceeded 417,000. Until 1987 the Nora Library consistently ranked first among all the branch libraries in the number of items loaned. In 1989, however, it ranked fifth with a circulation of over 435,000. The rapid growth in use of the Southport, Lawrence, Broad Ripple, and Warren Libraries had caused them to experience even heavier usage than the Nora Branch.

Nora Branch Managers
Helen Barron, 1971
Barbara Felton, 1971-1975
Ann Elliott, 1976-date

The use of the Nora Library was also adversely affected in 1988 and 1989 by major road construction work on 86th Street, and then by the renovation and expansion work of the branch itself. Both projects had made access to the building exceedingly difficult. With both projects completed in 1990, the use of the branch has increased substantially, with circulation of materials exceeding 548,000 that year, ranking second among all the branches.

As early as 1979 the library administration was in search of a suitable site for a new regional library in Warren Township. Although the township was served by Emerson, Brown, Northeast, and Lawrence branches, in addition to seven bookmobile stops, all of these four branches were far from the center of population in the township.

Selecting a suitable site for a new regional library in the township was one of the most difficult tasks the Library administration had faced since service to the county had begun in 1966. Factors which needed to be considered were the distance the majority of patrons must travel to reach the library, the density of population in the area, physical barriers, shopping centers and major thoroughfares.

The opening of the new Washington Square Shopping Center at 10th Street and Mitthoefer Road had influenced the normal pattern of movement of people in Warren Township, and its location had become a major factor in selecting a site for the branch library.

The problem of determining a satisfactory location was made even more difficult because Interstate 70 and Interstate 465 bisected the township, with the population density north of I-70, but the largest segment of the township lying south of the highway. The Library administration finally decided that the best location for the new branch would be east of Post Road, north of 10th Street, west of German Church Road, and south of 21st Street; and it was in this area that the search for a building site centered.

On October 21, 1972, the Library Board approved the purchase of a three-acre site from the Metropolitan School District of Warren Township for $30,000.00. The site was located at 9701 East 21st Street, adjacent to the Lakeside Elementary School, just northeast of Warren Central High School and midway between Post Road and Mitthoefer Road.

CHAPTER XVII

WARREN
BRANCH
LIBRARY

The Warren Branch, a "twin" of the Southport Library building, opened in Warren Township in 1974.

179

The spacious, colorful Children's Room has a stair-step story-telling area and unique pod lighting.

As mentioned previously, the Library Board selected the firm of Brandt, DeLap & Nice, Inc., to serve as architect for the new Warren and Southport Libraries, which were to be built as "twin" facilities. By using the same basic design for both branch buildings, and authorizing simultaneous construction, the Board saved on architectural and building costs. The site for the Southport Library had been purchased one year earlier.

Groundbreaking for the new library was on April 13, 1973. The building was completed early in 1974, and the staff and books were moved in on February 11, 1974. The library opened for service on March 4, 1974, with a dedication and Open House on March 17th.

Designed to be compatible with the adjacent Lakeside Elementary School, the buff-brick structure has a street-level entrance and narrow, smoked-glass windows at floor level to provide maximum wall space for library materials.

As the building is a "twin" of the Southport Library, its interior architectural features are the same as those described earlier for that branch. Only the colorful interior decoration used for furnishings, carpet and wallcoverings make each building unique. However, the architects "flipped" or reversed the floor plan of the two buildings to further create an illusion of uniqueness. The same technique was used in designing the "twin" Lawrence and Wayne Libraries. Special features of the 15,000 square foot building include an auditorium with fully-equipped kitchenette. The room seats 125 persons and is extensively used for community and library sponsored programs.

To reduce noise and confusion within the library proper, the circulation area is completely separate and is contained in an enclosed lobby. The Warren and Southport libraries are the only facilities in the library system to include this unique architectural feature. A well lighted and paved parking lot accommodates seventy-eight cars and is adjacent to the community room and main entrance. An island turnaround provides a convenient means for drop-off service at the after-hours book return depository. The cost of the new library was $626,846.88, including furniture and equipment, and the cost of the three-acre site.

The library was designed to house 70,000 volumes. It contained approximately 27,000 when it opened in 1974, but by 1990 the collection exceeded 90,000 volumes.

On Sunday June 3, 1979, a fire of uncertain origin started sometime before 4 p.m. in the interior book return area near the check-out desk. It caused extensive fire, smoke and water damage to the five-year-old building. Fortunately, most of the fire was contained in the lobby service area and the damage to books and equipment in the main part of the library was limited to smoke and mildew.

The branch was closed for seven months for clean-up and renovation. The books, furniture and equipment were cleaned, removed from the building and stored in a nearby warehouse provided by the Metropolitan School District of Warren Township. The renovation of the interior of the building was completed late in the year. Furniture, equipment and books were then returned to the building, which reopened on January 2, 1980.

Barbara Felton, the Branch Manager, indicated that more than 125 volunteers helped to clean the 45,000 smoke-damaged books, which took over 1,500 hours. Each book was vacuumed, covers were cleaned with liquid detergent, and smoke stains were erased from pages. Each volume was checked for dampness and a special drying process was used when necessary.

"We really broke ourselves," Miss Felton commented, "running around, and being on our feet nearly eight hours straight in many cases. But the very hardest part was accepting the realization that such a great deal of damage had been done." A bookmobile was moved to the Warren Library parking lot to extend limited service to the community during the time the branch was closed.

The Warren Library has continued to be heavily used since its opening in 1974. During its first full year of service, 1975, the branch loaned over 311,000 books and other library materials, and by 1990 the circulation was in excess of 507,000 annually.

CHAPTER XVII

Over 125 volunteers helped to clean 45,000 smoke-damaged books following the Warren Library fire in 1979.

Warren Branch Managers
Beverly Salzman, 1974-1975
Barbara Felton, 1976-date

Flanner House Multi-Service Center, built in 1979, contains a 3,200 square foot library wing. The library was the first to be opened in a city multi-service center.

FLANNER HOUSE LIBRARY

The Cross Country Cat holds a young reader's attention.

In 1898 Frank W. Flanner, a civic-minded philanthropist, donated two frame buildings located on Rhode Island Street to the Charity Organization Society. His specific instructions were to develop a "Negro Community Services Center." This organization was established and christened the Flanner Guild.

Mr. Flanner gave additional property in 1909 which enabled a larger building to be erected. In 1912 the institution was renamed Flanner House in tribute to his contributions. In 1918 the Christian Women's Board of Missions purchased, remodeled and equipped four buildings at the corner of West and St. Clair Streets for the organization. Flanner House was incorporated in 1935 as a not-for-profit organization dedicated to the delivery of human services to the growing Indianapolis black community.

On May 30, 1944, a new building was dedicated at 16th and Missouri Streets on land leased to Flanner House by the Department of Parks and Recreation, and in 1975 it moved to 2110 North Illinois Street.

Library service in the northwest quadrant of the city had been almost nonexistent since the Rauh Memorial Library had closed in August, 1973, to make way for the new Children's Museum. Earlier, in August, 1971, the Riverside Branch, 3101 Clifton Street, had closed. The Crispus Attucks Branch Library had been closed as a branch of the public library since July 1, 1959, when the library was transferred to the Indianapolis Public Schools to be used as the high school library.

The Indianapolis-Marion County Public Library has been associated with Flanner House for many years. In 1967 a library station was opened in Lockfield Gardens. When this building closed, a library station was opened in the Flanner House building at 2110 North Illinois Street. This service was provided in cooperation with the Library Committee of the Flanner House Board of Directors.

The Library Board was eager to have a branch library located in the Flanner House Multi-Service Center planned for construction in Watkins Park. The Library administration began as early as 1970 to become involved with the Flanner House Board in making plans for the new library. On September 9, 1978, following years of delay, ground was broken at 2424 Dr. Martin Luther King Jr. Street for the new multi-service center. In December of that same year, the Library Board approved a ten-year lease for a branch library to be incorporated into a wing of the new building. The center was dedicated and opened on October 28, 1979.

The Flanner House Branch Library opened for service on October 29,1979, the twenty-third branch in the library system, and the first to be opened in a multi-service complex. Housed in 3,260 square feet, the branch provides users with books, recordings, magazines, information, referral services and outreach programming. The library has a capacity for 23,000 books, provides twenty-nine seats for browsing and study and has five study carrels.

Growth in the community's use of the library has been steady, but slow. One of the most difficult tasks was publicizing the library's availability. Being the first branch library to be located within a social service agency did give it name recognition and visibility, but some area residents thought is was a library just for children and/or an in-house function of the multi-service center.

Semi-annual school visits, regular distribution of program flyers to area businesses, and a one-time saturation area mailing were done to alert the community of the library's presence. A "Friends of the Flanner House Library" group was formed in April, 1982, to be a support arm of the library for programs and publicity.

In 1980, its first full year of operation, the library loaned 15,657 items from a bookstock of slightly more than 7,000. By 1990 the collection totaled approximately 20,000 books, recordings, and other library materials and circulation for home use exceeded 40,000 loans.

It has not always been easy for some of its users to conveniently get to the public library. Natural and man-made barriers have channelled traffic away from many library agencies; patrons' needs and abilities to get to the library have changed. Sometimes the area served is in a pocket of the city or county too small to warrant a permanent facility. Other times the older libraries have been situated in rapidly changing areas where limited use of a larger facility does not justify its continuance. Bookmobiles, flexible little libraries on wheels, have become an essential part of service for the Indianapolis-Marion County Public Library.

Most important of all, the use and popularity of bookmobile service in the growing and expanding areas of the county have been major criteria for deciding whether a permanent branch facility is needed. Several of the branches owe their existence to the heavy use of the bookmobile in the area where the branch was ultimately located.

In the 1940s Librarian Luther Dickerson initiated the forerunner of bookmobile service with traveling libraries and story hours in public play-

CHAPTER XVII

Flanner House Library
Managers
Wilma Miller, 1979-1982
Gwendolyn Harden,
1983-1987
Marcia Woodard, 1988-date

BOOKMOBILES
AND THE
BOOKS-TO-
PEOPLE "GO-GO
VAN"

Library Service on Wheels—two new mobile units went into service in 1966 when service was extended to all of Marion County.

grounds, but the advent of real library service on wheels did not begin until 1952, when the first bookmobile was acquired. Its first stop was on September 23, 1952, at Tenth and Bosart Streets.

Gertrude Rhoades, an experienced branch librarian, was placed in charge of this new service. Its first "base" or office was located in the garage at the rear of the Rauh Memorial Branch Library. There a collection of books was maintained, so that the unit could be restocked before each day's trip.

Regularly scheduled stops were, and still are, made at shopping centers, churches, schools, nursing homes, markets, apartment complexes, and other locations.

The bookmobile headquarters was moved to the Central Library upon completion of the first phase of the Central Library annex in 1964, which included a garage for the mobile unit. Then the adult book collection was integrated into the Branch and Station Division collection then housed at Central Library.

A new bookmobile was acquired in August, 1964, to replace the ailing, original 1952 unit. When service to the county began in 1966, two additional units went into service in December. In their first year of operation as a combined city-county unit, the three bookmobiles serviced thirty-eight stops and loaned 177,385 books. Additional temporary stops were added during the summer months to accommodate vacationing school children. By 1969 inner-city stops at community centers and federal housing projects began to replace many of the suburban stops, as six rental branches had already been established out in the county, and bookmobile service was no longer needed in those communities.

Although the emphasis changed somewhat with the advent of permanent library facilities in the suburban areas, many "pocket areas" in the central city existed because of new highway development and redevelopment housing projects. Population density was high and cultural and educational levels low.

Use of one of the three bookmobiles was discontinued on January 17, 1974, when it suffered a severe mechanical breakdown. The remaining two units filled in the gaps in service. A new unit went into service on December

13, 1976, bringing again to three the number of mobile units in service. By August, 1977, two of the older units were out of service due to mechanical failure.

In November, 1977, bids were received for the purchase of two Beechcraft commercial vehicles to be designed for bookmobile use. The new units were received in early 1978. That year the three bookmobiles provided service at fifty-seven stops located throughout the county in areas where residents were not served by local branch libraries. Eventually only the two new Beechcraft units were being used for service on a regular basis, with the oldest bookmobile used only as a backup. By 1988 these two units were making sixty-two regularly scheduled stops and circulation was over 154,000. In 1989 the two eleven-year old Beechcraft units were replaced by two new units to be used for regularly scheduled stops. One of the old Beechcraft units was retained to serve as a backup. By 1990 the loan of materials from the two units approached 200,000 items.

From 1952 until 1975 the bookmobile was considered a separate library agency with its supervisor on the same administrative level as the administrator of a neighborhood branch library. Beginning in 1976 the administrator of the bookmobile operation was reclassified and came under the direct supervision of the Extension Division Manager.

Bookmobile Managers
Gertrude Rhoades,
1952-1957
Marilyn McCanon, 1957-1960
Marguerite Smith, 1960-1965
Jacquelyn Harris, 1965-1967
Sherrill Franklin, 1967-1968
Ruth Ann Power, 1968-1975

Extension Divison Managers
Ruth Davis, 1973-1975
Ann Brady, 1976-1978
Freedia Washington,
1979-1982
Barbara Wince, 1983-date

A bookmobile librarian shares a story with an eager group of youngsters at one of the mobile unit's many stops.

The Books-To-People service started as a federally-funded project developed by Harold Sander, and resulted from an Institute for "Public Library Service for the Inner-City Disadvantaged," sponsored by the Indiana University Graduate School of Library Science and the Indiana State Library.

A grant of $32,000 in federal funds was received to fund the project which began service on June 14, 1971. Its goal was to concentrate on neighborhoods where there was a high percentage of non-users and on locations not routinely served by the bookmobiles.

The colorful, flowered Books-To-People Van, popularly called the "Go-Go Van," took library service directly to the people, using mostly paperback books. The project staff reached adult learning centers, infant, pre-school and prenatal clinics, drug addition centers, community centers, Goodwill Industries, nursing homes, day care centers, churches, senior citizens groups, laundromats, beauty and barber shops, doctor's offices, taverns, Boys Clubs, YMCA, and other locations where people might gather. The Marion County Jail was also served.

Another service it offered was the distribution of "minikits" made up of such titles as *Everyday Etiquette, Name Your Baby, Good News For Modern Man, World Almanac, Home Medical Encyclopedia,* which were left at various locations which the van visited. Each carried the message:

> *Books-To-People*
> *Indianapolis-Marion County Public Library*
> *Mini Reading For You*
> *Please leave it here for the next person to enjoy.*

The project's well-chosen assortment of popular titles reached many people who would seldom make the effort to go to a library. Each person contacted was carefully told where the nearest library was located and was asked to return their books there. In this way his or her interest could be aroused to seek library service for the first time at a neighborhood branch library.

The van and its staff also participated in Black Expo, Junior Achievement Expo, the Fountain Square Festival, and a variety of community street fairs.

Although originally assigned to "street corner" service in under-privileged neighborhoods in the Center Township area, it gradually took on a variety of activities and ever-changing objectives. The project was terminated in 1980 as a separate service unit. However, many of its programs were retained and absorbed into the services of the Extension Division. The fact that the project was retained and funded by the Library long after the grant funds had been expended, attests to its success in reaching a large unserved segment of the community.

This brings to a close a marathon chapter on library service to the community neighborhoods of Indianapolis and Marion County. The historical sketch of each agency, by necessity, has been brief, but the total indicates the important part branch libraries have played in keeping the Library a vital presence in Marion County for nearly a century.

Since the opening of the first four branches in 1896, thirty-six libraries have been established outside the confines of the Central Library, including

The Go-Go Van and its staff promoted its materials and service throughout the community.

thirty-two neighborhood or community branches, and four "special" service agencies: Manual Training High School Library, Business and Teachers' Libraries, and the Wishard Hospital Library.

Several agencies have occupied numerous locations during their lifetime. Two of those four 1896 branches, Prospect and Haughville, are still in existence, and although they have relocated several times, still serve the same communities.

Of the twenty-one branch libraries in service in 1990, nine have been opened since county-wide service was established in 1966. Of these nine, five have been relocated from leased facilities into large new permanent buildings. Of the remaining twelve branches, all have either been relocated, rebuilt, or renovated since they first opened.

The roots of branch library services run deep. The record of relative stability and service seems remarkable, considering the innumerable changes which have taken place in the city and county since 1896. The ability of the Library to adjust its locations, techniques, and services to meet the needs of these changing times and demographic demands shows just how alive it has been to a variety of individual community needs.

Staff Education, Training And Development

When the Library opened in 1873, Charles Evans had a staff of three to assist him: Mary Bradshaw, Fannie Currie and Lettie H. Allen, with a fourth being added the following year. Presumably, Mr. Evans taught his staff the Library's policies, procedures, rules, and regulations. It is known from Eliza Browning's own account that she learned much from Arthur Tyler, who was Librarian when she joined the staff in 1880. But when William deM. Hooper became Librarian in 1883, it was Miss Browning who was to teach him, a rather unsuccessful effort, she later reported. Then, in turn, she had the opportunity to learn more from Mr. Evans during his second administration.

Perhaps as a result of her own keen observations of the importance of professional knowledge for all staff, it was Miss Browning who in 1896, four years after becoming Head Librarian, first introduced examinations for prospective employees—a four-hour written test covering general literature given to all applicants.

With the expansion of the system and the growing need for staff with some grasp of the various duties they would be called upon to perform, training classes were initiated in 1918. Charles Rush, in his Five Year Survey, describes the classes: "One half of the work is devoted to preparation of assigned work and to lectures on such subjects as classification and cataloging of books, book selection, reference work and ordering of books . . . The other half is devoted to required practice work in various departments and branches." These classes continued, except for a few years during the Depression, until 1941.

In 1887, under the directorship of Melvil Dewey, a New York State Library School had been founded in Albany. A few Indianapolis Library staff members later attended this school. As the years passed, more schools of library science were organized, usually as an adjunct of a major university. Some graduates of the Library's training classes went on to take these advanced studies and obtained degrees in library science. More and more librarians appointed to the staff were graduates of these schools, some without any previous experience, others with experience in other libraries.

In 1942 the State Librarian Certification Law went into effect. The law established requirements of training and experience for all types of public library positions in Indiana, although those already in such positions at the time the law was promulgated were allowed to be certified for those positions. The law created a need for more trained librarians, a need greatly alleviated when Indiana University established its School of Library Science in 1949. At the same time, the creation of the pre-professional classification in the Indianapolis Public Library provided those with an undergraduate degree an opportunity to try library work before beginning graduate study, and acted as

One half of the work is devoted to preparation of assigned work and to lectures on such subjects as classification and cataloging of books, book selection, reference work and ordering of books . . . The other half is devoted to required practice work in various departments and branches.

—Charles Rush

Training Class, 1938. On the top row, left is Mary Alice Brown who retired in 1983. She served as Westlane Branch Manager from 1967 until her retirement.

Facing page — Training Class, 1922.

Training class lectures covered such subjects as cataloging of books, book selection, and reference work.

a "feeder" position into the profession.

The job analysis completed in 1947 by Helen Norris delineated more clearly clerical and librarian duties and better assured "equal pay for equal work." It made possible the creation of more clerical positions requiring specialized training and experience but not graduate library school training and professional certification.

All competent librarians need on-going, in-service training and a broadening of outlook. Currently there are regularly scheduled meetings of the Library's Advisory Council, branch and division managers, and librarians working with children or adults, as well as meetings of the staff as a whole.

With the staff scattered over the county, and with a variety of schedules, it is impossible to bring the entire staff together at one time though it was and still is a desirable goal. In 1952, with this objective in mind, a Staff Training Institute or "Library Day" was established. February 22nd, Washington's Birthday, was chosen because it was generally considered a holiday, although the Library had not previously observed it.

On this day the entire library system was closed and all employees came to the Central Library for lectures, discussions, and a mutual sharing of experiences. The first program in 1952 was organized by a committee of the Staff Association, chaired by Florence Schad, at that time head of the Teachers' Special Library. The theme of the program was "Lagniappe," a discussion on how to give a little something extra in the way of service to the public. The program themes in later years included "Reaching the Unreached," "The Urban Library in a County Setting," "The Sociology of Indianapolis," "The Image of the Library in the Community," "The Library in the Future," "Human Relations in the Library," "The Role of the Library in the Communication System," and "Books and You."

The "Day" proved so successful that it continued until 1972, usually being observed in even-numbered years and featuring publishers, authors, and local business and social service executives. In 1970 buses were chartered and the entire staff went to Bloomington to tour the Indiana University libraries. The final "Library Day" was on March 3, 1972. The programs were discontinued because of the development over the years of other library in-service training programs.

There are currently a wide variety of staff training and development programs which have been implemented since 1972. Several of the more important ones are: New Staff Orientation, two half-day sessions planned especially with the new employee in mind; the Reference Workshops, currently planned for those clerical assistants working in public service agencies; the three CARE Plus programs, designed to develop more positive public service skills in all employees; the Page Supervisor Workshops; Head Clerk Workshops; Custodial Workshops; Page Orientation Workshops; and a series of computer training sessions designed to acquaint primarily new staff with the use of the computer system as a bibliographical tool and orient them to its use as a circulation control system.

In addition, staff members are sent to special workshops which deal with specific areas of library service, such as patents, database services, technical services and computers sponsored by the Indiana Cooperative Library

Services Authority, the Indiana Library Association, or CL Systems, Inc. The sending of two staff members annually as Library Board representatives to the American Library Association Conference, the sending of staff to meetings of the Indiana Library Association, the Special Libraries Association, the Music Library Association, and other library professional organizations, are all considered a form of staff development.

Along with the constant education, development and self-improvement of the Library's employees, other important, although more worldly, things have happened. With the clarification of job classifications, salaries began to improve and there were, and continue to be, annual increments in pay based on performance evaluations. Salary schedules are reviewed annually by the Library Board, and periodic evaluations and revisions of the Library's classification and pay plan have been implemented, as noted earlier in this text.

On July 1, 1946, Library employees began participation in the Public Employees Retirement Fund, established the previous year by the state legislature. With the Library's later participation in FICA or Social Security, both provided more adequate income for those staff members facing retirement and a better career future for those whose salaries had been meager for so many years. In addition, over the years the Library Board has provided a variety of "fringe benefits," including life and hospitalization insurance, overtime pay for hours worked on Sunday, compensatory time for those working the evening schedules, and other welcome benefits.

A staff group visits the Brown Branch Library as part of their New Staff Orientation program.

Manual of the

OF THE

Public Library

William B. Burford, Lith. Indianapolis.

OF THE

City of Indianapolis,

1896-97.

Policy And Procedure Manuals

When the Library first opened in 1873, there apparently was little reason or use for "published" rules and regulations to guide Charles Evans and his staff of three. Guidance and instruction in Library rules and procedures in those early days were, for the most part, passed on verbally to each assistant, with the Head Librarian doing the instruction. The Librarian formulated the rules under which the Library operated, which were then subject to review and approval by the Library Committee of the Board of School Commissioners.

The first printed rules and regulations found in the Library's archives appeared in 1896, although there may have been earlier editions which have since been lost. It was titled *Manual of the Public Library of the City of Indianapolis* and listed members of the Library Committee and School Board as well as members of the Library staff, which in 1896 numbered twenty-seven. The manual outlined twenty-one "Rules and Regulations for the Government of the Public Library, Branch Libraries and Delivery Stations of Indianapolis." This little manual also stipulated specific rules pertaining to the staff, such as reporting arrival and departure each day, time allowed for dinner, sick pay allowances, hours of work, and the salary for the various positions.

Facing page — Public Library rules and regulations, 1896-97.

The first *Practice Book* currently on file is dated August 1, 1919, and outlines in detail specific rules and regulations for seemingly every aspect of the Library's operation. The next manual, titled *Practice Book: Approved Instructions and Procedures*, is dated 1928. It is more comprehensive than its 1919 predecessor.

There is nothing on file to indicate that any later manual or practice book was published between 1928 and 1946, although administrative memos and directives from the Librarian served to supplement the 1928 edition. By 1946 the Library had grown to such an extent that a complete revision of rules and practices was necessary. In order to bring together the numerous directives issued through the years, and to provide or bring up-to-date uniform procedures throughout the entire system, in 1947 Miss McFadden compiled and issued a new manual titled, *Staff Rules and Regulations.*

A committee of the Staff Association was appointed to help compile the work and to make the new rules compatible with staff thinking. Covering most phases of library work, the committee used the basic outline of the previous Practice Book, with the addition of all the rules and procedures which had changed or been added since the 1928 edition.

In 1957 the *Policy and Procedure Manual*, as it is known and used today, was formulated. Harold Sander defined the theory behind its compilation:

> *For some years, there has been some need for a definitive manual of policy and procedures. With a staff of approximately 175 people, the Central Library, the Annex which houses the School Services and serves over 100 schools, the Business Library and the Teachers' Library located outside of Central, with a Bookmobile and 15 community branches, a definite policy and procedure manual is a necessity for a reasonably uniform operation. The orientation of new staff members will be greatly assisted by such a manual. With existing policies and procedures being set down and systematically noted, I believe when completed, this manual will be one of the finest library manuals in the country.*

Barbara Frantz was appointed Research Assistant in 1957. Working in cooperation with Nevin Raber, the Assistant Director, Miss Frantz was the first to compile and outline the Library's *Policy and Procedure Manual*, organizing it into nine sections covering all phases of the Library's work. As each section was written and distributed to departments and agencies, it was apparent that its use in a growing institution was invaluable. As policies and procedures changed or new ones were created, the manual was enlarged and brought up-to-date.

In 1958 Judith Sollenberger assumed the position of Reaseach Assistant, and took responsibility for the *Policy and Procedure Manual*. By then the staff had come to rely upon the manual as a vital guide to the Library's internal operations. A comprehensive index was prepared and included in the completed manual, which was officially approved by the Board of School Commissioners. Miss Sollenberger, a member of the Library staff from 1935 to 1966, had assisted Mary Emogene Hazeltine in revising and editing the second edition of *Anniversaries and Holidays*, published in 1944. She also wrote articles for *Collier's Encyclopedia* and for *Encyclopedia Britannica*.

Upon Mr. Raber's resignation, Raymond E. Gnat became Assistant Director in March, 1963, and continued as advisor to the manual project. Gene Berryhill, who had revised the index to the previous manual, was appointed Research Assistant in 1969 to completely revise the entire manual. As each section was re-written, pertinent changes were made, and an index created for that section. Before publication each section was checked by appropriate personnel for accuracy and detail, with final approval given by the Director. A short "Ready Reference" index, for specific policies and procedures covered the entire manual. The manual has remained a consistent procedural aid for current staff members, and a helpful guide for new employees.

When the revised *Policy and Procedure Manual* was completed in 1971, it was officially approved and accepted by the Library Board, as have all subsequent changes or additions.

Current practice reflects a policy of continuous revision. That is to say, specific pages are revised to reflect changes in policy and practice. The dates on the bottom of the pages indicate the latest activity date.

Readers' Ink
Indianapolis Library Service

| Number 8 | APRIL | 1923 |

Public Library in 1873

INDIANAPOLIS PUBLIC LIBRARY FIFTY YEARS OLD

On her fiftieth birthday, April 8, 1923, the Indianapolis Public Library finds herself in the very prime of life, full of vitality and health, but with no hint either of age or immaturity. Although her countenance may bear the marks of struggles and pioneering, there is stronger evidence of hope and confidence. In reminiscent vein she harks back to the days of her youth. She points out her many homes about town and likes to tell how fast she grew—so fast, in fact, that her elders were continually letting down her skirts!

Staff and Library Publications

For nearly ninety years both the public and the staff have been kept informed and up-to-date on what was, and is, going on both inside and outside the Library with a variety of publications.

The publication *Readers' Ink*, which lasted for more than ten years, was first published in 1922. In its new and enlarged format it was a continuation of the *Book Bulletin* which had been published from 1904 until 1917, made up chiefly of book lists.

Readers' Ink was appreciated by the public—it seemed to be one of the most welcome little periodicals which they received. Issued monthly, its purpose was to tell the readers, staff and public alike, of the Library's work, hopes, and plans—it was the latest on what the Library could do for the reader, and what the reader could do for the Library. It told of library services such as borrowing privileges, telephone service, library hours, book reserving and even how the reader might participate in book selection.

It also covered all varieties of subjects of interest to librarians, including formal reports on Central Library departments, branch libraries, stories of the openings of new branches, activities of staff members, both professional and extra-curricular, and lists of gifts to the Library. Beautiful bits of poetry, quotations from great authors, and pictures were added for leaven and spice.

Lighter events were included. When Queen Marie of Romania visited the Library in 1926, the publication described her as a "story book queen come to life, a most beautiful and gracious person, clothed in gold." The pet parade, a colorful event sponsored by the children's department, was described with all the details. Book reviews and stories about authors had their place too, like the one about the dearly-loved Hoosier sage Kin Hubbard, which appeared at the time of his death. Funny and unusual experiences of librarians as they dealt with the public added zest.

The first editor was Mary Dyer Lemon, whose talent and spirit were the greatest factors in making *Readers' Ink* what it was. This tribute to her, made when she retired in 1929, is worth quoting. "We salute you. We know that your like will not pass this way again. Your indomitable courage and gentle gaiety have helped us over stony ways. We will not forget." Edna Levey succeeded Mrs. Lemon as editor, a position she held until 1933 when the publication was discontinued.

A new publication began, called the *Antennae*, with Ethel Cleland as its first editor. The primary purpose of this news sheet was to publicize the activities, interest and work of the library staff members.

In 1942 *Ad Lib* first appeared. Its first issue on July 14, 1942, described it as "the brand new mouthpiece of the brand new Indianapolis Public Library Staff Association." Its first editors, Mary Wilson, Judith Sollenberger, Pauline

French, and Margaret Habich said, "It will not take the place of *Antennae*, which will continue to be published four times a year on staff meeting days . . . The committee hopes that *Antennae* may become more professional in order better to voice our library ideals and accomplishments. *Ad Lib*, to take up the slack, will develop along personal and newsy lines." Its editors advertised it as a "disseminator of information, both serious and, if it pleases, frivolous." *Ad Lib* has not ceased publication since. It was first issued weekly, then semi-monthly, and currently monthly.

Also through the years there were issues of the *Staff News Letter*, which was not published with any regularity—copies appearing as early as 1918 and as late as 1942. In 1929 it was labelled "Published when unnecessary," and later as the *I.P.L. Yellow Journal* or *Miss-Information*, although usually using its more dignified name.

In February, 1942, a rather unique issue came out titled the *I.P.L. Victory Flash*. Although described as an orphan sheet under the auspices of no one in particular, it says, "The staff has a successful paper called the *Antennae*. It shall continue to have a paper. We are a stop-gap merely." It announced, "Big things are coming. A staff organization looms." Until the staff organization was completed this paper planned to carry on "even if we have to go to press by hand, in a bomb cellar, so help us!"

Victory Flash was full of enthusiastic descriptions of the great Victory Book Campaign being put on by the library staff with the cooperation of many organizations, businesses and churches. The account of the successful book drive for the soldiers, and the role of the staff in selecting, discarding and preparing for it, is sometimes amusing, but always impressive.

As noted earlier, when Harold Sander became Head of the Business Library in 1948, he replaced their published book list with a new publication titled *Your Cue To Business*, which not only listed new business acquisitions of the Library, but presented the information in a chatty, readable style.

Throughout the years the library has published an extensive array of booklists, program flyers, handbooks, hours of opening schedules, and other miscellaneous publications for distribution to the public as guides to the Library's programs and services.

In October, 1972, *Reading In Indianapolis* was first published. It was designed to replace most of the Library's other miscellaneous publications, and to serve as its primary house organ for dissemination of bibliographic and program information.

Originally issued monthly by the library, and subsequently twice monthly, it contains a calendar of events taking place throughout the Library system, other information about various Library services, and a cover article contributed by a staff member, normally in the form of a bibliographic essay. The articles are usually Library or Library program oriented, but occasionally may discuss other topics in which the writer may be interested. In 1988 the publication was expanded in size, and from four pages to six.

Reading In Indianapolis enjoys a wide circulation. Schools, civic organizations, clubs, newspapers, radio and television stations, and any interested individual may ask to be placed on the mailing list, which in 1991 contained over 22,000 names. This well designed and attractively printed newsletter has provided another valuable communication link between the Library, its staff and the public it serves.

INDIANAPOLIS—MARION COUNTY PUBLIC LIBRARY

READING IN INDIANAPOLIS

March 15 - 31, 1990   116th Year of Service, #12

JOHN UPDIKE

A Writer for All

By Lenore Grossinger
Arts Division

"In Antarctica, everything turns left. Snow swirls to the left; seals, penguins and skua gulls pivot to the left; the sun moves around the horizon right to left; and lost men making a determined effort to bear right find they have made a perfect left circle..."
John Updike from the essay "Our Own Baedeker", in *Assorted Prose* by John Updike (818).

There are few living writers who have achieved the stature of John Updike. Many prizes and praises have been heaped upon him in the past thirty-plus years of his writing, for his beautiful prose, his penetrating insight into the modern human condition and his remarkable imagination and inventiveness.

He is a member of the American Academy of Arts and Letters, and was awarded a Guggenheim fellowship for poetry in 1959. In 1960 he received an award from The National Institute of Arts and Letters for *The Poorhouse Fair* (Fiction), and in 1963 he was given the National Book Award in fiction for *The Centaur* (Fiction). In 1980 he was nominated for The American Book Award for *Too Far To Go: The Maples Stories* (Fiction).

And now the Indianapolis-Marion County Public Library is pleased to present Updike as the 1990 Marian McFadden lecturer. On March 30 the people of Indianapolis will have an opportunity to see and hear John Updike in person — free, no less! As the new decade begins it seems fitting to pay tribute to a writer whose work has been prominent during the entire second half of the century.

Updike has been showing us our modern dilemmas in their various forms since the 1950s when he wrote light verse, vignettes and short stories from the New Yorker Magazine, where he was on staff. He has been a prolific writer and has not confined himself to one or even two forms. Instead, he has done almost everything a writer can do, including novels, short stories, poems, plays, essays, criticism, memoirs, and writing for children.

A major movie, *The Witches of Eastwick*, is based on his novel of the same name (Fiction). A computer search under the author's name takes up a rather large and pleasant bit of time and reveals a veritable smorgasbord of treats in store for the reader.

Witches, computers, art, opera, ashrams, centaurs, adultery, God, death, life, happiness, love... there seems to be no limit to the subject matter that Updike has transmuted into literary gold. But no matter how fanciful the subject matter may seem at times we always can recognize ourselves and our attempt to make sense out of our modern world. Though witches levitate and cast spells for good and evil in *The Witches of Eastwick* (Fiction), we

cont'd p. [2]

The Library's Newsletter "Reading In Indianapolis" is published twice monthly, providing a valuable link between the Library and the public it serves.

The Staff Association & The Staff Has Fun

In December, 1934, and June, 1935, articles appeared in the *A.L.A. Bulletin and Library Journal*, respectively, which extolled the virtues of staff associations as a means of promoting the common interests of the employees of public libraries through establishing of such benefits as "professional standards, pensions and annuities, loan funds, social and gift committees, new staff orientation, group hospital services, state certification, staff welfare, library news," and a myriad of other activities which could be of substantial benefit to the staff as a whole.

As a result of these articles, staff members Helen Brown, Edna Johnson and Vera Morgan sent a memo to Mr. Dickerson on September 11, 1936, asking that he consider such a plan for Indianapolis.

Mr. Dickerson appointed a committee on December 28,1936, composed of Marcia Furnas, Mary Gorgas, Atta Henry, Cerene Ohr and Evelyn Sickels, with Ethel Cleland as chairperson, to explore "the possibility of bringing about a closer acquaintanceship among members of the staff and a better knowledge of the resources and workings of departments and branches." Their tentative report was submitted to Mr. Dickerson on January 16, 1937.

Documents on file indicate that it was not until November 13, 1941, that Mr. Dickerson appointed a Staff Activities Committee to take over as one of its first duties the investigation of a form of staff organization . . . "to be responsible for conducting, organizing and encouraging meetings and other activities as the staff desires with the object of furthering staff acquaintanceship and friendship, social activities, staff welfare, individual and IPL professional awareness and development."

Marian McFadden, chairperson of the Staff Activities Committee, held the committee's first meeting on November 27, 1941, with its first job to ascertain whether the staff wished an organization. On December 10, 1941, an explanatory letter and questionnaire were sent to all staff members. The results showed that 122 staff members were in favor of an organization and 16 opposed. Miss McFadden appointed a committee to investigate Staff Associations in libraries of some what similar size and make recommendations for the type of organization best suited for the Indianapolis staff.

A tentative constitution was drawn up for criticism and approval. Five staff groups, organized in a manner to assure a cross-section of opinion in each group, met between April 14 and April 18, 1942, with twenty-five to thirty people attending each meeting. Following these meetings a digest of opinions and ideas was submitted to the Constitution Committee with recommended changes for the final revision.

On April 27, 1942, a general staff meeting was held in the Riley Room at Central Library. The final revised Constitution and By-Laws were read and

Facing page — Library Director Harold Sander lends his musical talents to the May Breakfast skit in 1958.

adopted. All who wished were given an opportunity to sign the constitution and then receive election ballots. Mary Wells was elected the association's first president; Hortense Kelly, Vice-President; Harriett Golay, Secretary; and Verna Hankemeier, Treasurer. Miss Cleland was Branch Representative and Edna Johnson, Central Representative. All members of the staff were granted membership upon the payment of dues.

A resolution was adopted asking the chairperson of the Staff Activities Committee to serve as "retiring President" on the new Executive Board of the Staff Association, thus forming a link between the new and old organizations. The first meeting of both was on May 2, 1942. Following this meeting, the Staff Activities Committee was dissolved by its chairperson, and its authority and responsibilities were transferred to the new association.

In 1943 the Staff Association established a Staff Loan Fund, begun in memory of Marcia Moore Furnas, Head of the Circulation Department from 1917 until her death in 1941. It was made up of voluntary contributions and a percentage of the association's annual dues. Its purpose was to help any member with education expenses or emergencies arising from illness or death in his or her family.

The association held a variety of fund-raising activities to support scholarships and the loan fund. One of the most popular was the publication of a series of cookbooks which were a collection of the "best" recipes contributed by members of the staff. They always became instant "bestsellers."

The Staff Loan Fund was discontinued after the Staff Association became a member of the Finance Center Credit Union in 1984.

Beginning in 1964 a staff committee appointed by the Director selected annually a staff member to receive the Distinguished Service Award for outstanding ability and leadership. The award consists of a citation and a check which initially was $50, increased to $125 in later years. This gift comes from the proceeds of a fund established by Helen Norris, and from subsequent gifts given in memory of several other staff members. The fund currently exceeds $3,300. Beginning in 1990 the Library Foundation presented the recipient a check in the amount of $875, bringing to $1,000 the total amount of this prestigious annual award. In 1979 the award was renamed the Helen L. Norris Distinguished Service Award in honor of her role in establishing the award and her generous initial gift to fund it.

Recipients of the award have been Leila Marquis, 1964; Mary Wheeler Wells, also 1964; Doris Plummer, 1965; Dorothy F. Lawson, 1966; Margaret O'Connor Cobb, 1967; Jacqueline Ek, 1968; Elizabeth Dorsey, 1969; Edith Griffin, 1970; Dorothy L. Gray, 1971; Betsie Collins, 1972; Robert Trees, 1973; Mary Burns, 1974; and Lillian Ryan, 1975.

Others were Bruce Aldridge, 1976 (posthumously); Anna Auzins Lagzdins, 1977; Rosalind Horner, 1978; Ernest White, 1979; William Barrow, 1980; Mary Alice Brown, 1981; Marian Hightshue, 1982; Beverly Salzman, 1983; Charity Mitchell, 1984; Sadie Scrougham, 1985; Dan Fast, 1986; Virginia Stroud, 1987; Jeanne Bridgewater, 1988, Rasheeda Randle, 1989; and Matthew Hannigan, 1990.

Soon after its founding the association began to send one of its members to the annual conference of the American Library Association, with all expenses paid by the association. The delegate is chosen each year by a vote of the association membership.

After she became Head Librarian in 1945, Miss McFadden began the custom of presenting a red rose to every staff member with twenty-five years of service to the Indianapolis Public Library. In 1972 for the first time ten to twenty years of service were recognized with the presentation of a pin awarded at the Staff Association's annual May Breakfast program. Currently pins are awarded for ten, fifteen, twenty and twenty-five years of service to the Library.

At the Library Board Award Ceremony, usually held in October of each year, awards are given by the Board for years of service. A congratulatory letter is sent to those of the staff with fifteen years; a certificate is presented for twenty years, and a distinctive bronze medallion on a cherry base is given for twenty-five and thirty years of service. Also at the awards ceremony the Library Board presents each Library retiree with an engraved silver bowl.

The Staff Association was established in 1942 "to advance the interest of the library, promote its professional and social relations and the economic welfare of its staff." This still remains the basic purpose of the organization. It has responsibility for activities such as the annual May Breakfast, which will be discussed in detail later, retirement receptions, gifts for weddings, and flowers for illness and deaths.

But most important of all is its role in forming policies of staff, administration and inter-library relationships. The association's Salary Committee meets annually with the Library Board, or as often as may be necessary, and many of the association's concerns and proposals taken to the Board have helped the Board understand and act upon staff concerns, and have initiated changes in salaries, fringe benefits, and personnel policies. The association has also established an excellent working relationship with the Library administration, and as a result holds an important role in the activities and policies of the Library, both professionally and socially.

Everyone loves a party, and the Library staff is no exception. There are no annals concerning parties in which the staff participated during the early years, but the employees probably did enjoy some sociable moments, which the imagination may be apt to reconstruct as rather staid affairs. It would be difficult to picture Mr. Evans being put on the gridiron by his lady librarians.

During Mr. Rush's administration the recorded and unrecorded tales begin to appear. The staff was small enough that they, along with the whole Rush family, would sometimes adjourn to the then wooded countryside for an impromptu picnic.

An account of at least one clandestine affair has been handed down by word of mouth. Some adventurous souls at Central Library decided to spend the night in the library—not because there were conscientious, but just for the sheer devilment of trying it. The dark hours were spent in examining the tunnels at the lowest levels and climbing the concealed spiral staircase to the upper reaches of the building. What Mr. Rush thought about the escapade has

CHAPTER XXI

THE STAFF HAS FUN

CHAPTER XXI

The "cast of characters" for a 1920s May Breakfast skit.

faded into oblivion, but apparently, as there were no broken bones, nor furniture, he preferred to look the other way.

At some time or other birthday groups were organized. There were four of them, each open to those whose birthdays fell within the three months covered. The month was the only concern and diplomatically, the year of birth was never asked. Yearly parties by each group have been held with more or less regularity for many years. Some groups are currently still active, while others have dropped by the wayside. Their chief value was, and still is, the bringing together of those in varied agencies of the Library who might otherwise not have the opportunity to become well acquainted.

The most traditional of all the informal celebrations is the May Breakfast, which has been held annually for seventy years. The idea originated with Mr. Rush, who felt that staff social activities bound the workers together into a close-knit, loyal group which would ultimately be of benefit for the Library.

The first May Breakfast was held in 1921 in the staff dining room at the Central Library, as the staff was small in those early days. Eliza Browning, then Assistant Librarian, presided and gave a "serious" talk on diets, particularly of red radishes, for short people. Equally seriously, Amy Winslow, who was more than six feet tall, talked on diets for the long, recommending only long radishes, green beans, bananas, and the like.

During the early 1920s the breakfasts were all held in the staff dining room. The event always provided the one great opportunity to kid "The Chief." In 1924 the program consisted of an uproarious burlesque of a Department Heads' Meeting, with Wilma Reeve impersonating Mr. Rush so successfully that she was destined to play the role many times afterward. In fact, to every Head Librarian has been granted at a May Breakfast what the poet once desired:

> *O would some pow'r the giftie gi'e us*
> *To see oursel's as others see us!*

Not even the long departed have been spared. One bright May morning a very scholarly looking "Charles Evans" with a skull cap and a tan duster-type coat appeared discussing book selection with two bustle-clad lady librarians. All went peacefully for a few moments as dull tomes were discussed and then there was a dead silence. The audience felt uncomfortable, certain that the personifier of the learned gentleman had forgotten his lines. He (she) had not. There was much hesitation and wiping of the brow and finally, "Uh—Uh—should we consider this zoological treatise on the—uh—uh, the sex life of the bee?" Whereupon one of the very prim lady librarians turned to the other very prim lady librarian and in a stage whisper remarked, "I'd rather read the Kinsey Report."

By 1926 the staff had outgrown the dining room, and the breakfast moved to Cropsey Auditorium, which would be gaily decorated with window boxes of yellow forsythia. That year each guest had been asked to send in her Kodak picture. To the staff members' surprise, at each place was a card with a cartoon picture topped by her own face and a jingle describing her virtues or foibles. The program consisted of a very professional Maypole dance and a floor show provided by the Library's youngest and prettiest. For variety the next year, a picnic was held in the Mooresville Gym with Isabel Russell as May Queen. There was even a jester with cap and bells, Edith Newlin, who delighted the crowd by turning handsprings. The last breakfast with Mr. Rush at the helm was in 1928 at the Propylaeum.

The first for Mr. Dickerson, in 1929, featured the dedication of the Rauh Memorial Library and the marriage of Miss Rauh to Mr. IPL. Louise Hodapp was the groom, Opal Foxworthy the bride, Millie Drane, the best man, and Jeannette Mathews the parson. An assortment of library beauties served as bridesmaids.

The early thirties took the breakfast back and forth between the Athenaeum and the Propylaeum. In 1935 at the L.S. Ayres' Tearoom, Mr. Dickerson was razzed unmercifully. Provided with halo and wings, and wearing asbestos gloves, the nervous impersonator of "Angel" Dickerson dropped the "dirty" books down a chute to a flaming hell below.

Throughout the years the staff has shown great originality in its programs for May Breakfast. Skits have ranged from pantomimes to revues, poetry, song and dance, all seasoned with a great deal of fun and laughter. One skit called "Quick, McFadden, the Aspirin" caused a great deal of mirth, and in another, "psychiatrist" Harold Sander administered to patient Dorothy Lawson.

One of the most unusual, perhaps, was held at the Medical Center in 1958. A skit written by Alice Payne carried staff members to the South Sea dream isle of Boola Boola. "Happy Hal" Sander and "Tired" Raber were faced with problems of teaching the native girls, attired in grass skirts and with pineapples on their heads, the meaning of the word "book." Performed in a setting of palm trees, fruits and flowers, with music provided by Mr. Sander's ukelele, the skit was never to be forgotten by those who saw it. After it was over Mr. Sander complained that the cost of production, which reached a grand total of thirty cents, was much too much.

The staff assemble in 1948—the Library's 75th Anniversary year. Front center, right, is Head Librarian Marian McFadden.

Several memorable skits of the 1980s centered on the world of computerization, with the cast of staff members posing as computer terminals, forever complaining about the "downtime."

The locale of the May Breakfast has varied from the Fishback Grille, the Propylaeum, the tearooms of Ayres and Block's to the Athenaeum, LaRue's, the Women's Department Club, and several hotels. But wherever it has been held, it is certain that no year would seem complete without this annual get-together. It not only provides fun for the current staff, but gives an opportunity for retirees, who come as invited guests, to renew old friendships.

In recent years members of the Library Board have also come as invited guests of the staff association and have had an opportunity to share in this traditional annual library staff "fun" activity. Beginning in 1990 the Library Foundation served as host for this perennial staff social affair, paying the cost for both staff and retirees.

Staff, retirees and Board members enjoy good food and pleasant conversation at a recent May Breakfast.

Staff member Alice Marcelleenna Smith receives the Helen L. Norris Distinguished Service Awards from Library Director Raymond E. Gnat at the 1991 May Breakfast.

Special Programs and Celebrations and Distinguished Visitors

The staff has not reserved all the parties and celebrations for its own enjoyment. The more important events are shared with the public.

One of the early colorful activities sponsored by the Library was a Library Pet Parade in 1924. In spite of dire predictions, nothing terrible happened. A dog chased a cat across the park, a goat balked, a few small boys nibbled dog biscuits, and a few lost pets caused temporary tears. More than 400 children participated. The Police and Firemen's Band led the parade and said they had never enjoyed themselves so much.

Prizes totaling $120.00 were given, the gifts of interested friends. A little girl who brought a snail won the prize for the animal lowest in evolution. The dog pound wagon rode along with its dogs scrubbed and be-ribboned for the occasion, resulting in new-found homes for many of them. There were Mary and her little lamb, a baby alligator in a pickle dish, and many little wagons decorated with bright crepe paper carrying pigs, kittens, and bird cages.

The parade became the inspiration for the book *The Pet Parade*, to be written by Evelyn Sickels, a member of the library staff, who later was to author several other books for children.

Special programs and celebrations for children of all ages have been a traditional part of the library's activities for over seventy years. Especially important have been the Summer Reading Programs, Children's Book Week, and the Family Festivals.

SUMMER READING PROGRAMS

In the summer of 1919 the first Vacation Reading Program was implemented, and its purpose has remained unchanged since then—to instill a love of reading in those who participate each summer by bringing children and books together, using a structured format. Although historically the purpose has not varied, the format has taken on many forms and has been reflective of the attitude and changes in young people over the years.

As early as 1920, librarians were making school visits to tell stories and talk about the Library and what students could expect to find there during the summer months. By the end of the 1920s, the Vacation Reading Program was receiving rave reviews from teachers and parents.

During the Depression years, the Vacation Reading Program continued, but less emphasis was given to publicizing the program, due to lack of materials and empty shelves caused by high circulation during the early 1930s.

The tradition of the Vacation Reading Program was carried on in the 1940s. What the child read was no longer an issue, but how much he or she read continued to be controlled, with each participant expected to read eight books over a period of eight weeks.

Facing page — Queen Marie of Romania visited the Library in 1926.

In 1946 the Vacation Reading Program was changed to the Summer Reading Club to attract those children who wanted to participate in a group activity.

The 1950s and 1960s brought the introduction of picture books, and younger children were encouraged to participate and report on the books they had read. However, the number of those who enrolled and actually finished the program began to diminish dramatically throughout the 1960s.

In past years reading certificates had been presented to those children who completed the Vacation and Summer Reading Programs, but in the 1960s and 1970s the program was no longer motivating in itself. Somehow, over the years, reading had lost its entertainment value with young people. Reading as its own reward was becoming a lost incentive. Accelerated lifestyles and the bombardment of multimedia alternatives were being blamed for the declining desire to read and ultimately the inability to read.

In the 1980s the issues changed dramatically. It no longer mattered what they read; getting children to want to read was the real goal. The program needed a higher profile to attract the attention of children.

In 1985 the Summer Reading Program was re-evaluated and restructured to reflect the interest and structure of today's youth. Changes included a flexible format that would blend with the busy schedules of the participants. The program also adjusted its focus from just the school age child to include the entire family. Those involved setting their own goals based on their interest, time and personal values. To create excitement and intrigue, the program featured a point system for the type of book read, a bonus list as an added challenge to satisfy those who like to read from lists, and a point redemption element which allowed the participants to select from a variety of prizes.

The program became so popular that it experienced a 786% increase in participation between 1984 and 1990. Book circulation increased from an average of six books per child in 1984 to seventeen in 1990, with 44,273 children and parents participating in the program in 1990. A funding campaign was begun to establish a one million dollar endowment to insure perpetuation of this vital program.

CHILDREN'S BOOK WEEK

When Franklin K. Mathiews, director of the Boy Scouts of America, expressed concern about children's books in 1919, the idea of Children's Book Week was conceived of to encourage the publishing and enjoyment of fine books for children.

The Indianapolis Public Library was quick to endorse and promote the idea. In 1921 librarians made visits to the local schools during Children's Book Week, displaying books, telling stories and setting up special displays in their branches. The tradition continued through the 1970s.

In the 1980s the branch libraries were encouraged to perform and implement programs related to the annual theme of Children's Book Week, but this was an independent effort made by each branch library. In 1985 a unified, system-wide effort was made by the Library Children's Services Office to coordinate programming efforts. The concept of Children's Book Week was also extended beyond one week to sufficently cover all of the programs and branch needs.

The revolutionary concept of implementing a systemwide Read Aloud Program was conceived in 1986 in celebration of Children's Book Week. The program was designed to encourage families to read aloud together in the home. The Read Aloud Program remains in effect today, with overwhelming enthusiasm from local families and teachers, and the program continues to grow annually. As part of the program, well known children's authors come as guests of the Library, providing families the opportunity to meet a favorite author in a neighborhood branch library setting.

In 1977 the Children's Division at Central Library planned a festival on the library's front lawn to celebrate summer. The "Sunfest," held in August of that year, consisted of music, crafts, special events, puppet shows and storytelling.

The "Sunfest" continued in 1978 and 1979, with the adult divisions at Central Library also becoming involved in the program's activities. Unique events were held in the various reading rooms, and included storytellers, ballet and folk dancers, local radio and television personalities and other activities.

The program was not held in 1980 and 1981 because it had become too time-consuming to plan effectively. However, the Children's Services Office wanted some kind of summer, family-oriented festival and in 1982 organized the "Family Festival." Activities similar to those of the original "Sunfest" were planned, but they also included many displays and exhibits. This was also the first year that a guest author was invited to perform and lecture. Steven Kellogg, author of *Pinkerton, Behave, The Mysterious Tadpole,* and other books for children was that year's guest.

In 1984 "Family Festival" was changed to "Celebrate Summer," which was conceived under the same objectives as the earlier programs, but held in June rather than August. Author Robert Quackenbush of the Miss Mallard Mystery Series fame was the guest that year.

In 1985 the summer festival took on the new name of "ArtWorks!" and it is still celebrated every other year on the library's front lawn. "ArtWorks!" takes a unique theme each year, and continues the tradition of inviting guest children's authors to participate, while also providing exciting activities and other forms of entertainment for children.

CHAPTER XXII

CHILDREN'S FESTIVALS

One of the musical attractions of the Library's 1978 "Sunfest" program.

DISTINGUISHED VISITORS

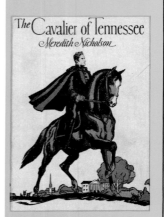

Four Indiana authors and frequent Library visitors: front row (left to right), George Ade and Booth Tarkington; (back row) James Whitcomb Riley and Meredith Nicholson.

Meredith Nicholson felt this was his best book.

The library has always been the mecca for authors, poets, illustrators, musicians, and artists. Some have been formally entertained, some invited as guest speakers, while others just happened to come into the building and end up having a cup of tea and a chat with staff members.

The late John Mason Brown, dramatic critic for the old *Saturday Review of Literature*, and several times a speaker at Town Hall lectures, would drop in for a cup of coffee. One day a staff member recognized Clarence Budington Kelland wandering about and took him in tow. A rather wizened, small and very shy gentleman, he seemed the antithesis of his robust *Saturday Evening Post* stories, but he did gather a group of excited boys around him in the Riley Room.

Meredith Nicholson came in quite frequently in his last years. On one of his last visits downtown, he spent some time in the Librarian's office reminiscing about the old days, when the brilliant coterie of Indiana authors gathered together to exchange their innumerable anecdotes. He said also that he felt his best book was *The Cavalier of Tennessee*, a fictionalized biography of Andrew Jackson. It seemed a strange choice, as it was one of the least recognized or remembered of all his books.

Ferdinand Schaefer, founder of the Indianapolis Symphony Orchestra, spent many hours in the Music Department, poring over musical scores. Behind him hung the portrait of him commissioned by the musicians of his first orchestra, painted by Simon Baus, and presented to the Indianapolis Public Library in March, 1945.

There are amusing stories of two who did not come to tea. One was dramatist T.M. Behrman, whose new play was having a pre-Broadway opening at the English Theater. An alert staff member noticed him looking assiduously through a drawer of the public card catalog. Afterwards, the curious librarian went to the same drawer and discovered he apparently had been checking how many of his works were in the Library collection.

The other uninvited guest was Richard Halliburton, riding at the top of the best seller lists at the time. He brought a call slip to the Reference Room on which he had written the bibliographical details of the book he wanted. "I signed my name to the slip," he said to the librarians, "as I thought you would want my autograph."

Autographs are by no means shunned, however. The Library's guest book has made its appearance again and again since its first appearance in 1922, a gift of Cerene Ohr. In it may be found such signatures as those of Hugh Walpole, Sir Gilbert Parker, William Beebe, Vachel Lindsey, Christopher Morley, Carl Van Doren, Dr. Wilfred Grenfell, Robert Tristrim Coffin, Louis Slobodkin, Marguerite Henry, Charles Finger, Hugh Lofting, Augusta Stevenson, Rosamond du Jardin, and Edward Holley, author of a fascinating biography of Charles Evans. Although Mr. Evans himself never returned as a guest, his three children, Charles Jr., Gertrude, and Eliot visited in 1964 and dutifully signed the guest register.

More recent guests have included Madeleine L'Engle, Saul Bellow, Elaine Konigsburg, Norman Mailer, Gail Sheehy, Jean Fritz, James Baldwin, Richard Peck, Kurt Vonnegut, Lloyd Alexander, Tom Wolfe, David Macaulay, and John Updike, all of whom came to Indianapolis to deliver the Marian McFadden

Memorial Lecture which has been given annually since 1978.

These noted literary figures have not been the only guests to bring excitement and prestige to the Library over the years. On November 17, 1926—Royalty came to town!

Queen Marie of Romania, the Crown Prince Nicholas, and Princess Ileana were including the city as part of a national tour. The beautiful Main Room of the Central Library had been chosen as the site of the party's first reception in Indianapolis.

Met at Union Station by Mayor John Duvall, the royal party proceeded first to the library, for as the Reception Committee noted, ". . . it is in keeping with the recognized literary tendency of the state and its many writers, to have a representative literary group to greet the Queen."

And they were there! Among the noted literary figures were Meredith Nicholson, Booth Tarkington, George Ade, William Herschell, Kin Hubbard, Elizabeth Miller Hack, Kate Milner Rabb, Chic Jackson, George S. Cottman, Elmer Davis, and numerous historical writers and educators from throughout the state.

The Queen, a granddaughter of Queen Victoria, arrived looking every inch as Indianapolis imagined a queen should look. She wore a long coat of cloth of gold with a matching cloche hat. With great ceremony the guest book was brought out and to Mary Gorgas of the Reference Department staff went the honor of handing the pen to Her Majesty. Into the Book went the Queen's resplendent signature, and there it remains to this day. For some unknown reason, the signatures of the other members of the royal family were not recorded for posterity.

Just before the royal party was to attend a banquet at the Columbia Club that evening, word was received of the serious illness of the King. The banquet went on as planned, but the tour was shortened and the royal party soon returned to Romania.

The anniversary programs in honor of James Whitcomb Riley's birthday were double celebrations, for the present Central Library had been dedicated in 1917 on October 7th, the poet's birthday.

On the first anniversary of the Library's opening, an open house was held for the public, with all members of the staff acting as guides. In the evening Mayor Charles Jewett spoke, Mrs. Demarchus Brown gave a talk commemorating Riley's birthday, and Mrs. James Gavin and Frederic Krull sang poems of Riley set to music by Mr. Krull. Each year, the pattern of the program was similar, with music sometimes provided by the popular Orloff trio, Mrs. Howard Clippinger or other musicians, and always Riley's poems were read or sung.

On the fifth anniversary in 1922, the speakers were William Herschell who read his poem, "Ain't God Good To Indiana"; Hoosier author and friend, Meredith Nicholson, who described Riley as the "Keeper of Lockerbie gate," and Miss Harriet Monroe, editor of the *Magazine of Poetry,* who gave a tribute, as did also William Dudley Foulke. It is uncertain if annual anniversary celebrations continued after 1922, but in 1938, when the Central Library

A program was held at the Romanian Christian Orthodox Church in honor of Queen Marie.

SPECIAL ANNIVERSARY CELEBRATIONS

"came of age," Mrs. Luther Dickerson, wife of the Librarian, cut an enormous birthday cake topped with twenty-one candles.

In October, 1946, the branch libraries celebrated the fiftieth anniversary of the opening of the first four branches. Newspapers gave them stories and pictures, and a full week of events at all branches noted the anniversary of Riverside Park, Haughville, Prospect, and Madison Avenue branches in December 1896.

Not to be forgotten are the dedications and open houses held for the opening of new branch libraries. Besides attracting the public, these events are a genuine testimonial of community pride over the arrival of each new library facility. With the expansion of the library into a city-county system in 1966, there seemed to be a never-ending number of dedication and open house events as new branches were opened or as existing branches moved into new or renovated quarters.

The golden anniversary of the Library's founding was celebrated on April 8, 1923. The April, 1923 issue of *Reader's Ink* commented that the Library was still "in the very prime of life, full of vitality and health but with no hint of either age or immaturity." The staff celebrated the event with a big party, which they attended costumed in old-fashioned dresses, many of them lovely gowns which their grandmothers had worn fifty years before.

The more formal celebration of the Fiftieth anniversary took place in the flower-decorated Main Reading Room, filled to capacity with distinguished guests. Mr. Charles Rush, the Librarian, presided. Introductory remarks were made by Charles W. Moores, Chairman, Citizens Library Committee, and former member of the library's night and Sunday staff.

> *The Program:*
> *"Memories of days gone by - their libraries, books and people"*
> *Responses:*
> *Charles Martindale, Son of Judge E.B. Martindale, Member of the first Citizens Library Committee*
> *Meredith Nicholson, Member of the Citizens Library Committee*
> *Eliza Gordon Browning, Assistant Librarian, Librarian, 1892-1917*
> *Jacob P. Dunn, former Member, Indiana Library Commission*
> *James W. Fesler, former Member, Library Night and Sunday staff*
> *Benediction by Dr. Frank S. C. Wicks, Member of Citizens Library Committee*
> Music was provided by Helen Harrison, harpist.

In 1948 the library prepared to celebrate another birthday, its seventy-fifth. And at age seventy-five it felt strong enough to spread the festivities over four days.

On Monday, April 5th, the great iron gates of Central Library were ceremoniously thrown open, and the members of the staff filed into the building. Tuesday evening the Junior Chamber of Commerce sponsored a program in the Main Reading Room with Richard James, former Lieutenant Governor, as principal speaker. Wednesday, April 7th, there was a tea for representatives of the women's literary clubs of the city. Mrs. Eldo Wagner and

Mrs. Clayton Ridge, former members of the Board of School Commissioners served, and Mrs. Louis Bruck, then a member of the Board, was in the receiving line. Mrs. Thor Wesenburg gave a witty talk titled, "Why Henry James, Now?" as Henry James was staging quite a comeback that year. On the afternoon of the 8th, distinguished Indianapolis author Jeannette Covert Nolan gave one of her delightful talks in Cropsey Auditorium to the Junior High School Reading clubs.

The evening of April 8, 1948, was a pleasant one compared to that of April 8, 1873, when "the flood which poured from Heaven deluged the streets." People came to the beautiful Main Reading Room of the Central Library to celebrate a reality that had grown for three-quarters of a century. The speaker for the evening was Mr. Luther Evans, Librarian of Congress. Preceding the meeting a dinner was held at the Propylaeum with Mr. Evans the honored guest, and with Board members, their spouses, and the supervisory staff of the Library attending. The climax of the dinner was the appearance of a huge, beautifully decorated birthday cake.

That evening at the Library Mr. Evans reviewed the history of the institution, paying tribute to its early librarians as "a precious heritage." Continuing, he said, "Respect for interests of the individual and faith in his ability to develop his potentialities and to assume his responsibilities as a citizen have been basic to the development of public libraries in this country, and this library has had them in abundance."

During the program, honor was also accorded to a citizen of Indianapolis. In the audience was a frail but charming lady, Mrs. Amelia L. Arndorff, who, at the age of fourteen, was one of the first 500 borrowers registered in April, 1873. Also during the program a telegram from Charles Rush was read which said in part, "On this . . . occasion, Indianapolis should rise up and call blessed its exceptional Public Library staff . . . I salute staff members of the present and the past."

The next morning, showing few signs of the elegent celebration held the night before the Library opened again to serve the public in the same dedicated style it had when it opened its doors seventy-five years earlier.

CHAPTER XXII

Mrs. Amelia Arndorff, who, at age fourteen was one of the first 500 borrowers registered in 1873. She attended the Library's 75th Anniversary Celebration in 1948.

75th Anniversary dinner held at the Propylaeum April 8, 1948. Attending were members of the School Board and Library administrative Staff. Librarian Marian McFadden cuts the cake.

Special Gifts and Memorials

The Library has benefitted substantially throughout the years through gifts of money, books, paintings, sculpture, and a wide assortment of other valuable assets. Even the iron gates at the entrance to Central Library were purchased through the generosity of the Indianapolis school children, who collected their pennies, nickels and dimes for a memorial to the Hoosier poet, James Whitcomb Riley.

Indianapolis citizens who are book lovers remember the Library with gifts of money. Some have left money in their wills with definite instructions as to the use of the bequests, such as for collections of books in some particular field which had been the benefactor's hobby. Clubs and other organizations have a plan for giving books instead of flowers in memory of deceased members, selecting for purchase subjects of interest to the person to be remembered. The generosity of the public has contributed greatly year after year to benefiting an increasingly greater number of people.

One of the prime moves in the establishment of the Library was the formation of the Indianapolis Library Association in 1869.

It developed a subscription library with the books purchased from funds received from its "stock holders," but volumes could be borrowed by non-members.

On September 1, 1872, the Association offered to transfer its entire collection of 3,649 books to the newly organized public library with the understanding that not less than 8,000 additional books be purchased, that suitable reading rooms be provided for the public, and that the Library be so established as to be free to all citizens of Indianapolis. These conditions were met and the final transfer was made on April 1, 1873. It was the first gift to the newly established Indianapolis Public Library and became the nucleus of its original collection.

The second significant gift, consisting of 184 bound volumes, was received in 1874. The following letter describes its worth and an early appreciation of the new library:

Gentlemen:

My father, the late Calvin Fletcher, left me by will quite a number of bound volumes of newspapers, all of which are useful for consultation and reference, and some of which are valuable in a historical point of view, from their age, rarity, and special records of passing events. These volumes I propose through you, its representatives, to donate to the "Public Library of Indianapolis." I do so; because I think the bestowal would meet with the approval of him, who at great pains thus preserved the current history of the city and state of

CHAPTER XXIII

Dr. John Stough Bobbs, founding member and president of the Indiana State Medical Society.

his adoption. I do so, also, with the hope that the volumes safely kept in an institution so liberal in its spirit, and so enlightenting in its workings, as the "Public Library of Indianapolis" may in some measure, be monumental of my father, who spent the best years of his life in promoting the educational, moral, and religious welfare of this city of his choice . . . .

E. T. Fletcher

In 1878 Mayor John Caven gave 264 volumes containing material on Indianapolis. With these two large donations Librarian Charles Evans was well started on his project of preserving local historical material. He received permission from the Board to advertise for material "however trivial" on local history. In 1903 the historical collection was further enriched by a gift from Judge Daniel Wait Howe which contained material on Indiana history and books by early Indiana authors.

On November 1, 1898, a medical collection was established through the efforts of Dr. George W. Sloan, President of the Board, and Dr. Frank B. Wynn, chairman of the Library Committee. Dr. James Ewing Mears of Philadelphia had presented to the Marion County Medical Society a collection of medical books. Also later in his will there was a bequest of $1,000, the interest from which was to be used for the purchase of books and periodicals. It was decided, probably due to the interest of the two doctors closely associated with the Library, to place the books in the Public Library until the Medical Association had suitable quarters to house them.

The Eli Lilly Company for several years contributed $50 annually for the purchase of periodicals. At the death of Mr. John Kolmer in 1918, his medical library of 220 volumes has given to what had become known as the Mears collection. Another generous gift came as a memorial to Dr. Lafayette Page, and the collection eventually grew to about 10,000 volumes.

When the new Central Library was opened in 1917, the medical collection was housed in the south end of the East Reading Room. A life-sized bas-relief of Dr. John Stough Bobbs was placed in the room's south end in memory of him. Dr. Bobbs was an early Indianapolis surgeon who was a founding member and president of the Indiana State Medical Society. In 1867 Dr. Bobbs performed the world's first gall bladder surgery.

The Bobbs memorial was designed and executed in bronze by the famous sculptor Gutzon Borglum, who also did the great works at Stone Mountain and Mount Rushmore.

In 1962 the Medical Society found "suitable quarters" for the Mears collection, and it was moved from the Central Library, with the latter retaining some volumes which were transferred to the Business, Science and Technology Division. In 1988 the bas-relief of Dr. Bobbs was removed and reinstalled in a prominent location of the new Medical Library and Research building on the Indiana University Medical Center campus in Indianapolis, with which he had a prominent connection.

Another memorial collection was the Lee Memorial Fund Collection of reference books. They were housed in an alcove in the West Reading Room of the Central Library behind doors inscribed "Memorial to H. H. Lee," presented by his wife, Elizabeth Wood Lee.

The library has received many gifts in memory of outstanding Indianapolis musicians. As early as 1900 Ella Sharpe Duncan gave the Library a collection of opera scores and oratorios in memory of her son Harry S. Duncan. The People's Concert Association gave money in memory of Edward Bailey Birge, and Mrs. Oliver Willard Pierce gave her husband's complete musical library. Other gifts were received from Max Leckner and friends of Ferdinand Schaefer. One of the finest gifts was the Alexander Ernestinoff collection, received in 1923, and consisting of over 100 volumes of orchestral scores.

A bust of Ferdinand Schaefer, founder and first conductor of the Indianapolis Symphony Orchestra, was given by Mr. and Mrs. Harper Ransburg and Mr. & Mrs. Herbert Woollen. Kept in the Central Library Arts Division for many years, Mr. Schaefer's portrait and bust were given to the Indiana State Symphony Society in 1984 when the Indianapolis Symphony Orchestra moved to their new permanent home in the renovated Circle Theatre on Monument Circle.

In 1924 friends of Mr. and Mrs. Clemens Vonnegut gave a gift of $2,500 in memory of Mr. Vonnegut so that books and scores could be added to the Library's collection. Stained glass doors were designed by Kurt Vonnegut, Sr. and inscribed with the words, "Clemens Vonnegut, Jr., 1853-1921, Ardent Lover of Music, Given by his friends." These doors originally enclosed the collection, but were subsequently removed as the collections grew and are now in storage.

Individual gifts of music and scores are too numerous to mention. Music scores have been given by many musical organizations: The Matinee Musicale, The Ensemble Music Society, The Mendelssohn Choir, and in memory of Indianapolis musicians Leonard Strauss, Friedna Klink, Olive Kiler, Edward LaShelle, Adolph Schellschmidt, Fabien Sevitzky and others. Mr. J. K. Lilly contributed a collection of Stephen Foster songs.

In 1930 Mr. Charles N. Thompson set up a fund of $25,000 in memory of his wife, Julia Conner Thompson, for a collection of reference books on "The Finer Arts of Home Making," to be available to any individual interested in the building, furnishing and decorating of a home, from cabin to castle. With the income used for the purchase of new books each year, and with other additions, the collection has become one of the most beautiful and outstanding in the state.

A generous gift of securities valued at more than $45,000 was given by Miss Margaret Shipp as a memorial to her sister, Miss May Louise Shipp, for the purchase of books "suitable to students of current history," especially because Miss Shipp had held classes in current events at the Central Library.

The death of an Indianapolis department store executive prompted his business associates to set up the Charles W. Jones Memorial in 1944. The fund was expended for the purchase of books "in the fields of personnel, social services, religion and government—for use by students interested in these areas of service to fellowmen."

In 1941 a bequest of $50,000 was left to the Indianapolis Public Library by Mrs. Maude H. Darrach for the establishment of a genealogical library in the name of her husband, Eugene Haslet Darrach. However, due to litigation in the

Charles N. Thompson established a fund in memory of his wife Julia Conner Thompson for books on "The Finer Arts of Home Making."

estate, it was not until February, 1948, that the bequest was received.

Although the public library had a good, but small genealogy collection, its expansion and maintenance presented problems of space and finance, as well as duplication of sources already housed in the Genealogy Division of the Indiana State Library. By mutual agreement of the two library boards, the public library collection went on permanent loan to the Indiana State Library on October 11, 1949. A plaque in the Genealogy Division of the State Library recognizes the Darrach Memorial Library of the Indianapolis Public Library as part of the Genealogy Division's collection.

The terms of the agreement designated that one-half of the bequest become an endowment fund and the remaining half be used for purchase of equipment, supplies, books, and microfilm. The interest received from the endowment continues to provide funds for the addition of materials to the Darrach Library. In addition, the public library contributes $1,200 annually from its own budget funds to supplement the personnel budget of the State Library Genealogy Division.

In 1948 a bequest of over $1,800 was received from the estate of Miss Jennie Jones of Indianapolis. According to information received from the executor of her estate, she wanted to give money to the Indianapolis Library because the staff of the East Washington Branch had always been "nice to her girls." As there were no restrictions on the use of the funds, some were applied to the financing of the Holladay Memorial Library for Young People. Over $6,000 has currently accumulated from the original bequest.

Many other rare gifts have added to the wealth of the Library's resources. A valuable gift of Shakespeare's Second Folio came from Judge Cyrus C. Hines.

Mrs. Frederic M. Ayres and Librarian Luther Dickerson discuss the memorial collection of 321 volumes published by Yale University Press. It was given to the Library in 1941 by friends of the University in memory of Mr. Ayres, a member of the Yale class of 1892.

The beautiful residence of Mr. and Mrs. Samuel Rauh was given to the Library in 1928 to be used as a branch library. It housed the Rauh Memorial Library from 1929 until 1973.

Other prized possessions include a fine James Whitcomb Riley collection from Riley's nephew, Mr. Edmund Eitel and other members of Riley's family, and a sign which Mr. Riley painted, given by Mrs. Marcus Dickey.

Books autographed by Riley, Booth Tarkington, Lew Wallace, George Ade, and others were given by Mrs. George Philip Meier. Letters written to May Wright Sewell, a leader in women's activities in Indianapolis for many years, were given by Miss Katrina Fertig. A gift of $500 was received in memory of Mrs. Sewall.

Mrs. Frank Darlington gave an excellent Andrew Lang collection belonging to her husband, and Mrs. William Allen Wood presented the Library with an especially rare collection of books on demonology which were given by the Library in 1986 to the Lilly Library at Indiana University in Bloomington. The Bill Welcher 1953 memorial gift of books on guns is one of the most fascinating, made up of rare books giving invaluable information regarding the nature and manufacture of high explosives. An interesting collection of letters of Governor Oliver P. Morton, written in 1863 and concerning a financial scandal, were given to the Library by Dr. William Niles Wishard.

From Mr. Wright Marble came a collection of cook books, gathered from all over the world and written in many languages. One, dated 1746, is authored "by an unknown lady." A book by a surgeon, who was doubtless an authority on the subject, was entitled, "Carving."

In many instances, funds have been established in memory of loved staff members or friends of the Library. Among these are those for Sarah E. Banning, Hortense Rauh Burpee, Jesse G. Crane, Eliza G. Browning, May Louise Shipp, Mary Dyer Leamon, Lyndell Martling, Bruce Aldridge, Florence Jones, and Mary Wheeler Wells.

The Library has among its prized possessions Babylonian tablets spanning over 2,000 years, the latest dating from 538 B.C. One of these dated 2350 B.C., is a bill for a temple offering—"45 goats, 59 sheep, 19 lambs and 6 kid goats." Among the interesting autographed letters held in the archives are ones from Otis Skinner and another from Louise de la Valliere, mistress of King Louis XIV of France.

An interior view of the Rauh Memorial Library showing the large Rookwood fireplace and a portion of the dark panelled woodwork found throughout the house.

Many scrapbooks long held by the Library gave fascinating local stories. Ones from the Indianapolis Symphony include memorabilia dating back to 1896. There is a chronological list of all the productions at the Murat-Shubert Theatre from 1910 to 1925, as well a history of the English Theatre, which also includes a list of productions of the historic theatre which stood for seventy years on the Circle. In the Spring of 1990 these scrapbooks were transferred to the Indiana Historical Society Library located at the Indiana State Library.

Not to be omitted are the gifts of library buildings or land on which to build them. First of all and most outstanding was the gift from Andrew Carnegie in 1909 of $120,000 to erect branch libraries, of which only $100,000 was actually received. Then came gifts from Michael Spades, Andrew Henry and Lemuel Trotter of land also to be used for the building of branch libraries.

One of the great gifts, of course, came in 1928 when the Samuel Rauh family gave their lovely home on North Meridian Street for the Rauh Memorial Library. A teacher, Miss Clara Holladay, also left her home for a library which, as described earlier, became a special library for young adults in the city. The latest gifts were the donations of land by Mr. and Mrs. Harrison Eiteljorg upon which the new Nora Library was built on 86th Street, and parcels of land given by Mr. Kurt Mahrdt, Jr., Mr. John Urbahns and Mr. Raymond O. Lee which were adjacent to and became a part of the 4.12 acres on which the new Wayne Library was constructed.

Numerous other gifts have been presented over the years, such as the Wayman Adams portrait of James Whitcomb Riley, which hangs in the Central Library Children's Division, a gift from Mr. Booth Tarkington; a bust of Riley by the famous sculptor John Prashun which stands in the east hall of the Central Library near the entrance to the Riley Room for Young People, and two original hand-colored etchings by Marc Chagall which hang in the Central Library Arts Division, presented in 1979 by Mr. and Mrs. John B. Winslow. Mr. Winslow was a nephew of Dorothy Adams, who was a librarian in the Arts Division for thirty-seven years, until her retirement in 1963. The etchings were presented to the Library Foundation in honor of Dorothy Sipe Adams.

These are but a few of the most significant gifts made to the library during its long history. A special "Gifts" file is maintained in the Library's Business Office, which fully documents these hundreds of fine donations and special gifts.

The Library's Centennial
One Hundred Years of Service

The Indianapolis of 1873 was a thriving city of 48,244, all potential customers of the fledgling library, who in that first year were to borrow 101,281 books from a collection of 14,560 volumes. By 1973 the population of the Library service area exceeded 765,000, and in that year 3,399,000 items were borrowed by 260,000 registered borrowers from a total collection of 1,103,000 items. One hundred years of growth and service was a milestone deservedly to be observed, not just for a day or week, but for the entire year.

The 1973 Centennial Year celebration was the most ambitious program ever undertaken by the Library up to that date, or since. It gave the Library an excellent, year-long public relations opportunity. During this year it was possible to sum up progress over the years and to impress upon the residents of Indianapolis and Marion County the contrasts between early Library efforts and the services offered by a vibrant and still-growing library system that enriched the entire state of Indiana.

It offered the opportunity to involve the commmunity in activities of celebration and observance that made them become more aware of the Library's functions and services and feel that the Library belonged to them.

Although programs had been planned throughout the year, the celebration began officially on Monday, April 9th, which Mayor Richard Lugar had designated as "Library Centennial Day." At 9 a.m. on that cold, windy day, he read his proclamation in front of the closed iron gates at Central Library, spoke a few words, and presented a framed copy of the proclamation to Mrs. Winifred Pettee, President of the Library Board.

She thanked him for participating in the event and said in part, "Today, the members of the Library Board, the Foundation Board and the staff pledge to you, Mr. Mayor, and to the community, that we will make the next 100 just as glorious and fruitful as the past 100."

Mrs. Pettee then quoted the words Meredith Nicholson had spoken, when in 1916, he stood on that exact spot, and helped with the laying of the cornerstone for the new Central Library. "The administration of our library first and last has been characterized by broad-mindedness and catholicity, and this is the true spirit in which the library of a great city must be conducted.".

Jim Simon, President of the Staff Association, said a few word, Mr. Gnat handed the scissors to Mayor Lugar, who cut the red, white and blue ribbon across the door, and the gates swung open to begin year 101. The first to enter were the staff and guests, who went to Cropsey Auditorium for a reception and refreshments.

Thus what we bear witness to today is that ultimately any library is a living testimony to someone's faith—faith that collection of the records of our heritage, the provision of information resources for all citizens, and the communication of mankind's knowledge and wisdom, will make an important contribution to man's continuing quest for a better world.

—Dr. Edward Holley, speaking at the Centennial Celebration, April 28, 1973

Facing page — Mayor Richard G. Lugar presents his "Library Centennial Day" proclamation as Mrs. Winifred Pettee and Raymond E. Gnat look on.

One of several publications prepared as part of the Library's Centennial year observation.

The White House, Washington, April 19. 1973

It is most appropriate that the Indianapolis-Marion County Public Library celebrates its one hundredth anniversary during the month of April. This is a time when all Americans focus on the vital role of our libraries as we observe National Library Week. As the people of the Indianapolis-Marion County area look back on the ten decades in which their library has carried forward the traditions honored during this special week, they have great reason to be proud of their contribution to its meaning in the life of our society.

I warmly commend the staff and patrons of the library and all those who have associated with its useful programs. May it continue to build on its fine reputation in the challenging years ahead.

Richard Nixon

The above might serve as a harbinger of what was to take place on Saturday afternoon, April 28th, at Clowes Memorial Hall. This was truly the day of remembrance; the proud review of "A Century of Service."

The program:

Welcome - Mr. Gordon Thompson, Chairman, Library Centennial Committee

Introduction - Mr. Lou Sherman, WFBM Radio, Master of Ceremonies

"Thanksgiving Day Sermon" - The Honorable William H. Hudnut, III, Member of Congress and former pastor of the Second Presbyterian Church, Indianapolis

"The Indianapolis Public Library—A Live Thing in the Whole Town" - Dr. Edward Holley, Dean, School of Library Science, University of North Carolina

"Indianapolis in the World of Books" - Dr. G. Thomas Tanselle, Professor of English, University of Wisconsin

"Now and Then" - Miss Emily Kimbrough

Dr. Holley, author of *Charles Evans, American Bibliographer*, that somewhat enigmatic first Librarian in Indianapolis, reviewed the growth of the Library during its first century. "Thus what we bear witness to today is that ultimately any library is a living testimony to someone's faith—faith that collection of the records of our heritage, the provision of information resources for all citizens, and the communication of mankind's knowledge and wisdom, will make an important contribution to man's continuing quest for a better world."

In conclusion Dr. Holley looked to the future. "Whatever . . . lies ahead we know that the library will continue to be responsive to the community's needs, and we trust also, in Miss Browning's happy phrase, that it will be 'a live thing in the whole town.' "

There is an apocryphal story often told that a visiting lecturer requested that if there were an author in the audience, would he please stand; whereupon the entire assemblage rose to its feet. Dr. Tanselle, an Indiana born author and bibliographer, recognized this Hoosier propensity for writing books, which flowered in the late nineteenth and early twentieth century, but his principal topic related to other facets of the literary scene, which have contributed to the cultural life of the city and its library.

> *What has been less widely commented on, however, is the connection which Indianapolis has had with other aspects of the book world: publishing, printing, book design, bibliography, and book collecting. One should not be surprised that such connections exist, for these are all related activities which nourish each other; and it is to be expected that an area which produces a large number of writers is going to exhibit other bookish interests as well.*

He then related the history of the Bobbs-Merrill Company, the publishing house which for many years was a near and good neighbor of the Central Library. This was followed by mention of Bruce Rogers, distinguished book

Miss Emily Kimbrough is greeted by Associate Directors Marilyn McCanon and Lawrence Downey upon her arrival in Indianapolis to participate in the "Century of Service" program.

227

Lord, what I learned about Indiana.

—Cornelia Otis Skinner

designer and native of Lafayette, Indiana, whose early, much prized work was done in Indianapolis.

There were also the Grabhorn brothers, who made the Grabhorn Press in San Francisco one of the most honored private presses in the world. However, their first work was done in Indianapolis where Edwin Grabhorn as a boy read avidly in the Public Library and also studied the physical makeup of the books, and where he first established his Studio Press, later to become the Grabhorn Press.

Dr. Tanselle then reviewed the noted bibliographers the city has produced, beginning with Charles Evans; the excellent book stores which have been patronized through the years; and, finally, the collectors, especially the Lilly family, who have given so much to the city and the state. Concluding, Dr. Tanselle said, "With a past of this kind to build on, the Indianapolis-Marion County Public Library has good reason to look to the future with confidence."

Miss Kimbrough, author of many delightful and popular books, such as *Our Hearts Were Young and Gay* and *Through Charley's Door*, it seems almost superfluous to say is, of course, a Hoosier, a native of Muncie. She spoke of her life in Indiana and also told of how, when she and Cornelia Otis Skinner were in Hollywood for the filming of their book, *Our Hearts Were Young and Gay*, they met Will Hays, at that time the "guardian" of movie morals, and also a Hoosier. Invited to his home, Miss Skinner looked forward to hearing all about the motion picture industry. Not so. As she expressed it to her companion later, "Lord, what I learned about Indiana."

Miss Kimbrough also spoke of and deplored the limited vocabularies in common usage today. Words, after all, are the wonderously flexible tools of literature; and she presented the best example of what language can do, carrying her audience with her by the sheer imagery involved by the beautiful choice of words at her command. Thus the main program of the year came to a close on a quiet, intimate and glowing note. It was followed by a reception in the Krannert Room at Clowes Memorial Hall, attended by many of those who had come that day to honor the Library and its "Century of Service."

Other events of the Centennial Year included open houses in most of the branch libraries, an essay contest, production of a twenty minute color-sound film about the Library's services titled "Its A Lot More Than Books," numerous radio and television programs and promotions, publication of a 1973 calendar in conjunction with the Marion County Historical Society, many special displays and exhibits, publication of the Library's "Historical Highlights" booklet, adult and children's film series, publication of "Authors of Indianapolis and Marion County," "Indianapolis in the World of Books," and a myriad of other special programs, publications, and services.

The first century of the Indianapolis Public Library had come to an end; surely it had served as a catalyst for the second. During the 1970s and 1980s the Library continued to grow rapidly with an explosion of new branch construction, the implementation of the computerization of most library functions, and a major renovation of the Central Library. By 1990 the loan of materials for home use topped 6,630,000 items, the number of registered borrowers exceeded 561,000, and the number of items in the Library's collection was over 1,646,000.

By no means does the Library resemble a static institution. Quite the contrary, it has been as Eliza Browning visualized it, "a live thing," strong enough in its ninety-fifth year to contract a marriage with its surrounding area and courageous enough to take on the longer and more fruitful name of the Indianapolis-Marion County Public Library.

This account, therefore, has merely been the chronicle of a young life; conceived in the dreams of a few, given birth through the practical motivation of others, nurtured by the needs of many. It has grown strong because of those who have crossed its threshold seeking recreation, information, knowledge and because of those who have willingly and ably served its public; and most of all because within its walls have gradually but steadily accumulated the resources that make that service possible. A library, a place of books, can never grow old so long as those books live in the minds of the people who need, desire and cherish them.

It was probably Miss McFadden who left this piece of wisdom in the Library archives:

"As the world continues to pass through rapid and even violent changes, it is well to remember that man from the beginning of history has recorded his deeds and his thoughts in pictures and in words. Most of these records have been preserved in caves, monasteries, libraries, preserved through years of greater upheaval than this generation now witnesses. It is as if some Infinite Wisdom has decreed they shall not be destroyed, for man's need for knowledge of the past has been and will ever be a pre-requisite for his intelligent coping with the present and his sane planning for the future."

With this thought in mind, the Indianapolis-Marion County Public Library has moved well into its second century of service to the community with the same courage and faith which blessed its birth over one hundred years ago.

CHAPTER XXIV

Program participants included (l. to r.) Dr. Edward Holley, Miss Emily Kimbrough, then Congressman William H. Hudnut, III, and Dr. G. Thomas Tanselle.

The Indianapolis-Marion County Public Library Foundation, Inc.

The Public Library has had a "Gift Fund" for many years consisting primarily of memorial gifts and some special donations, most of which are used for the purchase of books and other library materials. As noted earlier, the first "gift" came in 1872 from the Indianapolis Library Association.

Subsequent gifts over the years included other collections of valuable or rare books, bound periodicals, a collection of medical books from the Medical Association; paintings, sculpture, musical scores, recordings, and a large assortment of other memorabilia.

Monetary gifts made to the Library itself over the past 100 years have been substantial, largely unsolicited but nonetheless welcome. The Public Library itself currently has eighteen gift account funds dating as early as 1925, with assets totaling in excess of $700,000.

When Harold Sander returned to Indianapolis to be Director of Public Libraries in 1956, he brought with him the hope of establishing a foundation to encourage gifts, bequests and endowments to the Public Library. It would be similar to the library foundation in Roanoke, Virginia, where he had been director of the library for several years, an organization which could insure the continued growth of the library and provide for constantly expanding services and facilities.

He saw the foundation as a vehicle to stimulate public support for the Library, to disseminate information about the Library to the public, to increase the resources of the Library through gifts and bequests, to make current resources better known, and to encourage an appreciation of Library services. The gifts, bequests and endowments given to the foundation would be administered by it and would be separate from and in addition to the already established Public Library gift fund accounts.

It was not until the Indianapolis-Marion County Public Library was established in 1968, following the separation of the Indianapolis Public Library as an entity of the Indianapolis Board of School Commissioners, that Mr. Sander could proceed with his plan to establish a public library foundation.

Planning and organization for the foundation began in 1968, and on February 26, 1969, the Indianapolis-Marion County Public Library Foundation was officially established as a not-for-profit corporation, and its Certificate of Incorporation issued by the Secretary of the State of Indiana. The first meeting of the Foundation's Board of Directors was held that day. Mr. Sander chaired the meeting and had selected those who were to serve on the first Board of Directors. He chose a cross-section of leaders who provided a high community profile, and who could best advance the purposes for which the Foundation was established.

Facing page — Robert Hollingsworth, Friends of the Library Chairman and Committee Secretary Eve Fromin.

The first officers and directors were:

> *Mr. Kurt Mahrdt, President; Vice-Chairman of the Board, Indiana National Bank*
>
> *Mrs. W. L. Appel, Vice-President; former member of the Indianapolis Board of School Commissioners*
>
> *Mr. Harold J. Sander, Secretary; Director, Indianapolis-Marion County Public Library*
>
> *Colonel L. Robert Mottern, Treasurer; Retired, Army of the United States, and Plant Superintendent, Swift and Company*
>
> *Mrs. James Anderson, Public School Librarian*
>
> *Mr. Robert E. Houk, General Partner and Realtor, F. C. Tucker Company*
>
> *Mr. Jack B. Kammins, Attorney*
>
> *Dr. George F. Ostheimer, Retired Superintendent of the Indianapolis Public Schools*
>
> *Mr. Burton E. Beck, President, Eli Lilly and Company*

Others nominated and elected by the Foundation's Board of Directors who have served on the Board since 1969 include:

> *Mr. Raymond E. Gnat, Director of Public Libraries*
>
> *Mrs. Ardath Burkhart, Civic Leader*
>
> *Mr. Gordon H. Thompson, Retired Headmaster, Orchard Country Day School*
>
> *Mrs. Winifred Pettee, Civic Leader*
>
> *Mr. G. Wilbur Little, Vice President and Cashier, Indiana National Bank*
>
> *Dr. Joseph T. Taylor, Special Assistant to the Vice President, Indiana University-Purdue University at Indianapolis*
>
> *Mrs. Catherine S. Wallace, Teacher, Library Board Representative*
>
> *Mr. Joseph A. Rothbard, Investments, Civic Leader*
>
> *Mr. H. Roll McLaughlin, Architect, Civic Leader*
>
> *Mrs. Marjorie Tarplee, Executive Director, Central Indiana Newspapers, Inc., Civic Leader*
>
> *Mrs. Elizabeth M. Gunn, Civic Leader, Library Board Representative*
>
> *Mr. John R. Walsh, Senior Vice-President, INB Financial Corporation*
>
> *Mrs. Sarah W. Otte, Library Board Representative*
>
> *Mr. David L. Ratcliff, President, American States Life Insurance Company*
>
> *Mr. William J. Stout, Consultant*
>
> *Mr. David W. Knall, Branch Manager and Managing Director, MCDonald & Co.*

The by-laws adopted by the first Board of Directors on February 26, 1969, reads in part: "The purpose of the foundation is to promote the development, expansion, and improvement of library facilities and services . . . any person or organization interested in the purposes of the foundation and paying dues specified . . . shall be eligible . . . to membership . . . All members of the foundation shall be known as the 'Friends Of The Public Library.' "

It was the hope of Mr. Sander and that first board that gifts and bequests to the Indianapolis-Marion County Public Library Foundation, Inc. would demonstrate the public's belief in the future improvement and expansion of Library service, would provide a perpetual memorial to honor family or friends, and would assure that gifts of endowments and trusts, books, buildings, and land would continue to honor the individual memorialized.

With adequate resources the Foundation hoped to sponsor a number of major book related events, scholarships, exhibits and lectures and cultural programs to enhance community awareness and use of the library.

With Library Director Raymond E. Gnat are members of the Foundation's Board of Directors: Seated (left to right) Mrs. James Anderson, Mrs. Ardath Burkhart and Mrs. W. L. Appel, standing, Colonel L. Robert Mottern, Mr. Robert Houk, Dr. George Ostheimer, Mr. Kurt Mahrdt, Sr., and Mr. Gnat.

MEMBERSHIP AND THE FRIENDS OF THE LIBRARY

The "Friends of the Library" committee held its organizational meeting on May 22, 1973, with Mr. Samuel Montgomery and Mrs. Lester Fromin elected as temporary Chairman and Secretary respectively. The group was to serve as an entity of the Foundation to set up and run the booksales, and membership was provided for in the Foundation's by-laws, upon payment of dues. The annual dues range from $10 for the individual membership to $2,500 for a life membership. Mr. Robert Hollingsworth has served as Chairperson of the group since 1974, with Mrs. Fromin continuing as Secretary.

In 1974 a pamphlet, "Are You a Friend of the Indianapolis-Marion County Public Library?" was printed and distributed for the first time to stimulate interest and to attract a wider membership base. That year, its first to solicit

233

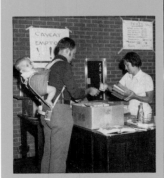

ARE YOU A FRIEND
of The
INDIANAPOLIS
MARION COUNTY
PUBLIC LIBRARY?

BOOK SALES

Booksale bargains are for even the youngest members of the family.

memberships, the total number of members was eighty and that number has continued to grow each year to 851 in 1990. Memberships have generated $131,569 in revenue since 1974.

As an incentive to memberships, a variety of premiums have been offered including book tote bags, reprints of pen and ink sketches of Central Library by K. P. Singh, note paper, posters, and umbrellas embossed with the Library logo and the words "Friends of the Library."

Several branch libraries have had chapters of the Friends of the Library with the first being established at Nora Library on March 4, 1980. A chapter for the Decatur Library was organized in March, 1982.

The Foundation Board of Directors has granted honorary life memberships to:

1975 - Mr. William Manthorne, for his presentation of many travel slide programs at the library
1980 - Mr. Harrison Eiteljorg, in recognition of his donation of the building site for the Nora Branch Library
1984 - Mr. George Newton, for his volunteer efforts in organizing the library's local music files, and annotating and grading the choral music collection.
1987 - Mr. Harold J. Sander, former Director of Public Libraries, for his work and vision in establishing the Foundation.
1987 - Mrs. Halene Smith, for her volunteer work at the Concord Community Center Library.

Sales of discarded and gift books no longer needed by the Library have been a primary source of revenue for the Foundation. The first Foundation-sponsored booksale was held at the Nora Branch Library June 3-11, 1972, with receipts of $2,596.55. The sales continued to be held only at the Nora Library until 1980 when Southport Branch Library also became a site. Public interest in the sales, as well as the revenue generated, has continued to increase each year.

Booksales were held at the Nora Library in June and at the Southport Library in November through 1985. The opening of the new Broad Ripple Branch Library in March, 1986, made the "Old" Broad Ripple Library building available as a discard center for the Library. Since 1986 a series of booksales have been held at the new site for no more than thirty days during each year.

Discarded books, for which the Foundation pays the Public Library, are now included in the sale. After being withdrawn from the Library collection, the books are arranged and stored for the sales, staffed in large part by "Friends of the Library" volunteers. Books donated to the Foundation are interfiled into the broad subject areas.

The substantial increase in the number of books available, the increase in the number of sales held each year, as well as the arrangement of volumes into popular subject categories, has significantly increased the sales revenue. In 1990 $119,253.78 was made in support of Foundation programs through these popular booksales, and since the sales were begun in 1972, they have generated over $565,000, and are now the chief source of support and revenue for the Foundation.

With the establishment of the Indianapolis-Marion County Public Library Foundation, Inc. in 1969 the Library now has a strong support umbrella organization for the actual solicitation of gifts and bequests and a Board to oversee the investment and expenditure of these funds for the purposes for which the Foundation was founded.

Since 1969 the Foundation has received a total of $762,412.69 in major gifts and bequests, in addition to those revenues received from memberships, booksales, memorial gift books, and other sources. Those gifts and bequests which have been in excess of $5,000 have been:

—$229,918.75 given by 1,061 contributors in support of the Central Library Restoration Fund Drive in 1984-1986.

—$200,000 given in 1984 by the Krannert Charitable Trust as a challenge grant, also in support of the Central Library Restoration Fund Drive.

—$200,000 pledged by the American United Life Insurance Company to establish the AUL Lecture Series to begin in 1991.

—$152,441.13 from the estate of Marian McFadden, Director of Public Libraries, 1944-1956, to be used "for objects and purposes of said foundation." The investment of these funds was used to establish an annual author lecture series.

—$150,000 grant received from the Lilly Endowment in 1989 in support of the library's summer reading program, with $50,000 to be given each year for three years.

—$20,000 given in 1985 by the law firm of Bingham Summers Welsh & Spilman to create an endowment as a memorial to Claude M. Spilman, Jr. The endowment income will be used for the purchase of current books and materials in the subject area of the Social Science Division.

—$5,052.81, given in 1982 in memory of Clarence T. Drayer.

—$5,000 given in 1974 from the estate of Marie B. Ostermeyer in memory of Carrie B. Scott, the Library's Supervisor of Work with Children from 1917 to 1943.

Other smaller gifts have included a total of $2,650 in grants given in 1978, 1979, and 1980 by the Dayton-Hudson Foundation; $1,000 to purchase an Audubon Print in 1982 in memory of Jeannette Covert Nolan, a noted local author and former Library staff member, given by her family; a film projector and $300 gift by the Alpha Nu Latrian Sorority to fund the purchase of films for the hospital library; and a gift of $200 given by the Pittsburg Plate Glass Company on behalf of Wayne Moss, a Library Board member, and an employee of the company.

In addition, hundreds of dollars are received each year from individuals and organizations for the purchase of books to memorialize a family member or friend. These purchases are processed by the Library's Adult Services Office.

MAJOR GIFTS AND BEQUESTS

Mrs. Claude Spilman, Jr., and Gov. Matthew Welsh present the endowment in memory of Mr. Spilman. Looking on are Robert E. Houk, Lawrence Downey, and Raymond E. Gnat.

CULTURAL, PROFESSIONAL, AND ENRICHMENT PROGRAMS

A young essay contest winner examines his prize, *A Wrinkle in Time*, written by the awards program speaker, Madeleine L'Engle.

Mr. Robert Hollingsworth, Chairman, Friends of the Library, presents awards to winners of the annual essay contest sponsored by the Public Library Foundation.

One of the primary goals of the Foundation has been to use its resources for library materials, scholarships, exhibits, lectures and cultural programs to enhance community awareness and use of the Library.

Some of its earliest efforts in these regards were in conjunction with the Library's Centennial celebration in 1973. The Foundation sponsored the Centennial Essay Contest using the theme, "What Books and Reading Mean To Me." There were 561 entrants and prizes of $25 and $50 were awarded to the winning essays chosen by the judges in the three categories—elementary school, high school, and college entrants.

The Foundation funded the publication of the booklet, "Indianapolis in the World of Books," which was issued in 1974 to commemorate the 100th Anniversary of public library service. The booklet contained a reprint of the Thanksgiving Day sermon delivered on November 26, 1868, by the Reverend Hanford Edson as his plea for a public library in Indianapolis. Also reprinted in the booklet were the talks presented at the Centennial Gala, April 28, 1973, by Edward G. Holley, G. Thomas Tanselle, and Emily Kimbrough. Reverend Edson's historic sermon was read at the gala by then Congressman William H. Hudnut, III, later Mayor of Indianapolis. A reception following the Centennial Gala was also sponsored and funded by the Library Foundation.

Creative Writing Essay Contests were sponsored by the Foundation, in 1974, "My Favorite Kind of Book," with 560 entrants, and again, in 1975,"Discovering Your Country's Past Through Books." The contests were held bi-annually thereafter.

In 1976 in cooperation with the Indianapolis Bicentennial Committee, the Foundation published a two-volume reprint of Jacob Dunn's *Greater Indianapolis*, originally published in 1910.

The Leonardo da Vinci exhibit of twenty-five working models was on display at Central Library in May, 1977, sponsored jointly by the Foundation and the Library.

In 1979 the Foundation purchased a baby grand piano for use in Central Library's Cropsey Auditorium, and it has subsequently funded the annual Spring and Fall Music Series "to enhance the quality of music programming planned at Central Library."

Since 1981, in support of the Indiana professional library organizations, and in conjunction with the Indiana Library Association and the Indiana Library Trustees Association, the Foundation sponsored and funded lectures related to library service as part of the annual ILA-ILTA Conferences.

In 1987 the Foundation inaugurated the "Light Up A Life" program to raise $2,000,000 in support of literacy, lifetime learning, children's programs, particularly the enormously successful annual summer reading program, and programming in Business and Science.

In November, 1987, the Foundation and the Library co-sponsored a gala reception at the Central Library, the highlight of the quadrennial conference of the Midwest Federation of Library Associations.

In addition to these committments, the Foundation has funded a myriad of other cultural and enrichment programs, including initial funding for the purchase of framed art prints and videotapes, which became popular new Library services now funded as part of the Library's regular materials budget.

In 1977 the Foundation Board approved the investment of the $152,441.13 received from the estate of Marian McFadden, with the income derived from that investment to be used to finance an annual author lecture to be called the Marian McFadden Memorial Lecture.

The Library administration recommended that a noted adult and juvenile author be asked to present the lecture in alternate years, with an adult author in even numbered years and a children's author in uneven years. Such has been the case since the first lecture in 1978.

Since there were no libraries with auditoriums large enough to accommodate the anticipated audiences for these lectures, it has been necessary to hold them in non-library settings. All of the programs since the first in 1978 have been held either at the North Central High School Auditorium, the Northview Middle School Auditorium, or the auditorium of the Indianapolis Hebrew Congregation.

Those authors who have presented the lectures are:

1978 - Saul Bellow, winner of the Pulitzer Prize in 1976 and the Nobel Prize for Literature in 1976. He is the author of Mr. Sammler's Planet, Humboldt's Gift, Adventures of Augie March *and other titles.*

1979 - Elaine Konigsburg, noted author of children's books, and winner of the prestigious Newbery Award, presented by the American Library Association. She authored From the Mixed-Up Files of Mrs. Basil E. Frankweiler, Throwing Shadows *and other books for children.*

THE MARIAN
McFADDEN
MEMORIAL
LECTURE

Tom Wolfe, American Book Award winner and author of *Bonfire of the Vanities*, presented the 1988 McFadden Memorial Lecture.

1980 - Norman Mailer, winner of the Pulitzer Prize for fiction in 1980, and the National Book Award. Author of Executioner's Song, Armies of the Night *and numerous other best sellers.*

1981 - Scott O'Dell, winner of the Newbery Award for the outstanding children's book of the year. Author of Island of the Blue Dolphins, The King's Fifth *and other noted children's books .*

1982 - Gail Sheehy, author of Passages, Predictable Crises of Adult Life, Pathfinders *and others.*

1983 - Richard Peck, winner of the Edgar Allen Poe Award. Author of Are you in the House Alone? *and* Ghosts I have Been.

1984 - James Baldwin, author of Notes of a Native Son, Fire Next Time *and other books.*

1985 - Jean Fritz, author of And Then What Happened, Paul Revere, Where Do You Think You're Going, Christopher Columbus, *and other books written for children.*

1986 - Kurt Vonnegut, a native of Indianapolis, and prolific author of titles such as Slaughterhouse Five, Cat's Cradle, Welcome to the Monkey House *and numerous others.*

1987 - Lloyd Alexander, winner of the Newbery Award and the National Book Award. Author of The High King, Marvelous Misadventures of Sebastian *and other books for children.*

1988 - Tom Wolfe, winner of the American Book Award for general non-fiction. Author of The Right Stuff, The Electric Kool-Aid Acid Test, The Kandy-Kolored Tangerine-flake Streamline Baby *and the bestseller,* Bonfire of the Vanities.

1989 - David Macaulay, author of The Way Things Work, Castle, *and* Cathedral: The Story of its Construction.

1990 - John Updike, winner of the Pulitzer Prize and the National Book Award. Author of The Centaur, Rabbit is Rich, Rabbit at Rest *and other titles.*

These lectures have been enormously popular, with more than 1,500 guests attending many of the programs, and with standing-room-only the rule rather than the exception for several of the more popular adult authors. The availability of Foundation funding has permitted the library to obtain many of the most outstanding and currently popular authors of the day. In all probability this most successful lecture series will continue for many years to come and will continue to serve as a fitting memorial to one of the Library's outstanding leaders.

AFRO-AMERICAN HISTORY LECTURES

In February, 1980, the Library sponsored the first Afro-American lecture as part of the county-wide observance of Afro-American History Month. The lecture, held in the St. Peter Claver Social Center, and attended by 850 persons, was presented by poet Nikki Giovanni. Based on the success and popularity of this first lecture, the administration recommended that the Foundation support and fund an annual Afro-American Month lecture each February.

The lecture has been held each year since 1980, with the exception of 1989, and the St. Peter Claver Social Center has continued to be the site of this important lecture series.

Those distinguished authors and personalities who have presented the lectures are:

1980 - Nikki Giovanni - poet and author of Black Feeling, Black Talk, Black Judgment, Cotton Candy on a Rainy Day, My House *and other titles.*

1981 - Maya Angelou - poet, author, playwright and professional stage and screen performer. Author of I Know Why the Caged Bird Sings *and* Just Give Me a Cool Drink of Water 'Fore I Diiie.

1982 - Ernest Gaines - author of The Autobiography of Miss Jane Pittman, *whose televised adaption won nine Emmy Awards. He is also the author of* In My Father's House.

1983 - Lerone Bennett - author of Before the Mayflower; *and* Shaping of Black America. *Mr. Bennett received the Literature Award from the American Academy of Arts and Letters and is also senior editor of* Ebony *magazine.*

1984 - Virginia Hamilton - author and winner of the Edgar Allan Poe Award for the best juvenile mystery and the American Library Association's prestigious Newbery Award. She is the author of House of Dies Drear, *and* M.C. Higgins, the Great.

1985 - Mari Evans - poet and winner of the first annual Black Academy of Arts and Letters Award. Author of I Am a Black Woman, I Look At Me, *and* JD.

1986 - Shirley Chisholm - First black woman to serve in the United States Congress. She served seven terms in the House of Representatives.

1987 - James Haskins - author of books for both children and adults. One of his titles for children is From Lew Alcindor to Kareem Abdul Jabbar. *For adults -* Diary of a Harlem Schoolteacher.

1988 - Ruby Dee and Ossie Davis. Miss Dee is an actress who achieved fame in the Broadway productions of A Raisin in the Sun *and* Purlie Victorious. *Her actor husband, Ossie Davis, won an Emmy Award for his performance in the television drama,* Teacher, Teacher. *He is also well known for his writing and starring in* Purlie Victorious *on Broadway.*

1990 - Etheridge Knight - poet and author of Born of a Woman *and* Poems From Prison.

Now in its twenty-first year, the Foundation has assets in excess of $700,000 and annual income in excess of $100,000. These support the on-going programs—developed to fulfill the purpose for which the Foundation is organized—to further the Library mission of service to city and county citizens.

Acress Ruby Dee, above, and her husband Ossie Davis, spoke at the 1988 Afro-American History Lecture.

Bibliography

Architectural Forum, "The Public Library of Indianapolis," September, 1918

Browning, Eliza G., *Report*, 1902-1909.

Cottman, George Streiby, *Centennial History and Handbook of Indiana*, M. R. Hyman, Indianapolis, 1920.

Draegert, Eva, "Cultural History of Indianapolis," *Indiana Magazine of History*, Volume 52, 1956.

Dunn, Jacob P., *Greater Indianapolis*, Volumes I & II, Lewis Publishing Co., Chicago, 1910.

Dunn, Jacob P., *The Libraries of Indiana*, W. B. Burford, printer, Indianapolis, 1893.

Evans, Charles, *1st Annual Report*, 1873-74.

Hoak, Edward, and Church, Willis S., compilers, *Masterpieces of Architecture in the United States*, Charles Scribner's Sons, 1930.

Holloway, William Roberson, *Indianapolis; a Historical and Statistical Sketch of the Railroad City*, Indianapolis Journal Print Shop, Indianapolis, 1870.

Hull, Thomas V., *The Origin and Development of the Indianapolis Public Library, 1873-1899*, Graduate School, University of Kentucky, 1956.

Indiana Daily Student, March, 1887.

Indianapolis City Directory, 1916.

Indianapolis Journal, March 22, 1873.

Indianapolis Journal, April 2, 1873.

Indianapolis Journal, April 6-9, 1873.

Indianapolis Journal, May 15, 1874.

Indianapolis News, January 22, 1912.

Indianapolis Public Library, *Annual Reports*, 1873-1968.

Indianapolis Public Library, Archives.

Indianapolis Public Library, *Five Year Survey, 1917-1922*, Indianapolis, July, 1922.

Indianapolis Public Schools, *Annual Report, 1915-16*.

Indianapolis-Marion County Public Library, *Annual Reports*, 1968-1990.

Indianapolis-Marion County Public Library, *Indianapolis in the World of Books*, 1974. Commemorative booklet of reprints of talks presented at the

BIBLIOGRAPHY

Centennial Gala, April 28, 1973.

Indianapolis-Marion County Public Library Foundation, Minutes of the Board of Directors, February 26, 1969 to April 10, 1989.

Indianapolis Star, March 3, 1916.

Indianapolis Star, January 28, 1945.

Indianapolis Star, October 25, 1946.

Kershner, Frederick Doyle, Jr., *Social and Cultural History of Indianapolis*, 1860-1914, University of Wisconsin, Madison, 1950.

Lewis, Dorothy F., *History of the Marion County Indiana Library,1844-1930*, Division of Library Science, Indiana University, Bloomington, 1954.

Library Journal, Volume 12, January-February, 1887.

Library Journal, Volume 53, 1928.

McFadden, Marian, *The Indianapolis Public Library, 1945-1955*, Indianapolis, 1956.

Marshall, John David, compiler,*An American Library History Reader*, Hamden, Connecticut, Shoe String Press, 1961 [c 1960].

Meridian Methodist Church, Indianapolis, archives.

Sentinel (Indianapolis), February 6, 1873.

Sentinel (Indianapolis), January 28, 1887.

Sulgrove, Berry Robinson, *History of Indianapolis and Marion County*, Evansville, Indiana, Unigraphic, 1974.

Thornbrough, Gayle, and Riker, Dorothy, compilers, *Readings in Indiana History*, Indianapolis, Indiana Historical Bureau, 1956.

Tyler, Arthur W., Minutes of the Board Meeting, Indianapolis Public Library, September 15, 1880.

PHOTOGRAPHIC ACKNOWLEDGMENTS

Gaus, Laura Sheerin,*Shortridge High School, 1964-1981*, Indianapolis, Indiana Historical Society, 1985.

Indianapolis News

Indianapolis Public Library archives, 1873-1968.

Indianapolis-Marion County Public Library archives, 1968-1991.

Indianapolis Star

Leary, Edward A.,*Indianapolis: The Story of a City*, Indianapolis, The Bobbs-Merrill Company, Inc., 1971.

Pakula, Hanna, *The Last Romantic: A Biography of Queen Marie of Roumania*, New York, Simon and Schuster, 1984.

Sulgrove, Berry Robinson, *History of Indianapolis and Marion County*, Philadelphia, L. H. Everts & Co., 1884.

Index

243